SOLO

SOLO

How to Work Alone
(and Not Lose Your Mind)

REBECCA SEAL

G

GALLERY BOOKS

NEW YORK   LONDON   TORONTO   SYDNEY   NEW DELHI

G

Gallery Books
An Imprint of Simon & Schuster, Inc.
1230 Avenue of the Americas
New York, NY 10020

First Gallery Books trade paperback edition February 2021

GALLERY BOOKS and colophon are registered
trademarks of Simon & Schuster, Inc.

For information about special discounts for bulk purchases,
please contact Simon & Schuster Special Sales at 1-866-506-1949
or business@simonandschuster.com.

The Simon & Schuster Speakers Bureau can bring authors to
your live event. For more information or to book an event, contact
the Simon & Schuster Speakers Bureau at 1-866-248-3049
or visit our website at www.simonspeakers.com.

Manufactured in the United States of America

1 3 5 7 9 10 8 6 4 2

Library of Congress Control Number: 2020952049

ISBN 978-1-9821-8091-1
ISBN 978-1-9821-8092-8 (ebook)

Contents

Preface

I'm writing these words in the middle of the coronavirus crisis. It's too early to say what it will do to the world in the long run, but there is one thing I am sure of: it will change how we work. It is now inconceivable to argue that remote or flexible work is impossible when people have been doing it, against all odds, for months. Millions, if not billions, of people have had their first taste of working alone. Some will have fallen in love with it. Others will have struggled. Many will have done both. Still others will have lost their employment and started something new, by themselves.

I started this project years before most of us even knew what a coronavirus was, but my hope, now, staring this crisis in the face, is that it will be more useful than I could ever have imagined. Because this book was always meant to be for anyone who works alone, whether for a few hours a day in the corner of a bedroom, once a week at a rented desk in a shared office, in a workshop, studio, van or garden, or all day, every day and everywhere, with a laptop and a phone. It's not about whether to become a limited company, how to set up a website or when to pay your taxes. Instead, I want to help you cope with the demands of solitary work, using the best and most recent ideas in psychology, economics, business and the social sciences to create a new and resilient way of thinking about and coping with working alone.

I want to help soloists work and live well.

Introduction

Working for yourself is wonderful. Going solo is one of the best decisions I ever made. Working for yourself gives you the opportunity to do whatever it is you've always dreamed of doing and the chance to choose how, when and where you work. Working for yourself means having no boss to stifle your big ideas. Working for yourself is creative, self-directed and potentially more meaningful than working in the same old company, with the same old team, and in the same way every day.

Working for yourself is also terrifying. Working for yourself requires dredging your soul to find wells of self-reliance, bravado, optimism, hope, patience and grit. Working for yourself is tedious and monotonous, tiring and nerve-racking. Working for yourself means always working, always being on, always checking your emails. Working for yourself means having dozens of bosses, all thinking they are your first priority. Working for yourself means working at the weekend, working on holiday, working when you're ill. Working for yourself is lonely. Working for yourself is very, very hard.

All of these things are true, often all at the same time. I've been solo for 11 years, after six years working as a journalist for the *Observer*. I have done or felt all of the above, as well as elated, desperate, despondent, confident, confused, fierce, scared, knackered, proud ... and 100 per cent committed to never going back to working in an office.

Five years into freelance life, I reached what felt like a terrible impasse. I had been working without pause, writing articles and books, often until eight or nine at night, or later if I was attending a work event. On Sundays, 48 weeks a year, I got up at 6am and made my way to a TV studio in north London, where I appeared on a live breakfast show (for the same reason, I hadn't been on holiday for several years). I'd be home in time for a late lunch, giving me Sunday afternoons to regroup (or, um, drink unhealthy amounts of wine) before an early night in preparation for doing the whole thing again the next week. The years were rushing by in a haze of deadlines and presentations (under-) prepared in the back of taxis.

I felt an overwhelming need to say yes to every bit of work that came my way – even work I hated; even work that paid badly – because I was desperate to become established and fearful of losing my precious clients if I ever said no, or asked for a fairer fee, or a deadline extension. I wanted all my clients to think of me as the person who always delivered what they wanted, on time and to the brief.

I was making pretty decent money, particularly for a freelance writer, but I wasn't very happy on my hamster wheel. I was neglecting all the good things in life – my friends barely saw me, my family felt left out and my partner and I didn't seem to be having much fun at all. Like me, he is self-employed, as a freelance photographer. Like me, he worked all the hours he could, and then some, bending until breaking point to keep his clients happy. Like me, he talked about work at the breakfast table, and we muttered about it when we turned the light off at night.

We finally talked about it one evening in our local pub.

Introduction

Over burgers and red wine, we made a plan; a set of rules about when we would work, in the hope that they would ease the pressure slightly: no working or talking about work before breakfast has been eaten; no working after 8pm; and no talking about work after 8pm either (we were allowed to break this one once a week, only if it was really necessary). No working at weekends (we were allowed to break this one once a month, and only in emergencies).

For a while, fencing in the time that we were allowed to do work and talk about work really helped. As anyone who has ever had to collect their kids from childcare, or care for an unwell or elderly relative, or had any regular and immovable commitment, will already know: you get more done when you have a finite and fixed amount of time in which to work. Conversely, as anyone who works alone from home will have experienced, when a working day can easily drift into being a working evening, with nothing in particular to stop it, it can be tough to buckle down and focus. (I later found out that enforcing start and end points on the working day, whether real or arbitrarily self-imposed, is a very popular topic in the productivity literature to which I am now happily addicted.)

As time passed, though, it was clear that the rules were not going to be enough – although they stopped us actually doing work, the rules couldn't stop me thinking about it, chewing it over, silently, alone or in the dead of night. In theory, I loved my job and outwardly it looked as though I was living a freelance dream, but it was getting more and more difficult to find joy in what I did – something which made me feel both ungrateful and, frankly, kind of cheated. I'd worked so long and so hard to get here – so why did it feel miserable? Why wasn't I revelling in the fact that I had a job I was supposed to love? Why was I incapable of taking time off? Why was my phone always in my hand or my pocket? Why did I need to check my emails before I'd got out of bed each morning? What was wrong with me? Why couldn't I be happy with what amounted to a really good life?

Meanwhile, several of my friends decided to try working alone as well. Some actively chose to go solo and some were made redundant. Others changed career and because of what they wanted to do, had no choice but to work alone, even if they might have preferred a regular pay cheque. In the current job market, it's almost impossible to find a permanent job if you want to be a personal trainer, tree surgeon, private chef or writer. A friend, a lawyer, started a consultancy business of one, because he couldn't see himself working in the cut-throat, corporate world of large legal firms for the rest of his working life. Lou, a friend from university, found that the only way she could control her career as a senior aid worker was to leave the international charity she'd joined and become a consultant, helping non-governmental organisations respond quickly to humanitarian disasters. A successful marketing executive retrained as a make-up artist. Colleagues from my time working on newspapers became fiction writers and copywriters, or jacked in writing completely to run bed-and-breakfasts by the sea.

We sometimes talked to each other about how tough we often found it, how remote we often felt, even though we knew that for most of us, it was still better than being traditionally employed. We wondered how to assess our careers when there was no one to give us a performance review; we tried to figure out how, apart from checking our bank balances, we could tell if we were where we should be, when we had no idea what our new and novel career paths should look like.

Introduction

I couldn't stop looking for answers. This seemed to be such a common problem, coping with the weirdness of working alone, that I was confident someone would have looked into it and written a helpful book already. But I was wrong. I love a good life hack, and thought I knew where to look for solo-working versions. But I couldn't find a single book or even article which could answer my exact questions. There are dozens which address one aspect or another of working for yourself – how to manage your time, how to chase clients who haven't paid, how to do social media ... as well as hundreds on how to be happy, how to pursue success or how to work mindfully, but none which looked at everything through the one lens which mattered to me.

Buried within all this material, as well as in articles by brilliant scholars but published in obscure or inaccessible academic journals – are the makings of a whole new way of thinking about working alone. But it is hidden from most of us, and that's a sad thing for solo workers. That's why I thought: I'm a journalist. Perhaps my greatest skill is gathering and synthesising information and making it understandable, navigable. I will write this book.

Today, at the time of writing, there are more self-employed people than ever before – since 2008, the number of self-employed British workers has increased by almost 25 per cent, according to the Office for National Statistics (ONS). Fifteen per cent of working Britons are self-employed. Thirteen per cent of working 25–49-year-olds are self-employed. In London, over 17 per cent of the working population is self-employed; in the south west it's 16.8 per cent and in the south east it's 16.2 per cent. In America, there are 15 million self-employed people today, and up to 68 million who classify in one way or another as freelancers (American labour statistics are notoriously tricky to pin down). Research by FreshBooks in 2018 predicted a further 27 million Americans would have left traditional employment and be working for themselves by 2020, which would make up over 30 per cent of the US workforce. Almost 17 per cent of the Australian workforce is self-employed. The most recent figures from the European Union date back to 2016, when 33 million were classified as self-employed.

That's an awful lot of people grappling with these problems on their own.

This matters not just because everyone who struggles with aspects of their self-employment could be happier, but also because we are at an important crossroads when it comes to how we work. In order to survive within the modern, rather shaky economic system, we need a productive workforce – we need people who have the capacity to make good decisions, who have the motivation to work well into their late middle age and who aren't crushed by their jobs. Unless we can help solo workers to do this, they – we – just won't meet our potential.

But what is the answer? How do we work alone and thrive, without feeling like we are losing our grip on our lives? One answer is ridiculously, absurdly, almost laughably simple (although harder than you'd think to put into practice). Just … don't. Don't work alone. Don't attempt to plough through whatever career or side hustle you've chosen on your own. Don't sit alone all day, don't stare at a blank page, a blank screen, a brick wall. We are not made for constant, rudderless seclusion. Don't be alone.

I'm not suggesting that we should all give up on freelancing and return to the grind of an everyday office – and even if I was, it would be pointless and no one would listen, since many analysts expect that within just a few years, half the UK's workforce will be freelance. Half! The trend is moving fast, which is why getting a handle on this stuff is so crucial.

It's a fact that most solo workers don't think about the *way* in which they work. If you're like me, perhaps you set up a spreadsheet for your income and expenses (crossing your fingers and hoping there would be some of both). Maybe, *maybe* you bought a desk. But the chances are, that's all you did. After that you just ... worked. Like me, you probably didn't think about support networks and emotional resilience. You probably didn't have a five- or ten-year plan. You didn't visualise, or goal set. You didn't think about the feeling of the space in which you work (the kitchen table? A desk under the stairs? A cafe? Or – please, no – your bed?). You didn't plan your hours, or your time off. You didn't strategise. Like me, you barely made a single, conscious choice. There wasn't time. There wasn't space. You just ... worked.

Most solo workers don't reflect on the impact of their solitude, but recent research by Epson EcoTank found that 48 per cent of self-employed people find working alone lonely, and 46 per cent find it isolating. A quarter had experienced depression. We tend to think, 'I work alone, so I am alone in this'. In writing this book I've learned how pernicious and – literally – dangerous believing ourselves to be alone is. I'd like to shout this from the rooftops: you are not alone. But it often doesn't feel that way.

When we work for a business or organisation, we slot into structures which existed before we arrived. Or, if you join a business at the beginning, you might be part of – or at least witness to – the genesis of its ways of being and doing. But ask yourself this: when you started working alone, did you think about the structures and processes you might need for your business to function? I didn't, and I don't know a single solo worker who did. When you work for yourself, no one writes you a contract, telling you what hours you should work, and at what time and where. No one chases you from your desk if you stay too late for weeks on end (according to the ONS, British freelancers work 40 hours a week on average, while the employed work 38). No one provides a free telephone counselling service, or reminds you to take your holiday days. There's no one to bitch to at lunchtime when things are going badly. There is no IT support, no social media manager, no office gym, no Friday drinks. There's nothing ready-made.

However horrible you found line managers and performance reviews, human relations appraisals, health and safety training, dreadful coffee and ugly, air-conditioned bunkers, however much even the idea of office life made you want to race towards the freedoms of freelancing, organisational structures do provide a safety net of sorts. Zealous office managers often enforce structure so rigidly that it becomes stifling, baffling or repressive, but it's a mistake to reject the idea of structure completely.

Because those structures, services or processes create communities – even if it's a community brought together by the shared belief that the office canteen's food will one day kill everyone, or that the accounts department is somehow populated by people who hate making payments, or that no one should be allowed to crunch through a bag of crisps at their desk. (A team I would join, by the way.)

When we stop working within organisations, and step out on our own, it's extremely rare that we think holistically at how we create our own tiny organisations-of-one. Admittedly, it is hard to do at the very beginning, because when you go freelance or start a new business, it's difficult to know exactly what you'll be doing. But as time passes, and as soon as you can – and maybe don't leave it five years, like I did – it's critically important to remember that it's up to us to decide what our businesses look like and even more so what our lives could look like. We have a responsibility to safeguard the welfare of our team (that is, you), just as you would if you were the forward-thinking CEO of a massive corporation.

When I talk about structures, I don't mean that you need to replicate the straitjacketed approach to work that many organisations use. But here's an apparently insignificant example. Obviously, you don't have to have a dress code if you work at home. If you left office life precisely so that you can work in loungewear for the next 20 years – if that really, truly brings you joy – then go for it. But if you consistently find yourself un-washed and under-dressed at 3pm, because you panic-rolled out of bed and straight into your emails, and if that makes you feel grubby, or guilty, or just desperately miserable, then you need to give your days a bit more form. Whether we realise it or not, everything we do in our working days, as soloists, is a choice – regardless of whether a choice is actively thought through, or not – and those choices create a framework for how we work, and how we feel about that work. Our choices have deep consequences for our mental and physical health, as well as the health of our businesses.

There's nobody else out there who can make these choices, except you. I don't care if you get dressed or not: the point is that you have a choice about getting dressed (and dozens of others every working day) and it's yours to make. If we are going to survive this really quite strange new way of solitary working, then we need to know when we are making choices, what other options might lie beyond what we think we know, and how to choose the things that work best for us.

How do we make those choices? My plan – my hope – is to convince you that they're important, and enable you to make good ones, that suit you, your life and the work you do. Wherever possible, I use data, or academic specialists and experts in their field to back me up.

You should definitely cherry-pick the bits of this book that suit you and your life the best – if I've learned one thing interviewing the dozens of people for this book, it's that every solo worker needs to design their own situation, and then constantly adapt and tweak it. The best way to do that? You have to really get to know yourself – what you need, what you want and who you are, because then you can build your work life around your personality, rather than butting up against things that will never really feel right to you. The soloists who really thrive are the ones who are most open to change, who can be most agile when it comes to how or where or when they work, or at least, who know who they are and what they need to manage themselves.

*

We also need to fight against our own and others' misperceptions, which can include believing we are totally alone, when in fact we are part of complex webs of work relationships; that every other soloist is succeeding completely by themselves, when they too are part of invisible, nebulous teams; and that we should, whenever we are asked to be, be infinitely, endlessly flexible. It's so easy, in those moments when it feels as though we cannot cope with solo working, to feel as though we are the only ones feeling that way – which just isn't true, and the more that we can help each other see that, the less painful those moments will be.

Introduction

The choices you make will be unique to you and the particular work you do. There's no one-size-fits-all for solo working (apart from: being utterly alone fits almost no one), which is why this book is packed with ideas and advice from people who have already been where you are today, as well as persuasive science about how our brains and bodies behave, both in work and beyond work. I will use my own life, my own vulnerabilities, wrong turns and idiosyncrasies to tell the story of how solo work affects us, but at the same time, I am very aware that my way is not the only way. Disagree with me – I want you to. All I want is for all of us to think about what will work for us, alone.

*

I think we can all agree that humans were not built for office life. We were not designed to sit at a desk for hours on end, in darkened rooms under artificial lighting. (If you've found solo work that doesn't require you to do this – excellent.) This book will try and show all of us ways that we can navigate the fact that sometimes, work doesn't work for us.

One more thing. I'm not here to tell you how to make a million quid. I'm not even here to convince you to go solo – if you are traditionally employed and love it, fabulous. I'm not here to encourage you to turn your side hustle into a full-time job. I'm not about scaling your business, or generating sales, or making this year the year-you-make-the-most-money-you've-ever-made, and nor am I here to tell you that you can become a billionaire working on a beach in Bali. A lot of the stuff in here is simply common sense that today's world of work has sidelined or forgotten. Words like wellness, optimisation and self-improvement make me feel slightly ill. I know there's a strange tension in that – this is a book about changes, but I don't want you to think I can or should change you! I don't want to fetishise your productivity or hack you into an entirely different person. I will talk a lot about productivity, but not because I want you to turn into a workaholic machine, shackled to your desk/workbench/easel/steering wheel all hours of the day and night. I want all of us to be able to work effectively, even happily, that's all. In fact, I probably think you should work a bit less. Make the hours you *do* work count for a bit more. Take time off. Try not to think about money. Don't obsess with success. Rest. Do other things you love doing. Place work a bit further from the dead centre of your life. Paradoxically, you will almost certainly get more done (although that isn't my main aim), and feel better about it too.

Are you ready?

Part 1

How We Work

1

The Good Bits

Since so much of this book is about addressing the difficult parts of solo work and examining how to mend or transcend them, I want first to make it clear that solo working is wonderful – that's why so many people are taking it as an option; it's why so few people, once given the chance to work independently or flexibly, go back to more traditional forms of work. At the time of writing, the world is navigating the implications of the coronavirus, one of which will almost certainly be a seismic shift in the way millions of people work. Given a taste of flexible or remote working, employees who have been forced to home-work due to coronavirus lockdown are extremely unlikely to meekly return to traditional office set-ups, having learned how much they can achieve, with little or no commute and far more control over their lives than they've ever had before. That conversation with a boss about whether you could work flexibly or remotely, where they tell you it's impossible because the tech doesn't exist, or that the team need you in person? After months of proving it can be done, is feasible and cost-effective, that conversation simply cannot happen any more.

Soloists have more chances to make changes and build the kind of lives we really want and can enjoy, and as problems arise, we can solve them, whether they are practical, behavioural or circumstantial. We can pivot in ways that are impossible for traditional workers and whether we recognise it or not yet, we all have deep wells of resilience and courage to draw on.

We also get the chance to be ourselves, as Dior Bediako, who runs Pepper Your Talk, a mentoring platform for young fashion creatives, pointed out to me. 'I go to work every day as myself,' she says. 'Whether I'm creating content, hosting an event or on a podcast, helping girls with their CVs, I'm just being myself. I don't have to be anyone else; I don't have to pretend. I can bring *myself* to work every day. It's my voice; it's my mannerisms; it is just me.'

All the soloists I've interviewed here are in love with what they do and how they do it. Because this is a book about how to cope with solo life, perhaps the focus is slightly skewed towards their more challenging moments. But none of them would change what they do. I met Alex Hannaford while I was interning on the *Evening Standard*'s features desk, aged 19, when he was a junior writer. He now lives in Texas and has an award-winning true crime podcast as well as an international freelance feature-writing career: his enthusiasm for his job was boundless (on which, more later). Even down the phone, I could tell that he still can't quite believe that he gets to do what he does.

Fundamentally, this is a positive book. Every solo worker can have a satisfying, fulfilling and even joyful work life.

The best bits

Self-employed people have 10 per cent higher levels of job satisfaction than employed people, even those in lower paid occupations.[1] (Much of the data out there is on self-employed people, but I think we can infer that it applies to most solo workers.)

Although the gig economy is often characterised as being all about Deliveroo cyclists and Uber drivers, it's actually much more nuanced, with many freelancers and solo workers working on a mixture of gig work (the same or similar tasks, done repeatedly) and project work. But that doesn't quite illustrate how varied and interesting the work out there is for soloists, how much of it is knowledge work, nor how high on the corporate ladder soloists sometimes sit. Big banks, for example, hire freelance senior managers, especially on infra-structure or change-management projects, who can be very well paid. Solo IT contractors might work on blockchain, e-commerce development or cloud computing.

Other freelance specialisms include mechanical engi-neering, brand strategy, bid writing, architecture and even dietetics and nutrition. Because a lot of this kind of work now happens remotely via specialist global gig work plat-forms like UpWork, younger or less experienced but still highly skilled solo workers can have the chance to work on projects they might never be allowed to touch if they were in-house. Often, this work is also comparatively well paid (and in some countries, more tax efficient, too).

The gender pay gap is less obvious among freelancers too, with some estimates suggesting it has closed to around 3 per cent[2] – still not perfect but far better than the 10–20 per cent gap in many other sectors.

Solo working isn't just good for the people who do it, it's also good for the broader economy. Highly skilled freelancers in the UK contribute £140–145 billion to the economy every year. Research by UpWork in the US estimates freelance income accounts for 5 per cent of US GDP … nearly $1 trillion.

Almost three-quarters of self-employed people have no intention of going into or returning to traditional employment. (That applies even to people who didn't choose solo working, but were forced into it by their circumstances.[3])

Not being tied to the old-fashioned career ladder is liberating. Outside the confines of an organisation, you can do anything with your career – whether you want to leapfrog out of your field and use your current skills in another one, or skip parts of the traditional ladder that you don't want to take part in, or change jobs entirely. Or you can, like me, keep the same job title for years, but do loads of different things within it.

You can take much more holiday time than many workers are able to – and once you've read this book, I hope you will feel more able to, if you don't already. Around 90 per cent of self-employed people feel they have some-to-a-lot of control over their daily tasks and how they do them, and 92 per cent feel they can choose when they start and end their working day.

Research by Gallup in the US showed that entrepreneurs, despite being a couple of percentage points more worried or stressed than employed people, were also more optimistic and more likely to be enjoying their work and aware of learning new things.[4]

Fifty-five per cent of self-employed people say remote working gives them greater flexibility, 34 per cent say it makes them more productive, 43 per cent think it saves them time and 41 per cent confirm that it improves their work–life balance.[5] (Ninety-seven per cent of remote work is done at home.)

The majority of self-employed people are not entrepreneurs, but individuals who happen to prefer doing what they do, on their own.[6] So you don't have to invent an app or be looking for venture capital investors (unless you want to).

Many solo workers can choose where they work. From cafes to co-working spaces, libraries to even the tiniest corners of our homes, we have the ability to tailor where we work to our preferences. (More on this in chapter 10.) No more strip lighting, bland cubicles, or sterile office grey.

You might also get to choose who you work with – not just who your clients are, but also your colleagues. Rare is the soloist who works completely alone, and there's more choice for freelancers about who they have to sit next to all day (if anyone at all), than there is for many employed people.

Many soloists avoid a daily commute, which at the moment stands at an average of an hour for UK workers (74 minutes for Londoners) and 54 minutes in the US (68 minutes in Washington DC). In the UK, that delightful journey costs full-time workers an average of £1,752 a year. While soloists will probably have to travel for work sometimes, much of that travel can be claimed as an expense or offset against tax, unlike employed workers' commutes, which function more like pay cuts.

In theory, at least – and often in practice – you get more choice: what to wear, what to eat and when to eat it, who to work with, what work to do and when, and where to be when you work. Those choices are there even when they're well hidden. Sometimes all this choice can feel overwhelming, but with the help of this book, it's nothing you can't handle.

2

The Tricky Bits

If the way you solo-work right now makes you feel like you've backed yourself into a corner, don't feel bad about it. Did anyone give you a road map at the beginning of all this? Every single solo worker, to a greater or lesser extent, is feeling their way in the dark. And, I promise you, every single one of us has had times when it absolutely sucks.

When we start a solo business from scratch, we are often so worried about getting work, then keeping work, that we forget to plan for the working life we want (and need). When we finally look up and take a breath, a year or two years in, often we find that life feels tangled, even broken. Maybe we are tired. Perhaps we've forgotten why we decided to do this in the first place, or what we've ended up doing feels a long way from the original plan. We might have worked too hard, for too long, with too little time away from work. Maybe we aren't taking care of our bodies. Perhaps we were so busy working we almost didn't notice that the systems which have developed in our solo businesses were encasing us, and don't seem to work that well. We might discover that we need skills we've never even thought of, and we can't think where to look for them.

To reassure you that challenging, confusing times are both normal and survivable, I want to tell you two stories. One of hard beginnings, and one of a difficult middle. Thomas Broughton is the founder of Cubbitts, a small group of ten beautiful, cool yet affordable spectacles and sunglasses boutiques. Although they do eye exams, it doesn't feel fair to call them opticians, as the shops and what they sell are so far removed from the traditional, rather narrow and clinical experience of getting glasses – which was exactly what Broughton wanted to stand on its head. He opened the first groundbreaking branch in Kings Cross, London, in 2013.

'I wish you had written this book seven years ago,' he told me. Did he find the beginning of Cubbitts hard? 'Unbelievably hard. Incredibly hard. I had no idea. Hard in ways that I had no real foresight of; no real understanding of. Just to start a business, you need to be extremely committed. You start with a plan and a mission and passion and all that kind of stuff. But you've never done this before, so you have no idea what works and what doesn't. You're at the earliest stages of starting this thing, which is a really stressful point. But you're also at the point where you know the least. And those two things combine to make a real confluence of uncertainty and pain! How many hours should you be working? When should you be working? When should you be taking holidays? How should you work? What is the balance? How do you recruit people?' For Broughton, stepping away from work time proved almost impossible for him to contemplate. 'Just working out where I, as a human being, ended and this thing began was really, really difficult,' he says.

The result? Very, very long hours, and no time off. 'It was out of a sense of perceived necessity. In hindsight, it wasn't necessary, but it's an innate human characteristic to focus on stuff that you can control, and I think your hours worked are a lever that you have control over. Whereas a lot of other levers, you don't. I do worry – I reckon my life expectancy is going to be a few years shorter because of that first year. It was insane for a while and I couldn't really see anything outside the bubble of my inbox, some files on my computer and a little corner of a room in my flat where I was doing it all.' At the time, he didn't have a partner or family to moderate his behaviour. 'I thought a really productive way to work was if I ever woke up in the night, I would get up and start working. I'd get woken up at two o'clock in the morning by a bird and start working. I did get quite a lot done, but it was absolutely ridiculous because then, of course, I'd crash by two o'clock in the afternoon, sleep, and wouldn't be able to sleep that night, so it was a vicious cycle of sleep imbalance. Also if you're sending emails at two or three o'clock in the morning, there's a good chance the person on the other end is going to think you're crazy.'

He even decided not to go to Brazil, to a World Cup football match for which he had saved up, because he felt there was no one else who could do the work he needed to do.

'It was going to be my reward after two years of slog, so it was a real low point.' It was at this moment that he decided he needed to change. 'I thought, I will literally go mad if I can't get away, as well as becoming resentful of the work I'm doing.'

On top of this were financial stresses, after splitting from a business partner well before the business really began. 'I spent ten years saving up the money to start the company with and then I had to pay off the money that he put in. So immediately, ten years of savings had been whittled down to not-much money, and then what was left, I managed to spend in three months. There was a two-week period where we very nearly went out of business. There was that classic thing of credit cards and selling everything I owned. It gets to your worst fears as a person: what am I going to do? How will I eat? I'll get thrown out of my flat.' This was at a moment where he had no proven business model and no customers. 'Just emotionally overcoming that sense of loss was hard. I think it was good for me as a person – you go into mourning a bit, and panic, and all the different stages of fear and depression, but then you come through that and you realise, it's only money. It doesn't really make any difference whatsoever, as long as I can scrabble enough money to eat and pay rent.'

How did he keep going? 'I doubted the project hugely, at a whole bunch of different stages. But it felt too far gone. There's the "sunk-cost fallacy" as well: I have put all my life savings into this, so implicitly I've put my life into this too. So I have to keep going. I can't give up. And there's a whole thing, frankly, about ego as well: I've got to keep trying, I've been telling all my friends about this for years. Can I really go and tell them that I fucked this up, and I spent my life savings doing so, in the process? They're all going to laugh at me. That really did play into it a lot.' Although Broughton says there were moments of flow, moments of pure adrenalin and achievement which he misses today, they often 'veered into something much weirder and stress-induced. I think I could have got the same results and been much more mentally stable.'

As for life outside work, 'for two years, there wasn't any. It was pretty unhealthy. I speak to my friends about it now and they're like, yeah, you were a dick. It was not nice to be around you.'

Ultimately, Broughton found a way through, partly by recruiting people to help with his wildly increasing workload, and partly by playing online chess, which was free – and he was, as he puts it, skint – and an excellent foil for the chaos of a new business. 'I hadn't played since I was 12 years old, but there was something about focusing on something where you know all the rules: all you're thinking about is 64 squares, and 32 pieces, and that's it. There are no surprises, in contrast to trying to start a business where there are no rules – no, actually there *are* rules, but you don't understand them!' he laughs. 'And there are much worse outcomes than you just being checkmated.' Being unequivocally good at something took on great importance. 'You don't know if you're doing a good job or a bad job when you start a business. But playing a game where there are clear rules, and the little serotonin release of getting a thumbs up or a little winning emoji in the game, made a huge difference at the time.' He also got into running. 'There's the runners' high stuff, which I definitely think is true, but it was also about realising that it is difficult to do an Excel spreadsheet or reply to emails while you're running.'

Over time Broughton developed far clearer boundaries – where once he received updates from every store every evening, which could make or break a whole night, now he only looks at those emails on a Monday morning, when he's prepared for their impact. He realised having his email address as the point of contact for things like invoices was also making him unhappy, as he had no agency over when requests for money arrived in his inbox. So he set up a new email address: finance@cubbitts.co.uk. 'Honestly, it sounds stupid now, but it had a huge impact on my mental health – suddenly I was in control because I could go into that inbox once a week, when I was mentally prepared, and pay all the invoices in one go.' Today the company – and Broughton – is thriving.

For the TV presenter, explorer and writer Levison Wood, it was after he achieved apparent success that he started to struggle. 'It was once I got to where I wanted to be that it started becoming difficult,' he told me. After his first TV series took off, suddenly he found himself on a hamster wheel of work and work-related events. 'I was saying yes to everything, every opportunity, to build on success, keep momentum going, grasping at everything in a desperate bid to make it all work. And it did work from a career point of view. But it didn't give me any time for anything else. I had this big financial success but I found myself getting sucked into this media vortex of bollocks. I would think "Everything's going so well, but I've got no time for myself".'

It was painful because it was at odds with what he expected from 'success'. 'I was in such a fortunate position to have achieved my boyhood dream, but it was really tough because I did question what on earth all this success was for. There were really hard moments for me and it made me question what I was doing. It only changed when I started grappling with the old cliché: life's about the journey, not the destination. I focused so much on the destination that I forgot to give myself time to enjoy it.' Finally, he started to exercise control over his time, aware that his work was edging towards making him miserable. 'I got to the point where I said, enough's enough, I'm going to say no to everything! You can see why some people [who succeed] will lose their shit, because they lose touch with reality. I've seen it with some people I know. I was determined to take a step back and realise what it's all for in the first place.' Today, as we will discover in chapter 7, he is territorial with his time, scheduling work and time off in blocks of days, and is happy and able to enjoy his achievements.

Later in the book, we will look more closely at how and why the strategies both Broughton and Wood used can work for all soloists. Right now, I'm telling you these stories so that you know that whatever happens in your solo life, you're not unusual. On TV, Wood comes across as charming, immensely capable, handsome and completely unflusterable. We have no idea what backstories other soloists are living through. Even people who appear totally in control of their solo work, who seem to be leading fulfilling and rewarding lives with exciting, dynamic, adventurous purpose-filled careers, have had, will have or are – right now – having a crap time. But they got through it, and so will you.

3

Loneliness and Solitude

Despite the rise in co-working spaces, most solo work still takes place alone – as much as 90 per cent, according to some estimates. Many soloists spend a lot of time in relatively unusual solitude, and that can take a bit of managing. Solo workers aren't the only people who can feel lonely – you can feel lonely in an office, or at a party – but 40–50 per cent of soloists feel lonely some or a lot of the time, and I think that's more than understandable.[1] Our work can physically isolate us from other people, while for others feeling lonely is less about not having people around, and more about the loneliness of running a business by yourself. We all have a deep, almost primal need to be connected to other people – we need to feel heard, understood and cared about.

Loneliness can have far-reaching consequences, including for our health, which is why we need to face it head on and not ignore or bury it. Hard though it may feel at first, acknowledging and facing up to it means loneliness can be dealt with. If you feel lonely, don't feel ashamed. Not only is it common, it is also useful. As John T. Cacioppo, professor of psychology at the University of Chicago and a loneliness researcher, put it in an article in the *New York Times*, loneliness is like hunger or pain. It's an aversive signal that is just our body's way of telling us something is wrong and needs to be attended to. 'Denying you feel lonely makes no more sense than denying you feel hunger.'[2]

Loneliness is on the rise in Europe and America, with 9 million Britons and almost half of Americans feeling lonely.[3] As well as the desperate sadness of these statistics, loneliness has serious repercussions when it comes to work: lonely workers (solo or not) perform less well, quit more, have lower levels of productivity and take more sick days.[4] Loneliness costs UK employers £2.5 billion a year – it doesn't take a maths whizz to extrapolate that lonely soloists will also be paying a price. Beyond the world of work, studies by Professor Julianne Holt-Lunstad showed that long-term loneliness can be as dangerous for health as smoking,[5] and increases our risk of death by 26 per cent.[6] Another study suggested loneliness may be a preclinical marker for the development of Alzheimer's disease and cognitive decline.[7] Loneliness looks as though it's a better predictor of early death than obesity, and a potential cause of inflammation throughout the body.[8]

Research done on loneliness among American workers by Betterup, a coaching platform and research hub, showed those who have more people around them in their private lives were less likely to be lonely at work, regardless of race, gender or ethnicity. People working in law, science and engineering felt greater loneliness, as did people with advanced qualifications (medical and legal degree holders scored highest, experiencing 20 per cent more loneliness than PhDs, and 25 per cent higher than people with bachelor's degrees).[9] Identifying as anything other than heterosexual was also linked to greater loneliness at work. The study concluded that in America at least, workers who were highly educated, single or childless, non-religious, or non-heterosexual were at the very greatest risk from what they also call a 'loneliness epidemic'.

This is not meant to scare you. Being solo doesn't have to mean being lonely. The word solitude means the state of being alone; it's not the same as loneliness, which is about feeling an unhappy lack of other people. Being physically alone for some or a lot of the time does not automatically lead to loneliness. The research about the harmful effects of isolation and loneliness are not about solitude. It is totally possible to take deep joy in solitude, and if that doesn't come naturally or you hate being alone, then that's something we can manage, too.

Solitude itself doesn't really have a negative or positive value, but historically there have been two ways of thinking about it. On the one hand solitude has been and still is used as a punishment for crimes or as a way to exclude unwanted people from society. Solitary confinement is still one of the most extreme punishments a prison can deliver. People who chose solitude were – are – seen as weird, or even as a danger to the communities they chose to leave. (Think of hermits, or stories about witches living alone deep in a forest.)

On the other hand, there is the idea that great art, litera-ture or scientific breakthroughs have been tugged into being by solitary figures hunched over desks or easels. Cheerlead-ers for this point of view include the thirteenth-century poet Rumi, the nineteenth century essayist Henry David Thoreau, the twentieth-century monk and mystic Thomas Merton (who wrote a book, *Thoughts in Solitude*), and the nineteenth-century German philosophers Schopenhauer and Nietzsche (although Nietzsche had a famously complex relationship with being alone, despite craving it). Religious leaders – Buddha, Moses, Jesus, Mohammad – routinely trudge off into a literal or metaphorical wilderness and come back full of personal growth and spiritual communion.

If you feel negative about solitude – your own, or just the idea of it – then you're more likely to experience loneliness from it too, because you're liable to interpret your situation as though you are very isolated, regardless of whether you actually are, or not. Our perception of how solitary we are really matters. (And if you don't like being alone, you're not alone: a recent study in the journal *Science* showed – bafflingly – that most participants in 11 studies would rather give themselves an electric shock than spend 15 minutes on their own in a room with nothing to do.)

Living with solitude is a skill we all need and one we can improve, but being alone all day, every day or even most days, can be tough. It is much harder to drown out your inner critic when you don't have other, noisier people around to shout over it, or quieter ones to talk you down, and though it might spur on creativity and innovation, it's also much easier for unwanted thoughts to bubble up and overtake you. 'It is what one takes into solitude that grows there, the beast within included,' wrote Nietzsche in the 1880s. What you might gain in autonomy and focus, you can lose to self-doubt, or worse.

Extended solitude is less likely if you rent a space in a co-work office, workshop or studio. (See chapter 10 for more on where to work, especially if you find solitude particularly hard.) But, even if you'd prefer a shared space, they can feel expensive, and many solo jobs, like taxi driving, mobile hairdressing or plumbing, can't be done in a co-working rental, or divided-up shared office. You may find that you need or prefer to work by yourself even if you could share. I like silence when I'm writing or interviewing, which makes paying for shared space feel pointless. I'm too nosy to get much work done in a cafe or library – I spend too much time half-listening to conversations, spinning stories in my head about the couple in the corner, whispering over their coffees – and have to use noise-cancelling headphones to drown out all the interesting life going on around me.

Having a rough idea of where you sit on the introvert-ambivert-extrovert spectrum may help you understand your reaction to solitude, and how to manage it. Because many introverts often need a certain amount of solitude, some look for solitary work, and others struggle in contexts which don't allow for their particular needs, like hot-desking offices, and large or loud meetings. Susan Cain, in her book, *Quiet: The Power of Introverts in a World That Can't Stop Talking*, notes that introverts have a 'creative advantage ... introverts prefer to work independently, and solitude can be a catalyst to innovation.'[10] If you want to find out where you sit, there's a quick online personality test on Cain's website, www.quietrev.com. Although extroverts need quiet time too, they also seem to draw energy from other people. Not all extroverts struggle with solitude (and not all introverts love it, either), but if you are one who does, it might be a relief to know why.

When I started freelancing, I moved a desk into Steve's home office. After less than a week, he told me that I had to stop endlessly talking. I was used to an open-plan newsroom, full of very chatty journalists. Having been freelance for years already, he was used to monastic solitude and complete silence, in which he could focus on his post-production work. Ten years on, we've abandoned working in the same room. He is a sociable introvert, and loves social interaction but needs quite long periods of solitude to recharge, and doesn't find solo work lonely at all. I'm more of an extrovert, less prone to overstimulation from social interaction; I need less recovery time. (Also, I mutter to myself when I'm writing, an unrelated issue, but one that could lead to divorce. So: separate offices.) Solitude comes a bit less easily to me – like anyone, I need it sometimes but I don't often yearn for it. Although my solitude is productive, it sometimes blurs into loneliness. As the early twentieth-century writer Colette put it, 'There are days when solitude is heady wine that intoxicates you, others when it is a bitter tonic, and still others when it is a poison that makes you beat your head against the wall'.[11] Been there.

Technology, as well as being life-changingly useful for soloists, can lead to greater isolation if it stops us getting out and being around real people, even for mundane reasons. We need to make sure that the technology we use in our businesses to make our lives easier doesn't also rob us of the social interactions we thrive on. If we delegate too much to bits of AI technology, or to apps or websites, then we lose out on even the shallow connections we make just by doing things like going to the post office or visiting the bank.

In his book, *Solitude: In Pursuit of a Singular Life in a Crowded World*, writer Michael Harris tries to get to grips with alone-ness, having rarely experienced it, while examining whether it's even possible to be alone in the era of the smartphone. He writes powerfully about human's need for social grooming, conversations which are just a small step up from the physical grooming undertaken by our primate relatives. They are conversations which, layer upon layer, build up to create deep relationships, cultural and social ties, and historically, a sense of belonging. Social grooming allows a social group to function, and it allowed our oldest human ancestors to form small communities, groups which rarely included more than 150 people.

Today, because of instant messaging, social media and email, we are hooked on endless superficial social grooming as part of much, much bigger groups. Most modern social grooming involves little or no face-to-face interaction at all, just millions of tiny blurts of text or icons, constantly flitting between us, tying us together virtually, but not actually.

Regular in-person social contact decreases the risk of depression, but emails and telephone calls without in-person contact do not.[12] When there is no choice due to coronavirus lockdown but to rely on digital communications for social contact, they become incredibly valuable, and almost certainly have a positive effect on mental health. In a world where there is no choice between in-person and in-digital, and everyone is more or less equally alone, then Zoom, Skype and FaceTime can be the difference between abject loneliness and just-about-bearable solitude. But in-person contact is what our brains crave – and even though digital is better than nothing during a lockdown, we all know it is a poor substitute for conversations where you can see the other person's eyes, in focus and with no delay, and read their body language.

Smartphones and social media are addictive because the old, real-life version of social grooming is hard-wired into us. Every time we share something online or in a message, our brains flood with dopamine and other feel-good neurochemicals. This would have been helpful 100,000 years ago, when early humans were developing language and sharing information which might have helped a small group survive. Unfortunately our brains have evolved very little since life was lived in forests, caves and on savannahs and have not caught up even slightly with digital communications. We innocently love the rush we get from tweets and retweets, Instagram likes and floods of phone notifications, and bounce from one source of dopamine to the next. But many of the connections this kind of social grooming creates can be shallow, easily broken, or non-existent. Not all, of course: there are some rare-ish but brilliant examples of digital communities which really do support their members; and sometimes real-life relationships emerge from the digital world. (Not just on Tinder and Hinge.)

Social grooming and smartphone chats can happen in total isolation. Calling it 'social' media is a trick, really. The urge to get involved in social grooming lies as deep as our instincts to gorge on sugar, salt and fat, which, like safety, were also in short supply for early humans. In his book, Harris wonders if we have now become 'compulsive social groomers ... gobbling the fast food equivalent. Has social media made us socially obese – gorged on constant connection but never properly nourished?'[13]

Too much time distracted by social media or messaging is the equivalent of empty calories – and it can make us feel lonely, despite (or maybe because of) appearing to be connected to many, many people. A study published in the *American Journal of Preventive Medicine* showed that adults with high levels of social media use experienced three times the level of perceived social isolation to that of the rest of the population.[14] We all need people, real people.

Given all this, how can soloists make our solitude work for us, without our being alone drifting into loneliness? The keys are perception, practice, reduction and appreciation. By keeping an eye on how we perceive our alone-ness, whether we think of it as a bad thing and whether we really are as alone as we think we are, we can stop negativity creeping in. By consciously practising solitude, we can get more used to spending time in our own heads, and we can learn what triggers might prompt us to experience it negatively. Reducing the amount of time we spend alone or including small but valuable social interactions as ways to break up long periods of alone time, can help us feel more connected. And by understanding the power of solitude when it comes to creativity we can appreciate it, which is one of the most powerful ways to improve how we perceive solitude too.

Perception

Solitude can be a very good thing, but only if it's something we choose. Choosing solitude completely changes how we feel about it.

The film composer Nicholas Hooper is probably best known for his work on several of the Harry Potter movies. He is now a writer and musician and he echoed this when we talked about how he felt about solitude when he was writing film scores. 'I craved company,' he told me. 'It almost drove me mad – I used to go on about how I couldn't cope with it. But I had to be on my own to do the work, and so every other time I got a chance to meet people or be out, then I would take it. Now, lots of my time is taken up with family things, I crave time on my own. I'm much happier on my own now than I was when I was film composer and I *had* to be on my own.'

As Hooper experienced, even though being solo is a choice (we are not prisoners), it can feel like it isn't, especially if we don't naturally enjoy it, or if we feel we have to be alone to get our work done. How we feel about being alone is really important – much more important than the real-life facts about our solitude are to our brains. Chronic *perceived* social isolation is as dangerous to mental and physical health as *actual* social isolation.[15]

Although that sounds dire, it's really not, because knowing

this gives us a solution: reframing how we think and feel about being alone is enough to nudge ourselves into feeling better about it.

That might not be easy, but it's worth it. For me, working alone has contributed to periods of desperate loneliness, when I felt that no one understood how hard I had to work, or the pressures I was under, financially and emotionally. (It's how I came to write this book; if I felt it, surely others felt it too.) In retrospect I wasn't emotionally, socially nor physically isolated. But my feelings were very, very real, and so was my sense that I was trapped in my loneliness, when in reality, I was surrounded by other people, either geographically (in London), or digitally. People who were working in the same way and experiencing the same things, and who were available and willing to support me. I didn't know they were there at the time, but they were. (For more on creating support networks, see chapter 15.)

If loneliness is about how isolated we perceive ourselves to be, and how sad that makes us feel, then could we argue ourselves out of feeling lonely by assessing how *actually* isolated we are? Our work doesn't exist in an empty vacuum – unless you are a potter who has chosen to live in the Outer Hebrides, in which case you probably chose that level of isolation because you want and like it. You might think of yourself as alone in your work, but are you? It's common for freelancers and soloists to perceive themselves as more alone than they are, and it's a hole I've often fallen down. But every bit of work you or I do happens because of a web of other people.

Plumbers have suppliers. Painters have gallerists, agents, assistants. Novelists have proofreaders, copy-editors and publishers. Garden designers have builders, stone masons, plant suppliers. Decorators need shops to buy paint and brushes.

Drivers have passengers. Almost all of us, one way or another – jewellers, web designers, milliners, private chefs, administration assistants, social media managers, life coaches – have clients and colleagues.

In my work life there are editors and publishers, interviewees, photographers, proofreaders, press officers and other writers. Less obviously there is also a virtual assistant who does some of my research and transcribing, my accountant, a bookkeeper who chases my invoices, a cleaner, the nursery which looks after my youngest child and the childminder who has my eldest. I may be alone a lot of the time, but I am part of an enormous, nebulous, growing team. Repeatedly telling ourselves that because we work by ourselves, we are alone, does no good.

The image of a solitary genius isn't truthful. Although inventions and ideas are often named after one person, they rarely come about without the help of a large supporting cast, often unnamed and unsung. Thomas Edison, inventor of the light bulb, is easy to picture alone in a Victorian workshop, but he had a team of at least 30 people working with him. Charles Darwin may have done much of his writing alone (although even then he was married, had children, and frequent visitors), but the research voyage which kicked off his work on evolution meant spending five years on the *Beagle*, a 28-metre ship holding 68 people – it was so crowded Darwin had to sleep in a hammock hanging over a drafting table. Even Einstein, perhaps the most famous (apparently) lone genius, wasn't a loner at all, and had a valued network of friends and colleagues, like Michele Brasso, Marcel Grossman, Adriaan Fokker and Gunnar Nordström, who all contributed to his eventual general theory of relativity.[16]

Like Einstein, soloists are rarely lone wolves, and thinking of ourselves as such just ramps up our levels of perceived isolation. None of the solo workers you know in real life work are truly alone – for every entrepreneur you see on a stage winning an award, or speaking on a panel, there are dozens of people in the background who've helped that person appear (alone) in front of you. They are not doing it by themselves, and you don't have to either. As the author of *The Gig Economy*, Diane Mulcahy put it to me, 'I think this is one of the most damaging perceptions. Don't be a hero. You can't do this all by yourself.' She has what she calls 'team talks' whenever she meets other independent workers, to constantly reaffirm how interconnected this way of working is. 'Who do you have around you? Who's on your team? Who are you adding? Who have you added recently? Who do you need?'

The television explorer, writer and photographer Levison Wood concurs. I assumed – because he does things like walk the length of the Nile by himself – that he would often be alone. But he's not. 'The important thing for me is to have a team. You have to make sure you have the right people on board, because you can't do everything yourself. You've got to learn to delegate.'

Reduction

Taking a break from work and being around other people can prevent loneliness and mitigate it when it does happen. You might feel as though getting your head down and cracking on with your work, every day, is the best way to get as much done as possible – it's a completely normal point of view to have, and it's how most of us feel about work. Unfortunately, it's also completely wrong. As we'll get into a bit later, working long hours, especially without breaks, slows and then ultimately reverses our productivity. Leaving our work behind, getting outside and ideally into nature, recalibrates our ability to focus. Taking breaks and getting out into the world – which is usually full of other people – has even more value than just helping to curb loneliness.

Many of the small jobs which would have previously dragged us from our work are now do-able on apps or online. This is a problem, because the loneliness-curbing power of even small social interactions in real life is huge. One famous study from the positive psychology world is by Ed Diener and Martin Seligman – they figured out back in 2002 that the happiest people, in general, just spend more time around other people than the rest of us.[17] The really fascinating thing? You don't have to know, or even speak to other people in order to get some of the benefits.[18] Happiness researchers started further research into whether other people make us happier by looking at what happened when study subjects were made to talk to a barista they didn't know in a coffee shop (result: they left in a good mood).[19] But further research showed that even just making eye contact with other people, even total strangers we pass on the street, can make us feel connected.[20] (An odd side note to this research – people are really bad at remembering how good this kind of socialising makes us feel, and behave as though it would be preferable to avoid it, especially in situations involving strangers.[21] This is especially true in the UK where we behave as though we would rather die than speak to someone else on public transport. I recently watched an artist doing sketches on postcards and handing them out on a train. She had brief chats as she handed them out and everyone seemed overjoyed to receive her work – it was clearly something she did all the time, and she told them she does it all over the world. And yet. I still felt glad that I was half a carriage away, and wouldn't have to get involved.)

Soloists are particularly vulnerable to tech-induced loneliness. Soloists who run their businesses from their phones, using email and messaging, app-based banking and accounting software, easily get sucked in – how many times have you picked up your phone to pay an invoice, only to find yourself numbly scrolling through social media half an hour later? And how many times have you justified that to yourself by saying you're doing social media management and online marketing, so it's OK? I so often adopt the latest bits of technology which apparently make my life easier, without ever thinking about what the associated costs might be. It's not only that using apps and websites means I'm on my phone more than ever, but also it cuts down my already rare opportunities for human contact.

The nicest way to spend a break from work would be a leisurely and delicious lunch with a friend in a restaurant, or playing tennis with someone you know well, in the sunshine. But since those opportunities are usually thin on the ground, let's settle for more mundane ways to reduce the amount of time we spend alone. Going to a real-life shop to buy stationery instead of ordering it online. Having a swim at the local pool or taking a lunchtime break in a park. Chatting briefly to a neighbour as they pass, instead of rushing to get to your desk. Each small interaction builds into a more socially connected life.

You may live and work somewhere too remote to make this straightforward; you may find breaking from work partway through the day hard to even consider. If that's the case, then it's even more important for you to create or maintain other social ties. If your days have to be spent completely alone, then you need to invest energy into other relationships. We all need – to a greater or lesser extent – relationships to act like scaffolding around us, holding us together, helping with repairs. If it feels like you don't have time for such things, hold this in mind: loneliness is bad for your body, your brain and your business.

Practice

Over time, I have got better at seeing my own solitude more clearly, and better at being alone without being lonely. Today, solitude, and its accompanying silence, isn't something I just tolerate, and about three-quarters of the time, solitude and I can sit together, calmly. But that is something I had to learn to do. This is because to get at any of the potential benefits of solitude – Susan Cain's 'catalyst for innovation' – we have to learn how to be comfortable being by ourselves. The influential psychoanalyst Donald Winnicott wrote widely about what he called 'the capacity to be alone' and who does and doesn't have it, arguing back in the late 1950s that anyone who has developed the capacity to be alone, is never truly alone.

Anna Blackwell is a 26-year-old explorer and public speaker who has taken a year off from her regular solo expeditions to complete a master's degree exploring the effect of the natural environment on our brains and well-being (her first degree is in psychology). Last summer, she spent five weeks alone, trekking through the Swedish Arctic. She believes that we can train ourselves to enjoy solitude and develop our capacity to be alone.

'I had been building up to it,' she says of her year-long trek in 2019. 'On my first couple of long trips, I went solo but had

41

a lot of exposure to people along the way. By easing myself into it, I got used to spending a lot of time by myself and in my own head, but then had the opportunity to talk to people along the way.' By last summer she was comfortable being by herself. 'I was going five or six days at a time without seeing any people whatsoever. I knew that I'd get on well enough with myself. That might seem like a strange thing to say, but I think I'm an alright person, and that means that I can go off for that amount of time without getting too much into my own head and driving myself insane.'

Is the trick to start with little and often then? 'Do it in small chunks to start with, and also work out what the things are that might set you off on a negative spiral. Note when you're more vulnerable. One of the big risks of being by yourself is getting into a negative headspace, and then it can be a struggle to get out of it. One of the easiest ways would be to go and hang out with other people, but if you don't have that option, then you need strategies to pull yourself out or protect yourself against getting into those headspaces. I know that if I'm tired and hungry, for example, I am much more prone to being grumpy, and questioning why on earth did I bother to go on this trip? Now, I know that as soon as I have started to have those thoughts, I need to eat something. Then I take a moment to say, "I'm choosing to put myself into this situation. I want to do it, maybe not in this minute, but I do want to do it." And I know that once the food kicks in my perspective will change again – so it's about not letting myself put too much weight on those thoughts.'

Her advice applies whether you are sitting at a desk in a room on your own, or hiking in the Arctic. We can all get better at solitude if we practise it, thoughtfully and, if possible, gradually, looking for the moments when it feels the worst and unpicking what causes them. Few of us will ever need to spend six or seven days completely alone, as Anna does, but training ourselves for solitude is just as important. Start with a half-hour walk by yourself, or take yourself out for lunch alone. Gradually increase the time you spend alone until you can handle a couple of hours in one go. Accept the fact that you, like most people, might find being alone hard, but that it will get easier.

Do you have triggers which make you feel worse about being alone? They might be things like spending too much time alone, getting too little exercise, not enough daylight and fresh air, not eating or drinking enough, not having enough stuff going on in your life outside work, or having too much stuff going on outside work (if you're having to deal with emotional, family or financial issues that have nothing to do with work). For those of us at the mercy of hormones, their rise and fall can really mess with your solo head, too.

By figuring out what pushes us into a negative spot when we're working alone, grabbing the problem by the metaphorical shoulders and staring it down, we can think more clearly about how to get past it (or with hormones, endure and wait for them to pass). Sometimes, just knowing what's set you off is enough to override it: being able to say to ourselves, here it is again, but I know what the problem is and where it came from and that it will go away. The writer Elizabeth Gilbert talked about doing something similar with the fear that she says goes hand-in-hand with her creative work, on NPR's *TED Radio Hour* podcast. She created an image which has stuck with me: 'What I've had to figure out how to do over the years is to create a sort of mental construct, in which I make a lot of space to coexist with fear, to just say to it, "Hey fear. Listen, creativity – your twin sister – and I are about to go on a road trip. I understand you'll be joining us because you always do. You don't get to decide anything about this journey that we're going on, but you can come. I know that you'll be in the backseat in panic, but we are going anyway".'

I think 'we are going anyway' has great power. Whatever the feeling is – loneliness, fear, inadequacy – sometimes the best thing is to say, OK, I see you're here again, but *we are going anyway*. It's certainly not an easy thing to do, but in the long run it's a lot easier than spending a long work day staring into space, on your own, paralysed by negative thoughts.

Appreciation

Solitude is incredibly precious. It has the potential to make us more creative – and creativity is good for all of us, regardless of the job we do. Creativity is about problem-solving, idea-generating, new thinking. It's not just about whether you can draw a picture or make a quilt. Studies show that solitude can actually facilitate creativity in a number of ways, partly by lowering our inhibitions – we are less self-conscious when nobody is watching. Other studies show that extended periods of solitude can increase our feelings of self-reliance, intensify our ability to become deeply involved in a task, aka absorption, and that it can encourage measurably more fluid and imaginative thought.[22, 23]

Anna Blackwell is living proof of this. 'I wanted to see how I would cope with a prolonged period in a very remote wild barren landscape,' she tells me from Cornwall, where she is studying. 'And how I would deal with that emotionally and mentally. I discovered that I absolutely loved it, and I really thrived in that sort of situation. It was the most freeing and creative period I have ever had. I was writing about the trip as I walked, and immediately, as soon as I woke up every day I would have all these words in my brain. Although I'd always loved writing, that was something that I hadn't experienced before.'

What was it that worked on her so powerfully? 'I think it was a combination of different things. Part of it was being an environment that I find inspirational. I'm very moved by the environment around me, even if that is just patterns that the sun is making on the ground's surface through the leaves; I can be blown away that.' Did she feel less self-conscious because there was no one there to watch or judge? 'Yes! Disinhibited, definitely.'

That lack of other people was just as key as the environment. 'Not having people around gives you the opportunity to pay more attention to what's going on around you, because you're not focusing on making conversation with the person next to you or listening to them, or noticing what they're doing. Part of the brain does completely shut off and I could tell that was happening: there are days where I have very few memories from the trek because my brain had just gone somewhere else. But then there were other days where it was as though my senses were heightened, because I hadn't seen anyone in a couple of days or had any sort of interaction.'

Blackwell had chosen to remove herself from other people; she was alone, but didn't perceive herself as isolated. Because solitude was something she could enjoy and make huge creative gains in, it wasn't frightening (even when she got stung by a hornet and nearly had to have a finger amputated. Even then).

Alexandra Dariescu is a world-famous concert pianist, who travels the world giving solo recitals. 'I just do concerts for a living,' she tells me. 'I don't teach; the main thing I do is perform. And as a pianist, I am always alone. I practise alone. I travel alone. If I do a recital, I just see the promoter for a few minutes before the recital. And then I perform and that's it. If I play with orchestras it is nicer because there are people involved at least in the rehearsal process, which is usually the day before or on the day of the performance, so even then there's not a lot of rehearsing together. I would say, 90 per cent of my work is alone.' This level of solitude could be extremely isolating. 'When you're alone on tour, and you give everything on stage but then you have no one to go out for dinner with afterwards, you're completely alone in your hotel room, there's no more room service because the hotel doesn't serve it, and you're starving ... it can be crushing.' Dariescu quickly realised she needed to find a way around it.

'Very early in my career, I had an experience which made me change things. I had just finished a concert for a music society in a small town, and I went backstage to find there was absolutely no one there, and almost all the lights were off. The promoter wasn't there; nobody. I knew I had to walk at least 20 minutes on my own to my hotel room, because it was a small town and there were no taxis, and I just thought, oh god, this is dreadful.' Her fight-or-flight response fortunately kicked in. 'You go into this "feeling-sorry-for-yourself" or you do something about it,' she said. Instead of staying in the shadows backstage, she immediately found her way out and to the front doors of the theatre.

'People were leaving the concert so I started thanking them, "Thank you so much for coming. Thank you for coming". People started talking to me and all of the sudden, instead of feeling really, really down, I felt uplifted. Suddenly I had a whole community of people around me. That was the starting point of me, always, always going out after concerts to say thank you for coming, whether I play with big orchestras or in tiny little venues. I really consider this therapy. It has helped me enormously.'

It wasn't just the sense of community. 'Hearing people say things like, "I had the most horrendous day. And your performance has really uplifted me." Someone else said they had never been to a piano recital before and had never thought it would be so enjoyable. When you hear things like that, you feel that you're making a difference in people's lives.'

Even though she spends just 10 minutes saying thank you at the end of a concert, it's enough to get her through the evening and beyond. 'It puts me in such a great mood that I am absolutely fine to go to my hotel room and watch TV, instead of feeling alone and miserable. It's about my perception – because at the end of the day I am still alone. But I am in such a good mood and I have that positive energy from everyone that everything seems better.' And the rest of the time, the remaining 90 per cent of her work time, when she's alone, she still holds the audience in mind. 'I treasure the audience the most because they're the ones that make me be a performer. Otherwise I would just be performing for my chairs.'

If Dariescu doesn't go and meet her audience after her concerts, she runs the risk of her job feeling like it has no relationship to anybody. She needs her work to mean something to someone else, in order for it to mean something to her; she needs to feel like there's a connection between the music that she makes and her audience. Only then can she appreciate solitude for what it gives both her and her audience.

Solitude is far, far more bearable when it's meaningful. If the work you are doing while you are alone has meaning

47

for you, then that nasty inner critic has less to shout about and we feel less socially or physically isolated. There are a lot of different views about what makes work meaningful and how to figure what meaningful work is for you (see chapter 4), but the TED-talking organisational psychologist Adam Grant puts it this way: 'At the heart of meaningful work is the belief that your job makes other people's lives better. When that belief gets shaken, ask, "'Who would be worse off if my job didn't exist?" The names you generate are the reason your work matters.'

Appreciating what we can do in solitude, and what solitude can do for us, is a powerful way to make sure there's no room in it for loneliness.

4

What is Meaningful Work?

Before we try and get to grips with the idea of meaning-ful work, I first want to say this: you don't *have* to find your work meaningful. If you are quite happy doing your thing, or even if you hate your job but really aren't bothered by that (perhaps because it affords you something else of far greater value to you, like more time with your family, or the chance to be in a city you've always dreamed of living in, or that you can go paragliding every evening), then that is more than fine. Not everyone takes meaning from their work. It's not compulsory. And in many ways, finding meaning elsewhere in your life is far healthier and desirable than the modern trope that work gives us most of our value as people.

There is one great thing about having meaningful work though. It gives you the intrinsic motivation to keep on doing it. Since our careers are going to be longer than ever, we might as well enjoy them. Being intrinsically motivated means you aren't solely doing it for cash, status or rewards. We will see how powerful that is later, when we talk more about money and how it messes with our brains, but there is a big difference between being intrinsically motivated to do something because it feels right or good to do it, and being solely extrinsically motivated by outside factors, like a pay cheque. Purpose reminds us that we are part of something bigger – the focus is not just on us, our capabilities or inadequacies, which relieves us of our normal, human tendency to look inwards.

Thinking about this stuff is a pretty luxurious position to be in. Most people worldwide work just to pay the bills, because they have to. Not having work at all can make life feel meaningless. That doesn't mean we should feel guilty for pursuing meaningful work – I think it should be something everyone has the right to experience. The stats are depressing: in North America the research shows that 30–50 per cent of people are profoundly dissatisfied with their working lives.[1] In 2017 Gallup did research in 160 countries that found 85 per cent of the world's one billion full-time workers are dissatisfied with their working lives, and part of this must be about a lack of meaning.[2] Work shouldn't be something you have to grit your teeth and endure. (But that still doesn't mean you have to chase meaning, if you don't want to.)

As a solo worker, you are more likely to find your work meaningful already, but it's certainly not a given. Being a solo worker doesn't necessarily mean you're doing your dream job, but that's the assumption which is often made about us, and one we often make about the other soloists around us. But being solo doesn't automatically mean you're doing something deeply fulfilling, and it doesn't automatically mean you absolutely love what you do, even if it looks from the outside as though you 'should'. It's easy to get in a tangle about what meaningful work might look like for you – especially given that when you're solo, there can be a feeling of infinite – and therefore paralysing – choice. For some soloists, it's easier because a few of the right ingredients are in the mix, like autonomy, but for others it's no more autonomous than any other kind of work.

What is Meaningful Work?

When I talk about all this with Tom Morin it's minus 37 degrees Celsius outside his house. It's 8.30am and he's at home in western Canada in the depths of winter. We joke about how much nicer it would be to be in a London tea shop, rather than video calling. We chat about the weather, and I have no idea that Morin is about to give me the beginnings of an answer to one of the central questions of this book, one I've been struggling to get my head around. The topic of meaningful work has come up again and again in my research, but all too often all I read was 'try to find meaningful work', or 'workers are happier/more productive/more creative/less absent if they find their work meaningful', or 'look for meaning in your work'. Which has led to me scribbling HOW? in the margins of an awful lot of books.

When we speak, Morin is just about to publish his first book, *Your Best Work*, based on his years of experience as a business coach and speaker. His schtick is all about how to find meaningful work – it's what he's based his highly respected coaching practice on, and what big organisations and leadership conferences ask him to speak about. But Morin is no ordinary coach. He didn't step neatly from the corporate world into coaching. Morin has nearly died at work. Twice. In two different jobs, both of which he thought of at the time as meaningful.

As a young man, Morin joined the Canadian military, which took him to the conflict in the former Yugoslavia. While on duty, his unit was violently shelled, and as Morin puts it, the first thing he thought once they got the all clear was that he needed to get another job. His next role was on an oil rig in northern Canada – also a job where he felt the hard graft and team environment was meaningful. He wasn't safe there either, and was nearly cut in half when another worker accidentally dropped a tonne of steel equipment onto the pipe where Morin was working. Understandably, Morin left that job too, went back to college, and then started a corporate career. He found it physically safer, leading teams and project-managing for multinationals, but it didn't fulfil him like his earlier, more hazardous work, so he pursued a meaningful hobby instead: mountaineering. No prizes for guessing what happened next: in a single summer he suffered terrible hallucinations and breathing difficulties at 18,000 feet on a mountain in Peru, then just weeks later had to be rescued from a mountain in France.

At this point, with mountain climbing off the cards, and a burning need to leave his corporate job behind in the pursuit of something more meaningful, Morin went back to school again, completed graduate studies in social science and executive coaching, and started his own practice. He has spent the last 13 years thinking about meaning at work.

'Dissatisfaction with our working lives often comes from a lack of meaning,' he says, and there is plenty of data on this. 'But meaning is a thing developed by humans,' he tells me. 'It's a social construct. I always ask people, "What is meaningful work?" And they start reciting certain jobs. And I say, "No, no, no. Don't give me a list of jobs. Tell me what meaningful is". We use "meaningful work" as a kind of noun. Google "list of meaningful jobs" and up will come a list of 10 or even 20 jobs that are considered meaningful. Nursing, charity work, medicine and so on. That's fantastic, but what if I don't like any of those jobs? Does that mean I'm never going to find meaningful work?'

As he says this, I'm suddenly transported back to being about 15. I was a bright kid and expectations were high for me. My parents were social workers, and so were most of their friends (those that weren't were probation officers, teachers, therapists, librarians or academics – they overwhelmingly worked in the public sector). My sister and I were surrounded by grown-ups whose work measurably improved other people's lives. Looking back I'm not sure all of them enjoyed their jobs, for all sorts of reasons, but we grew up implicitly understanding work as something you do in the service of other people's welfare, as a public good and not necessarily something that brought you personal joy, because we really didn't know anyone else who worked in any other way. I was socialised into a very particular understanding of what meaningful work should be.

So when it came to choosing what I would do with my life (as if that's a decision a 15-year-old can or should make), I went for the grandest version of public service I could imagine: I would work for the United Nations. Most of what I spent my time doing over the next five years was in pursuit of this idea. I did everything I could to create a near-perfect university application form – taking five A-level qualifications instead of the usual three (which resulted in lower grades than if I'd taken a more sensible number); being voted onto the student council; attending a schools version of the model United Nations and taking the role of Secretary General; teaching gymnastics and sports camps at the weekends and in the holidays; getting extra tuition in French. I did anything I thought would make me look like a cookie-cutter high achiever, so that the London School of Economics would take me in to study International Relations, after which I would slide right into a job at the United Nations. In New York, hopefully, but Geneva would be OK, if necessary.

God, it was boring. And exhausting. I constantly did things I didn't particularly want to do, but thought I should.

(Not that I would ever, ever admit that. My boyfriend at the time constantly teased me for my entrance-form obsession, which I found infuriating. Because he was right.) Although I was in a privileged position, I was highly strung, and highly stressed, and got anxiety-related irritable bowel syndrome in the middle of it all. And when I finally, finally – after being wait-listed for five excruciating months – made it onto the course at LSE ... it was shatteringly dull. Devastatingly so.

I can only confess it now. I was so hell-bent on doing meaningful (but also impressive) work that I made a load of really important, *really* expensive decisions based on a socially constructed idea of meaningfulness, an idea I'd pieced together watching my parents and their friends. The problem is, I'm not interested in how governments and non-governmental organisations interact. I don't really care about the differences between the political theories of Hobbes, Locke and Hume. The politics of international economic relations course confused me so entirely that I was sent to remedial economics lessons in my lunch hour.

(There were bits I enjoyed: international law, especially about migration and refugees, was fascinating; so was reconciliation and justice after conflict. Modern international history was like reading an endlessly unfolding thriller; I took a wild-card year-long course in social anthropology and I loved that too. I made good friends and kissed some boys. I'm proud to have an LSE degree.) Attending was a privilege.

I graduated to discover that no, the UN did not want me. Nor did any intergovernmental or non-governmental organisations. Nor international charities. Nor, desperate now, UK-based charities or think tanks. I never even got selected for an interview. My applications must have been riddled with reticence, or something else which shouted loudly about my unsuitability, my lack of genuine interest and commitment. And if the UN had taken me on? I would have hated it.

Somehow, what Morin is explaining to me scratches away at this experience. It rushes back to me, and I have to tell him about it.

'For every job out there, there is someone who finds that job meaningful,' he replies. 'But the fact is, there are probably many people who would say, "Oh, my God. Working at the UN would be the worst job in the world". We know there are people working at the UN who find their job deeply meaningful, but statistically we also know that there will be some people working at the UN who are deeply dissatisfied with their jobs.' His point is, it's not the job in and of itself which has the meaning. I didn't, couldn't understand this when I was 15. Meaning is or isn't experienced by the person doing the job. It doesn't exist independently – it's only in our heads. We think of public sector jobs like nursing or teaching as being meaningful, for example, but because meaning is a construction, an idea we have created and attached to certain things, any work can potentially be meaningful, if that's you feel about it.

'I always tell people, if you're looking for meaningful work, there's really no such thing,' says Morin. 'Whether it's the meaning of being a good parent, the meaning of winning an Olympic gold medal, the meaning of having the biggest collection of cookie tins in your garage, the meaning of becoming a CEO, or being the best gardener. All meaning is made up. And that is a bit of a dark spot,' he adds, with a wry smile. 'The idea of living in a universe with no meaning is impossible for humans,' says Morin. 'We're always going to construct something. [Cultures] provide an orderly view of the universe and a way for us to be valued within that orderly view,' says Tom. 'One of those cultures is called work. We invented this system of commerce. We invented this way to participate in it.'

See how it feels to accept the idea that meaning is something different cultures create, and that therefore it's not an objective, binary thing. No single activity is any more meaningful than any other. In the abstract, nothing is meaningful. Or everything is.

That doesn't make meaning any less real, and the data is still clear – meaningful work gives people more satisfaction than work they don't find meaningful. It also doesn't mean you could find any job meaningful – you are still you, with your particular skills, priorities and interests. And as I experienced, you can't force meaning onto something where it doesn't fit, for you.

'I ask people just to realise that all jobs are equal,' says Morin. '*Your* meaningful work is the work you still want to do, in the face of that equal meaninglessness.' His experience is that most people, having got to grips with this quite confounding idea that everything is equally meaningless or meaningful, can say, 'I recognise that work is all kind of the same, but I still want to be a CEO'. Or 'I still want to be a writer'. They can say, 'I know that technically the person processing driving licences has a job that is equally meaningful as the person who's weeding that garden. But I only want to do one of them'.

But how does this help us figure out what meaningful work looks like for us as soloists? 'If we can see that we're taught meaning by our culture, that we are taught [our beliefs about] which work is meaningful, if we can cut through that as best we can, then our authentic, meaningful work will eventually bubble up,' says Morin. 'It happened for me, in the end. I love speaking, I love writing. I love helping people with leadership. I've found my role. But somebody else [using this way of thinking] might say, "Well, I decided to open a portrait photography business, but I just realised that's not really what I want to do. I was socialised into doing it. My mother was a photographer. I had all these cousins who used to take me to fashion shows and I was socialised to believe this job is meaningful. But now I'm doing it, I don't like it.'"

Having that knowledge might be painful, but it's also powerful and potentially liberating. If you dislike some or all of your job, especially if it's a job you feel that you are *supposed* to love, then knowing both why you feel that way, and that it's OK to feel that way, is incredibly reassuring.

Instead of wandering about in a fog of unhappiness with no obvious way out or through it, you can start to think more clearly, and make some reasoned, perhaps hard choices. Armed with this knowledge, you can start to make changes – not necessarily massive close-down-the-studio-and-take-up-windsurfing type changes, but perhaps the sort which could bend your work in a direction you find more satisfying. And if you can't make changes right now you can start to plan for changes further down the line.

Fifteen-year-old me had been socially conditioned to think about my future by two quite overwhelming sets of ideas. At my very ordinary comprehensive school, I was taught to believe that I was exceptional and whatever I did next would be exceptional. (There are loads of reasons why this kind of thing is bad for people, and it was very, very bad for me.)

At the same time, my parents and their friends were unwittingly teaching me that work was something that should be done as public service. So my 15-year-old assumption was that I should do something exceptional in public service. If I had been able to peel away the onion, and see that all those layers of meaning had not come from me but from outside me, then I probably wouldn't have found myself sitting in the first course of the first year at the London School of Economics, in a lecture on basic political theory, looking around the room and thinking, shit, *what am I doing here?*

With a bit of luck I may have another 20–30 years of work ahead of me. At 39 years old, I might not be even halfway through my career. I want to be able to make decisions about the work I do, and in fact, the way I live, that are based on what I actually believe to be meaningful, rather than those onion layers of meaning that culture, society and family have piled on top of me.

No job is inherently meaningful – not nursing, not medicine, not charity work. We cannot force ourselves to find meaning in work which isn't meaningful for us as individuals – I would be a terrible, terrified doctor; I would be a miserable human rights lawyer. Such jobs have enormous value, but the people who do them well and take satisfaction from those jobs, love their jobs – they don't endure them. You can't fake that.

You can't hold meaning in your hand. It's not a thing. It doesn't have constancy. It varies from person to person. It's subjective. What has meaning for your parents will be different to what has meaning for you. Things which are meaningful for your next-door neighbours won't have meaning for you.

For my parents, public service work was deeply, deeply important. I don't feel the same way, perhaps that's because I saw the pressure and the strain that public service work put on them. My dad's work had to do with child protection in contexts where children were being abused or neglected, and my mum's involved supporting incredibly vulnerable children and adults. Later, she worked on research projects looking at things like the impact of abuse, or drug-addicted parents, on children. They were constantly exposed to all the harmful ways in which families can fracture and fold in and destroy themselves. Their work was never going to be my meaningful work, probably because I could see how harrowing and troubling it was. None the less, I absorbed the idea of public service, practically from birth.

No one else can tell us what our meaningful work is. Talking to the renowned wine writer Victoria Moore, I happened to mention that I was researching this chapter. And she said, 'I'm not sure I've figured out what meaningful work is for me yet'. And I started to say, 'That's pretty surprising because I would have thought you ...' And then I realised what I was doing. Just because she has a job which I have admired for years, and envied even, just because she appears to be happily successful – even though I didn't know her at all – I had assumed that what she was doing felt meaningful to her. I immediately imposed my idea of what meaningful work was onto her life. Which is crazy, because I have no idea what her life looks like on the inside. How can I possibly know what meaning would look like for her?

I can't know what your meaningful work is. (Be wary of anyone who tells you that they do.) If you feel that you need to find out what your version of meaningful work is, the very first thing to do is sit down and figure out with yourself what you've been *told* is meaningful and what *actually* is meaningful for you.

Meaningful work is simultaneously a luxury and a right. Not all of us get to do meaningful work, and not even a meaningful job will feel full of purpose all the time. Sometimes we do the jobs we do because we just need the money, and for many, it will never feel possible to pursue meaningful work. So in that sense, let's not drive ourselves crazy if our solo work doesn't *always* feel meaningful. Perhaps we can aim for work that just feels meaningful some of the time, if possible.

For a couple of years after I left LSE, it felt like nobody would ever employ me to do anything except wait tables, a job which had started as a way to earn money during university holidays. I was pretty good at it. I even ended up assistant-managing a restaurant. Hospitality is full of people who love their jobs, but front-of-house wasn't my meaningful, which was what – along with cleaning the loos and working until 2am – made it so hard. The longer I did it, the more stuck I got. At the time (which coincided with the UN and every other international organisation not wanting me) it was the one place in my life where I was praised and could excel, unlike the endless job and internship applications I was apparently hurling into a silent void. I'd like to be able to write that I finally came to the smart conclusion that I had to leave hospitality and do something I really liked, but in fact it all came to an end when a more senior member of staff got drunk and was so insanely, revoltingly rude to me that I refused to go back to work for him after that shift had ended.

The bandage had been torn off, but that wasn't the end of the story. It took a lot longer – and a master's degree in International Peace and Security which I have never actually used – to abandon the UN idea. After a lot of unpaid work experience, I ultimately got a job on a national newspaper, which felt closer to my version of meaningful but was still partly driven by a need to meet those early expectations set at school: that I would do something impressive, and visibly so. I have now been a writer for more than 15 years, and freelance for 11, but I haven't always written about things I really cared about. I always cared about the writing itself, and doing the job well, but not always about the topic. I grappled with how that made me feel: I knew I was incredibly lucky to be paid to write anything at all and sometimes I really disliked myself for feeling so dissatisfied, for my lack of gratitude. I'm not sure people around me found it all that bearable, either. There was a lot for me to learn: that sometimes, at the beginning of your career, you have to do bits of work you don't love, in the hope that it leads to work you do. That it can take years to fall in love with the work you do have. That the process of becoming good at what you do can make you love it. And that you and you alone can craft your job into what you want it to be.

It took years to work out that the only person who could help me write about things I care about was me. This book has more meaning than any work I've done before because – I hope – it has a chance of helping people. Perhaps that makes it, finally, my very own version of public service.

*

At the end of the last chapter I mentioned Adam Grant. His TED podcast on, as he puts it, 'how to make work not suck', is brilliant, as is his writing. I am somewhat underqualified to quibble with his theories. He is, after all, an organisational psychologist at Wharton with more than 300,000 Twitter followers, and I am a journalist with a mischosen postgrad under my belt. Anyway, here goes.

Grant suggests that one of the best ways to find meaningful work is to find meaning in the work that you already have. On first reading – and still in pursuit of a way to work out what meaningful work even is – I thought this was spot on.

And up to a point, it is. If you can look around your current solo work and see ways to make it feel meaningful to you, then that's a huge win. It's an extremely worthwhile thing to attempt if changing your solo work is financially or circumstantially impossible – if you're gritting your teeth through a recession, for example, or if existing responsibilities, bills and debts make gambling on a new venture too understandably daunting to contemplate.

An example from my life: my husband and I run a photography studio, and recently, at weekends when it's usually empty, we've started inviting local businesses, like florists or photographers who wouldn't otherwise be able to afford a studio for a whole day, to use it for a few hours, for free. (In return, they mention the studio in a few social media posts.) I had no idea how profoundly this would affect how I feel about the studio. It was really Steve's dream to have a studio, but after a year or so running it on his own it became clear that he needed help, and that I had skills which would be useful. But until recently, even though it makes money for our family, I haven't felt particularly connected to it. If I'm really honest I've sometimes resented the time managing it has taken away from my own work. Today, though, we are giving people in our local community the opportunity to do something they probably couldn't afford to do anywhere else, and that makes them happy, which makes me happy.

Grant is right. If you can find meaning in a job that you're currently doing then that really will elevate how you feel about it.

To do this, sit down with a pen and paper (or better yet with someone whose views you respect, but who isn't so close that disagreement will hurt you or them) and think about the aspects of your solo work which you feel best about. Not which you do the best, but which make you feel the best. They don't have to be things which serve other people, although they might be, directly or indirectly. Make a list. Then examine whether one or two of those activities or skills (if you have that many) could be turned into a bigger part of your working life. When talking about employees, this process is known as job-crafting, a process and theory elaborated by Amy Wrzesniewski, Justin M. Berg, and Jane E. Dutton in the early 2000s.[3] The tools they suggest are just as applicable to soloists who are looking for more meaning in their work.

They divide the job-crafting process into three parts, which I'm simplifying here. First, the focus is on tasks: what tasks could you do more of, or do less of, to make your job more loveable? So a freelance PR consultant who wants to do more events management might look for clients about to launch a new product which would require a party. A set builder who wants to do more prop styling on photo shoots could offer herself as an assistant to a more experienced stylist, to begin building a portfolio. Alternatively you can change the way you do certain tasks – you could design a more efficient system to do something you find tedious, or outsource it, or batch it (do all the least pleasurable tasks at the same time so they're not forever hanging over you). The apparently minor act of figuring out a way to outsource my invoicing ten years ago, totally changed the way I viewed my job. I found invoicing and chasing overwhelming and it bothered me every day. By changing that one task, my whole job became more meaningful and enjoyable

The next thing they suggest looking at are the relationships which develop through your work. Could you make some of the most valuable ones into stronger relationships?

Or could you create mentoring relationships with people more technically junior than you, or less experienced? Could you leverage some of them better – without being fake or exploitative – to help you move your career in the direction that you want?

And finally, they refer back to Grant's policy of looking for meaning in what is already there, reframing the way we think about our work by looking for and accentuating the positives. This is kind of chicken-and-egg though – consciously crafting your job will almost certainly help you change the way you think about it.

Although job-craft theory is designed to help people in organisations, arguably soloists are even better placed to engage in a bit of crafting – it's not like our work lives are free of all restrictions, but for many of us, we aren't hemmed in by an existing organisational structure or an inflexible senior manager.

However. Job-crafting requires a certain amount of time, a fair amount of grit and the right circumstances. Not all of soloists can find meaning this way. Sometimes, despite all our best efforts, it will feel impossible to find meaning in a certain job. Grant's advice may be helpful for a lot of people, but I think it raises three potentially sticky questions, so I emailed him.

First, I asked him if I can't find meaning in my existing work, am I failing somehow – should I look harder and harder, even if I'm miserable? 'No!' he wrote. 'In the data I've gathered over 15 years, a lack of meaning is rarely a failure on the part of a person – it's a failure in the design of a job and/or the leadership of an organisation … meaning is hard to find if a job doesn't have a significant impact on others, [workers] have little contact with the beneficiaries of their work, or their manager fails to articulate the purpose of their work.'[4]

To be fair, Grant's focus is not on solo workers, but on organisations – he wasn't really talking to soloists. Most organisations include managers, and many soloists don't have a direct manager. None the less, Grant's point holds: since many of us are effectively our own managers, perhaps it's up to us to 'articulate the purpose' of our work, and keep ourselves connected with the beneficiaries of our work. Much like solitude can turn into loneliness if it feels as though what you do in your solitude doesn't benefit anyone else, so too can work feel meaningless if you don't get to experience how your work improves someone else's life. Think back to Alexandra Dariescu shaking hands with her audience as they leave the concert hall – the behavioural change she made was tiny, and didn't require her to do anything differently at work, day to day, but it profoundly changed the way she feels about her work, because it gives her purpose and connection.

But is looking for meaning in a job which doesn't have meaning for me just a way to trap me in the status quo? 'I'd say it depends on the person and the situation,' he replied. 'If it's important to you to experience work as a calling, you might want to look for it. If you're more content to see work as a job, it's more likely that your sense of meaning will come from other domains of your life.' Meaning doesn't have to come from the work we do, so whether you want to pursue it is up to every individual. Ideally though, surely no one should experience the darker flip side of this, in which they manage to convince themselves a horrible job is meaningful just because it does something meaningful, like paying the bills, or setting aside money for a child's future university education? We have to be careful that we don't trick ourselves into finding meaning where there is none.

My final question for Adam Grant: should I endlessly jump from job to job, in the hope that at some point I will find the one which is meaningful for me? 'If people are lacking meaning, it probably makes more sense to start with a smaller move of job-crafting. You can become an architect of your own job by adjusting your tasks and interactions to create more meaning.'

We all know people who are on a long-term, restless and never-ending quest to find the perfect job, and I think it's probably here where the waters get a bit muddy when it comes to meaningfulness. While being trapped in a job which isn't meaningful is horrible, so too is never being in a job long enough to discover whether it could be meaningful.

If you're lucky enough to have found meaningful work, that's an achievement, but for many of us, finding meaningful work is about a combination of trying to figure out what the right job would be, and then shaping that job so that it matches our needs as closely as possible; a process which can take a while. Pursuing meaning too hard, too fast, can be just as destructive as not having any meaning at all. Which probably means we need to settle for some meaning, some of the time.

The passion problem

How many times do you think you've heard someone say they were passionate about their work or their job? It gives me a bit of a shiver every time I do – and since I work with a lot of chefs, for whom passion is as compulsory as knife skills, I hear it a lot. There is, in work, a passion fashion. But saying you're passionate about your work shows a warped understanding of the word. (The Oxford English Dictionary's first definition of it is 'strong and barely controllable emotion'. Others include 'a state or outburst of strong emotion' and 'intense sexual love'. Not exactly office-appropriate.) And from a surviving-your-career-intact point of view? It's unhealthy. Like busy-ness and working long hours, we have glibly adopted the idea of passion right into the core of modern thinking about work – find your passion! Follow your passion! Discover your passion and get someone to pay you for it!

Well, no. I am not, in fact, passionate about writing. Or journalism. Or this book. Or writing about food (which is a big part of my job). I love it all. I'm deeply interested in my work and want very much to do it well. I know how lucky I am to have this job, but it's not my passion. I am not obsessed. In fact, I don't even know what my passion is. I don't think I have one. And that is 100 per cent, completely and utterly normal. Doesn't sound it though, does it? Because we've been led to believe that successful people are following their passions, and that therefore, the two things always go together.

They don't. Some successful people are intensely and overwhelmingly obsessed with their work (which when you put it like that, doesn't sound fun), but many, many others, are just very good at theirs. They like it enough, and find enough meaning and purpose in it, to carry on doing it, to persevere, until they are really very good at whatever they do. Along the way, they might become passionate about it too, but many didn't spend their childhoods dreaming about whatever their eventual career looks like. Getting to do what you wanted as a child is rare – and should be. I would be either a hairdresser or a mechanic. Work expert Cal Newport has written a whole book, called *So Good They Can't Ignore*

You, about why pursuing what he calls mastery, over following a passion, will lead to a happier, more satisfying work life. Other writers, like Angela Duckworth, suggest that discovering your passion can take years, which I think is almost the same thing – both are about taking the time to get really, really good at something. And when humans have learned to be very good at something, we tend to feel deep affection for and connection to whatever it is. If you want to call that passion, then fine. (In fact, in the academic literature, this is known as harmonious passion.)

Believing you should have a passion in the first place, follow it, and then get paid for it, creates a smog of muddled thinking. What if you – like me, and most people – don't have a passion? What if your passion (ice skating, the French horn, oil painting) is for something you enjoy but you're not that good at? What if it's impossible to make a living from it? What if you don't want to spoil your passion by dragging it into your work life?

Thinking you should follow a passion can send you down blind career alleys, and not having one can make you feel like a failure, like you're missing something.

You're not. In fact, people who do have a proper passion for their work may be at a disadvantage. If you're seen as passionate about your job, you're more likely to be exploited while doing it. It makes people think it's OK to ask you to work longer hours and over weekends, to take on demeaning tasks and ones not in your job description or brief, and to work unpaid. (This was found in a review of eight major studies by researchers at Duke University.[5]) Being exploitable is not in the interests of any soloist.

Those chefs who say they're passionate are expected and expect to work some of the most punishing hours of any profession, often in hot, windowless and occasionally even dangerous conditions. More than half report depression due to overwork, and a quarter say they drink to get through their shifts.[6] These things are not unrelated. Thinking of ourselves as passionate about our work blurs the line between work and not-work. If you love your work so much – or behave as though you do because that's what everyone else does – then why would you need time off? Why wouldn't you work those extra hours? It's your passion. It's practically not work at all!

That way, burnout lies. One of the few downsides of purpose-driven work (that is, meaningful work) is that it can make burnout more likely, by encouraging what's called obsessive passion (the academic opposite of harmonious) to bubble to the surface. It happens when we identify so strongly with our work that we can't find the dividing line between it and us (like Thomas Broughton as he launched Cubbitts), which leads to ever higher stress levels, lower resilience and much, much lower levels of general well-being, as well as a higher likelihood of proper, potentially career-altering burnout, and mental health problems like depression, anxiety and insomnia.[7] The more mission-driven the industry, the higher the risk is that burnout will lead as far as suicide – medicine has the highest suicide rate of any industry.

Glorifying passion at work isn't just etymologically ridiculous. It's also dangerous.

5

The Problem of Long Hours

There is an insidious idea about work and it's this: you are only as good as the hours you work. It's not true, and it's harmful, but still it persists. We are not meant to work this hard and this long. We've been sold a lie.

Understanding that overworking damages our ability to perform, excel and think creatively, is critical to making the most of our solo-working lives. How did we get to a point where long hours at work are how we judge our work? Knowing how this idea shoved itself into the centre of human life over the last few centuries, will help you let go of the idea itself. In turn, you will feel less pressured and panicked about work, which will enable you to do all the work you need to do in less time, and better. The practical solutions are in the second half of the book, but we need to know how we got here, first, and before we can work out how to get away.

Sometimes, I can almost feel time rushing through my fingers like sand, making a panicky lump rise up in my throat. And other times, it slows to an inescapable crawl. It's slippery fish, time. But what is not slippery are these two facts: hours spent at work are a terrible way to measure productivity, and working excessively long hours will harm you. Long hours should not be a badge of honour.

A Harvard study in 2017 suggested that lack of leisure

time is now a kind of status symbol, shown off on social media, particularly now that having loads of expensive stuff has become a less palatable way to brandish our money and status. Researchers found that fictional social media posts reflecting high levels of busy-ness made people think the fictional characters behind them were higher in social status and wealthier than characters whose made-up posts were about leisure, and more likely to be in demand among employers. As the author Anat Keinan says, 'When we talk about traditional conspicuous consumption, it's about consuming scarce and expensive things like jewellery or money or cars. But the new conspicuous consumption is about saying, I am the scarce resource, and therefore I am valuable'.[1] Perhaps this explains the popularity of products and services which broadcast our busy-ness, like part-prepped meal-delivery services for people who want to cook but don't have time to measure spices, or the seven-minute workout plan. Not only do we want to save time, but we want to appear busy for the status it confers.[2]

As the business and leadership expert, entrepreneur and TED-talker (11 million views and counting) Margaret Heffernan said to me, as she sees it, our over-commitment to working hours is not getting better. 'If anything it's got worse. The investors I work with work late every day and Sunday is spent preparing for the shit-storm that is going to be the next week. I think that's why we're seeing this explosion in mental health issues: everybody is working too late, too hard, too long, under too much pressure. They can't think but they're still at their desk. And I think it's as bad for freelancers as it is for people in ostensibly more secure jobs. The science says more hours doesn't equal more productivity. It never has; it never will. The brain is a physical instrument that is used for thinking and it's like everything else physical about you: it gets tired and it can get worn out.'

A 2017 study undertaken by the University of Lisbon showed a clear correlation between long working hours (defined as working more than 48 hours a week) and a subsequent lack of sleep or sleep disturbances.[3] Another followed 2,000 British civil servants for five years, and revealed that overwork (defined as 11-hour working days) led to a 2.5-fold increase in major depressive episodes, even in people with no mental health issues at the beginning of the study.[4] A third defined long working hours as anything over 40 per week, and showed links to depression, anxiety, sleep problem and heart disease, as well as general 'significant adverse effects on most health outcomes'.[5] It is such a major problem in Japan and South Korea that there is even a word for sudden death caused by overwork: *karoshi*.

If you're solo, you're at far greater risk of overwork because – unless you have a very persuasive partner or housemate – you are likely to have much lower barriers than workers in an organisation, whose long hours might (hopefully) be noticed, and (hopefully) managed. For both employed and self-employed people, the always-on culture that we currently live in – thanks, smartphones – can make the boundary between work and not-work extremely fuzzy. Your brain is still at work if you're answering emails while watching television on the sofa; it's still at work if you're managing your social marketing from the bench in your kids' play park; it's still at work if you're answering client WhatsApps over brunch on a Saturday or in a taxi going to dinner.

In 2017, the gig work job site Fiverr's ad campaign simultaneously enraged and energised commentators. One of the many taglines within the #InDoersWeTrust campaign was:

'You eat a coffee for lunch. You follow through on your follow through. Sleep deprivation is your drug of choice. You might be a doer'. This splashed across a poster of a woman who was surprisingly – irritatingly – well put together for someone who is meant not to sleep. Some commentators felt it rightly glorified hard work – you just keep on slugging! Whatever it takes! You'll get there in the end! There's no time for real life when there's work to be done! Coffee all the way!

If you hadn't noticed, I'm not one of those commentators. It made me and many others feel as though we live in a work-centric dystopia, not helped by the accompanying video ad, with Fiverr gig workers conference-calling in toilet cubicles in nightclubs, and being stalked by – literally – the grim reaper (Fiverr tells us to ignore him). It was all kinds of unhealthy, and only one tiny step away from you-can-sleep-when-you're-dead. It's an extreme example, but Fiverr's current marketing continues to emphasise that if you're a business person, you don't have time for *anything*, especially not interviewing real people for jobs. When 'so much work, so little time', becomes an online cat meme, and you can buy pencil cases decorated with the phrase, I think we have reached a dangerous moment in working culture.

Overworking isn't just bad for our health. It makes us less intelligent, worse at our jobs and – the ultimate paradox – less productive, sometimes even damaging the work we've already done. Overwork can contribute to something behavioural scientists call tunnelling. Convinced that time is scarce, but that work is never-ending, we feel panicky, hectic and frantic. When the feeling lasts – which it often does – we get into a psychological tunnel, where all we can think about are the closest tasks at hand. Those tasks are often not the ones which will get us out of the tunnel, or enable us to prevent the tunnel closing in on us again another day. They tend to be fires we can fight quickly, easy jobs we can tick off the list. As Brigid Schulte, who runs the Better Life Lab think tank and whose *New York Times*-bestselling book is called *Overwhelmed*, said to me 'Just as if you're in a tunnel, your vision narrows and you're so panicked that you can only see the things directly in front of you. They tend to be low-value tasks, like "Oh I gotta finish cleaning out my email inbox". What it does not enable you to do is take a breath and step back and think about the larger, bigger picture, the long-term strategy. It keeps you in that tunnel, thinking and acting small. When you're working on your own that could be one way to ensure that you won't be successful being on your own. As counterintuitive as it might seem, you really need to create space to get out of that tunnel if you're really going to survive as a solo venture.'

The things immediately in front of us are rarely creative, rarely grand in scale, and rarely to do with anything beyond the very near future. They almost never solve real problems, even if you appear to be solving multiple, immediate, smaller ones. (It's why I think inbox zero is a pointless pursuit – it's a low-value item, which adds little of substance to your work. But it makes us feel in control; a fire we can easily pour water on.) Once in this psychological tunnel, it's very hard to allow ourselves to step away from our work, change gear and get some fresh air – it feels too scary, we feel too squashed. Because we aren't effective, just physically present, the work doesn't get done. We stay later; or, if we can't work on, we worry more. The next day is about catching up after yesterday, and so the tunnel closes in again.

This is an issue for me. I couldn't even count the number of days when I have been theoretically working on an article, but – intimidated and panicky – have lost all the hours up to 4pm pointlessly, frenetically answering emails, fielding phone calls, flitting from task to task, feeling the day uncontrollably ebb away, leaving me with 55 useless minutes before I leave to pick up my kids. It's not procrastination – I can do that too, and frankly it's far more relaxing – and it's not avoidance either. I've always felt that it's as though, despite my racing heart, my brain has slowed right down.

And now I know that that is exactly what it's doing. In their book, *Scarcity: Why Having Too Little Means So Much*, Sendhil Mullainathan and Eldar Shafir show that this inside-a-tunnel mental state uses up so much of what they call our mental bandwidth that we lose a measurable 13 or 14 IQ points.[6] That's a lot. It's enough to push you up a bracket from average to exceptional, or down. They show that experiencing time as a scarce commodity, and feeling that we need ever more of it in which to get our work done, makes our work harder to do. This feeling makes us less capable of solving problems and saps our patience, tolerance, attention and concentration. These effects are not just limited to work life, and in fact they show up whenever we experience scarcity. There are similar consequences for our mental bandwidth when we experience dietary scarcity (studies show people on diets lose the mental capacity because their bandwidth is used up by thinking about the scarcity of food) to financial (I'm not sure we even need studies to tell us how cognitively impairing financial scarcity can feel, but there are plenty) and even auditory (kids whose bandwidth was used up by a noisy railway line by their classroom were a full year behind their peers). It's a very particular kind of distraction, scarcity, with surprisingly profound effects for solo workers. (Ones we will look at again in chapters 16 and 17.)

In 2018, Gallup showed that 80 per cent of US workers felt they 'never had enough time'. This is a distressing finding, because feeling time-rich is directly linked to higher levels of psychological well-being, as well as lower levels of things like divorce and obesity.[7] In fact, according to a paper by Laura Giurge from London Business School and Ashley Whillans from Harvard Business School, 'time poverty may be as important as material poverty in shaping human welfare'.[8] More distressing still, a very rare paper examining time poverty among entrepreneurs and freelancers (in Germany), found that solo workers tend to be more time-poor than traditionally employed people.[9]

The weird thing about all this is that people who are actually time-rich (and often money-rich) feel time-poor. In theory, among the relatively affluent worldwide, our leisure hours have doubled, to eight or nine hours a week, in the last 50 years. But we don't feel it, because as commodity theory partly explains, even though there is more time, it feels like less; the hours feel scarce because of what we could earn if we were using the time to work. Our earnings allow us to apply a specific value to our hours, and the way soloists work often means that this is more intensely true than for people like salaried workers (people on an hourly wage also feel this stuff very keenly). And to humans, valuable things feel scarce. And scarcity uses up our bandwidth. Which makes us less productive, as well as less happy.

The very same research showed that the happiest people, who felt the most time-rich, were able to transcend commodity theory: they either used their money to buy themselves time (doing things like spending money on outsourcing stuff they don't like spending time on) or they actively chose to earn less in order to spend less time working, although obviously everyone has a bare minimum they need to earn, which they can't fall below. People who value their time more than the money it could earn them share other traits which enhance well-being, too: they are more sociable, and importantly for soloists, are more likely to choose jobs they find intrinsically rewarding, rather than chasing a big pay cheque.[10]

It's a startling truth, but one which is repeatedly confirmed: we really do get more done when we work less. (Indeed, that is the subtitle and central message of Alex Soojung-Kim Pang's fascinating book, *Rest*.) Study after study has shown that limiting working hours boosts productivity, most famously in the four-day week experiment undertaken at Perpetual Guardian, a wills, trusts and estates management company in New Zealand. Perpetual Guardian not only made the policy permanent, but also created a not-for-profit, 4DayWeek.com, to help other firms cut their hours too.

Does it follow then, that if shorter hours mean higher productivity, longer hours mean lower productivity? It really does look that way, especially over a longish period of time. OECD data gives us a few clues: Greek workers do more hours than almost anyone in Europe, around 2,000 a year. German workers do about 1,400. But German productivity is up to 70 per cent higher than that of Greece. Obviously, there are lots of reasons for this that are not related to working hours, but it does add weight to the idea that more-hours-at-work doesn't necessarily lead to more-getting-done. Even Adam Smith, writing in 1776, had a handle on it: 'It will be found, I believe, in every sort of trade, that the man who works so moderately as to be able to work constantly not only preserves his health the longest, but, in the course of the year, executes the greatest quantity of work.'

Heejung Chung and I got so involved in our conversation about this that I ended up with thousands and thousands and thousands of words of transcript. She is a reader in sociology and social policy at the University of Kent, specialising in – among other things – working time flexibility and work–life balance, comparing the situations in different countries. 'What I see is that countries like the Netherlands or Denmark, which have very low working hours across the population, have the highest productivity levels,' she told me. 'Whereas if you look at the US and Korea which have very high levels of long working hours, they have very low hourly productivity rates.'

An individual's productivity is extremely hard to measure in a knowledge-based economy, so it is hard to say with absolute certainty that long hours will definitely impact on personal productivity over time. But research done by John Pencavel at Stanford University in 2014 and 2016 is persuasive. He found that among the workers he examined, output was actually higher in a 48-hour working week (eight hours a day for six days) than the output from a 70-hour week (ten hours a day for seven days).

Let's unpick that: the extra 22 hours work a week resulted in absolutely no productivity gains. Twenty-two completely pointless hours spent working, or as Pencavel puts it, *10 per cent less* output than a six-day week.[11] That shows that working extra-hard doesn't just flatline productivity, it actually lowers it. It reverses it. Twenty-two extra hours drove productivity into the negative. Not because the workers were smashing up everything they'd made earlier in the week, but because they were so exhausted, they could barely work at all.

His research also highlights that the effects are cumulative and go far beyond merely the week in which the hours were long: a long-hours week continued to damage output as much as two weeks later.

Older research, from the 1950s, backs Pencavel up. An Illinois Institute of Technology study revealed the strange effect of long hours on scientists, with an M-shaped productivity graph emerging: productivity peaked at 10–20 hours a week (*ten hours* – that's not a typo!), then dropped to about half the peak level for anyone doing 35 hours a week, before rising again if scientists did 50 hours a week, and dropping like a stone as soon as staff started edging close to 60 hours a week. Those who did 60 hours a week produced the least of anyone in the study.[12] (Alex Soojung-Kim Pang, in his book *Rest*, shows that most people – including geniuses and very high achievers – cannot and should not do deep work for more than four hours per day, 20 hours per week.)

Along with all the productivity, physical and mental health impacts of long hours, other measurable side effects of working long hours include being less able to read other people, especially non-verbally, and that our decision-making skills fall through the floor when we are tired.[13] This is partly due to tiredness and partly because long hours don't give us enough time to recover, physically and mentally, from work itself, robbing us of the chance to sleep or have much in the way of downtime, or a social life. (In the UK, recovery time is legally mandated for the employed, with 11 hours required between the end of one shift and start of another.)

We are also more likely to make mistakes. As Heejung Chung told me, 'There are studies that show that after a certain amount of hours you have negative impacts on not just your productivity but your performance outcome as a whole. The example often given is in the case of doctors [for whom mistakes due to overlong hours] can lead to very, very severe consequences. But even for, say, an [overworked] programmer, you see mistakes happen that take so much more time to find and correct, rather than if you just didn't make them.' There's plenty of evidence that we also injure ourselves more often and more seriously when we put in long hours, which matters for all of us, but is especially relevant if your solo job is inherently more risky (gardening, driving, cooking, tree surgery, carpentry).[14]

*

How many hours a week a person should formally work has been an issue for generations, but it's only recently become a conversation about mental health and productivity. From the late 1700s onwards, millions of people were slowly but surely absorbed into hard, repetitive and often strenuous work as the Industrial Revolution swept across the world, and as partial automation and reliable and bright artificial lighting meant that for the first time in history, work no longer had to stop when it got dark.

Over the previous six millennia, lighting relied on relatively dim oil lamps and candles, and although there were night-time jobs like fishing or innkeeping, the majority of people lived and worked in rural or agricultural settings, with the rhythm of their days and their work set by the sun. In the late medieval or early modern era, even for those who lived in towns and cities, work was still mostly agricultural or strongly linked to rural industries, the rural economy and its seasons. Only in bigger cities or ports, like Paris, Europe's largest urban centre in 1550, with 350,000 inhabitants, would you find more diverse industries, like book-printing, or cloth dyeing.[15] And even in bustling Paris, with its late-night taverns, cabarets and brothels, the night-time streets were notoriously dark and dangerous – walking through the dark meant carrying a burning torch or hiring someone to bear it for you.

But in the late 1700s the Genevan inventor François-Pierre-Amédée Argand created a much brighter form of oil lamp, which could burn for up to 16 hours. William Murdoch, a Scot, was simultaneously working on gas-powered lighting. During the first decade of the 1800s, Humphrey Davy created the first electric arc lamp, and by the end of the century, incandescent and fluorescent lighting was illuminating streets, homes and workplaces.

Work changed forever. Where once most people had worked seasonally, with longer hours in the summer and shorter hours in winter, now factories and offices could run all night, if they wanted to. Let's not pretend pre-industrial life took place in a pastoral idyll: rural poverty was high, and many families and especially women would have had a lot of what we would now consider additional unpaid work to do – keeping animals, growing food – just to subsist, while domestic staff had long been exploited by their wealthier employers. People were overworked even when there was only candlelight by which to do it. The Industrial Revolution was not an unequivocally bad thing, but in many ways (smog, slums, child labour, polluted water, diseases of close proximity, laissez-faire capitalism) and for many people, it made life a lot worse.

For some workers, there was almost no life outside work, as men, women and children were drawn like moths into city-based factory work, which often lasted 12–14 hours a day, with rare days off. Legislation tells the story: a barely enforced British law from 1802 banned children in work-houses and textile factories from working more than 12 hours a day. In 1833 a fractionally more successful law was enacted, limiting 10- to 13-year-olds to 48 hours a week and 14- to 18-year-olds to 69 hours a week. Not even Sunday was a guaranteed day of rest – in 1830s France, when Catholicism ceased being the state religion, workers were expected to do a seven-day week; having Sunday off didn't come back in to law until 1906.[16] Before long, most workplaces had adopted factory-like working hours, meaning clerical workers were just as liable to experience overwork.

Throughout the 1800s and into the twentieth century, labour movements in industrialised countries fought doggedly against horrific working hours and conditions, desperately hoping for an eight-hour working day or 40-hour week. Early adopters including Finland, Uruguay and the United States, where initially some individual businesses, then industries as a whole, and finally governments adopted limited working hours in the years leading up to 1920. (My less enlightened home country, the UK, took until 1998 to bring in the still-controversial working time directive, which limits the working week to a very long 48 hours. Barring a few high-risk professions, any worker can opt out – or be pressured to opt out – with just a signature.)

In 1930s Britain's average working hours were still an exhausting 48, but that didn't stop the influential Cambridge economist John Maynard Keynes coming up with a radical and novel idea. He argued, in a famous essay titled 'Economic Possibilities for Our Grandchildren', that as technology – particularly in agriculture, mining and manufacture – increased in speed and capacity, future economies would only need a 15-hour working week. One hundred years from his time of writing in 1930, he thought, it would be feasible to produce everything being made in the thirties with 'a quarter of the human effort'.[17]

Writing in the uncertain, confusing and economically precarious period between two world wars, Keynes was probably the most important economist of the twentieth century. He concocted his predictions even though when he was born in 1880s, Britons worked a staggering 56 hours a week (which was still fewer than most of Europe and the United States).[18] As we slip closer to the 2030s, there's no sign of Keynes' golden age of leisure arriving, although current weekly averages have improved to around 37.5 hours in the UK, 34 in the USA, and a high of 43 in Mexico. (Mexico, Costa Rica and South Korea currently have the longest working weeks in the OECD group of countries.)[19]

Dozens of economic, geo-political and philosophical arguments have been put forward about why Keynes' vision never unfolded, despite advances in technology he could never have foreseen. But for me, a large part of it is because of our ideas around the morality of work. Most of us live in societies rooted in a Judeo-Christian or Islamic tradition, regardless of whether we follow a religion ourselves. For each of these three religions (and many others) to work is an act of worship in and of itself. To work is to make the best use of divinely given gifts. Work is dignified and meaningful.

The nobility of work runs like a thread through each belief system, and was particularly emphasised by the Puritans and Calvinists who fled Europe and settled in what would become the USA, in order to practise a pretty extreme version of Protestantism. For sixteenth-century theologian John Calvin, prosperity was one of a set of possible (really quite complicated) signs that you were one of God's chosen people and would ascend to heaven on your death (everyone else was going down). It is not hard to see how this philosophy bled into American society as its economy developed. In other words, the Protestant work ethic, the religious centrality of hard work and success, is not limited to Calvinist Christians, despite requiring some creative reinterpretation of many of the messages in the New Testament, and a mangling of the Garden of Eden story, in which Adam and Eve were sentenced to labour, to work, as a punishment for their apple-eating sins. (This was later repurposed as evidence that work was in fact divine.)

My own family members often talk of their Protestant work ethic, despite two generations of atheism, lapsed Christian grandparents on one side, and a grandmother who dabbled in early twentieth-century communism on the other. Four hundred years after Calvin was writing, his is an idea with profound effects: a recent study revealed that unemployed people in Protestant countries suffer more acute psychological distress than those in non-Protestant countries, leading the researchers to conclude that the Protestant work ethic is still alive and kicking, and painful for people who don't have work to do.[20]

We remain in thrall. I am an atheist who had a brief teenage fling with arms-in-the-air evangelical Christianity (better than taking loads of drugs, but only just) and I studied religion for a couple of years, too. I can see where I got my own buried ideas about work, its value, and my value as a working, contributing member of society, and I don't even believe in the systems which generated them. I'm still on the hook, because ideas about the indisputable goodness of hard work are so pervasive in how we live today. We deify hard work. We celebrate hard workers. Our work ethic no longer has much to do with organised religion. Numbers of religious adherents may be dropping off, but we adhere to a very particular creed when it comes to work.

I know I'm walking a difficult line. Work is essential, for almost all of us. Work can be meaningful, which is all the more important since work is so necessary a part of life. We can't escape work, and nor should we. We probably all know people who for whatever reason haven't needed to or haven't been able to work, and often, they don't look like they are leading fulfilled lives, even – especially – people who inherited enough money that they never have to work. (I have a couple of super-rich friends. And it turns out that when you could do almost anything with your life, more often than not, you do nothing, and are unhappy about that.) Work can be dignified. Work can be noble. But I think we have taken these ideas far too far, and let the primacy of work, and the idea of ourselves as a particular kind of worker, expand like foam to fill almost every part of our lives.

Keynes' essay was all about challenging the double-helix of laissez-faire capitalism and Victorian-era Christianity; he was driven by a profoundly moral – but not religious – view of economics. He could see how religion as practised in Europe and America over the preceding four centuries had created a moral framework in 'which we have exalted some of the most distasteful of human qualities into the position of the highest virtues', although he found traces of the same instincts – hoarding and avarice, as he put it – in far older, pre-Christian societies. (And in fact, his critique of older religions, Judaism in particular, reads unpleasantly today.)

'We have been trained too long to strive and not to enjoy,' Keynes lamented. Which is just another version of that popular piece of graphic art, which hangs in homes, schools and offices all over the world. 'Work hard and be nice to people.'

However, it turns out Keynes was not the first person to come up with a 15-hour working week, his wild, fly-in-the-face of at least four centuries of work-oriented, Calvin-tinged Christianity and centuries more of conservative, hierarchical Judeo-Christianity. In order to find its real inventors, you have to escape the reach of the Protestant work ethic, and travel far further back in time. Thirty years after Keynes wrote 'Economic Possibilities', and 22 after his death, anthropologists began publishing papers which suggested pre-industrial – perhaps more importantly, pre-Biblical – hunter-gatherers had nailed the 15-hour working week well before establishment of agriculture, the Industrial revolution, labour movements and working time directives.

The first was published in 1968 by anthropologist Richard B. Lee, and examined the life of the !Kung Bushmen in Botswana. 'In all, the adults of the Dobe camp worked about two and a half days a week,' Lee wrote. 'Because the average working day was about six hours long, the fact emerges that !Kung Bushmen of Dobe, despite their harsh environment, devote from 12 to 19 hours a week to getting food. Even the hardest working individual in the camp, a man named ≠oma who went out hunting on 16 of the 28 days, spent a maximum of 32 hours a week in the food quest.'[21]

This was followed by time-use studies written in the 1970s by Marshall Sahlins, following Ju/'haonsi' people in Namibia and Botswana, which mirrored Lee's findings but also showed that the Ju/'haonsi' actively and joyfully use their comparatively long periods of leisure time for things like craft, socialising and music. This research was done with existing hunter-gatherer societies but, according to the anthropologist James Suzman, who has worked with Ju/'haonsi' people since the 1990s, there's strong genomic and archaeological evidence to suggest that the Ju/'haonsi' people's way of life has been broadly the same for at least 45,000 years and perhaps as long as 90,000. Which, as he points out, would make their culture a significantly longer-lasting and more successful one than those of the Greeks, Romans and Mayans, and certainly longer than us industrial and post-industrialists have been around.[22]

Hunter-gatherer communities did not work hellishly long weeks. They may have had to work extremely hard in times of crisis or starvation, but given their lack of food storage options, generally they simply worked until they had enough, then stopped, and got on with something else.

Why are hunter-gatherers important for soloists? Because we behave as though to work is to be human. But is it? Anatomically modern humans first appeared around 300,000 years ago. We didn't start farming until 10,000 years ago. That means that for more than 96 per cent of modern humanity's history, people primarily lived and worked as hunter-gatherers. For 15 or 16 hours a week.

It's not sensible nor desirable to even think about returning to a hunter-gatherer lifestyle – don't worry. As if we soft-bellied, hyper-modern humans would survive without vaccines, antibiotics and wifi. But what might earlier ways of life tell us about work and humanity's relationship with it? For most of our documented history, work has been placed right in the middle of everything we do. But what if that's not the case for our much longer, less documented prehistory? What if work as it has come to be, is nothing like what work was for most of the humans who have ever lived?

The other critical bit of those 1960s papers, and many that followed, is that being a hunter-gatherer turns out not to be awful. Thinking that hunter-gatherer lives must be or have been basic, miserable and short lets us dismiss their less work-obsessed cultures – we can shrug and say, they may have worked less, sure, but they all died young and painfully.

In fact, this seems to be wrong. Hunter-gatherers' average age of death only appears incredibly low if infant mortality is included. Infant mortality is horribly high in hunter-gatherer societies, and if you include it when calculating life expectancy as a mean average (add all the ages of death together and divide by the number of deaths), then it drags life expectancy down by decades. But if you strip out infant mortality, and instead look at the modal average age at which most hunter-gatherers die, it's close to 70. (Modal averages are the numbers which occur most often in a set of data.)

If a hunter-gatherer makes it through infancy, they have a strong chance of reaching an age only ten or so years younger than the average life expectancy in the so-called developed world, which is now pushing 80.

We have a tendency to look at less work-focused, less driven, less stressed modes of living, as if they are primitive and lower down on some kind of intellectual scale. Assuming hunter-gatherers lived grim lives, which ended early and painfully, allows us to think of our own work-imbalanced culture as the most developed, when really, it is only the most recent.

Life and work would gradually change when the first farmers switched from nomadic or semi-nomadic ways of life to form settled, fixed communities around 10,000 years ago. It was a precarious lifestyle then, and still is for farmers in economically and ecologically impoverished regions today. When farming conditions were good, they were very, very good, and farming populations grew rapidly, but they suffered occasional catastrophic famines and population collapses.

Farming meant that for perhaps the first time in human history, it was both possible and desirable to create a surplus, which could keep you safe if the climate turned against you, your crops failed, maybe even if your land was taken. Work was suddenly no longer about having just enough, but about having as much as possible.

Hunter-gathering might be or have been a hard life in some ways, by current standards, but it might also have been a good, long one, with plenty of leisure, rest and fun. Work is valuable, and gives us meaning, as well as a means to survive. But for most of human history, it hasn't been our sole reason for being.

*

Work is *new*. To work, it turns out, is not necessarily human. We soloists need to remember that the work we do – however valuable, meaningful and hopefully remunerative – does not have to be the central thing around which the rest of our lives must rotate.

This stuff is so deeply embedded in our thinking about work and time and achievement, that you may be in its grip even if you've never worked in an office. I slipped into judging people by the hours they spent visibly working when I had a job on a newspaper. An editor on a nearby desk always came in early. Our official hours were 10am until 6pm, but on the very rare occasions I went in especially early, he was always there. He left work at about 4pm.

I thought that was shocking.

I would stay at the office until 7pm, a lot, and often later. I very rarely took a proper lunch break, either eating at my desk or diving into the canteen for 15 or 20 minutes. I felt that being visibly at my desk showed how serious I was about my job. I was a grafter, and everyone could see me grafting. I had a colleague who would answer the phone mid-mouthful of cereal in the mornings. Frankly, we all answered the phone as though we were working at the Pentagon. (Now I'm freelance, and on the other end of those phone calls, I know how mean we sounded.)

After I left I quickly realised that office life is full of enormous time sucks, and that like most office workers, I was probably functioning for no more than half the time I was actually there, with plenty of long, panicky hours getting not much done (research suggests that full-time, eight-hour-a-day office workers are productive for as little as two hours and 53 minutes a day).[23] That editor was probably making much better use of his time than I was, producing more work, far quicker than me, even though he was leaving two to three hours before me.

I was a tiny part of a much bigger culture that values time spent at work much more than the work that results in the end. Heejung Chung calls these long hours performative work. She understands why I felt the way I did. 'You rarely have HR managers [in offices] telling people to stop work at 5pm. What you have is managers saying, "You know what, we're going to promote one person – and we're going to promote John, because he's been really giving his all by working on the weekends and working till late, and burning the midnight oil". Without understanding that John's probably making a ton of mistakes and also damaging the company by perpetuating the culture of long hours, which is not conducive to productivity at all.'

Time spent at a job and on a job, cannot be, will never be, a good measure of how well that job will be done. It might have worked once, in a few very particular contexts before today's large-scale automation – when an hour equalled a hundred rivets hand-made on a factory line, or 360 calls manually connected through a telephone exchange, or six pages of type-writing. But how many soloists do you know who do nothing but fit rivets? Unless you work billable hours for your clients, more often than not, the only person keeping track of when you clock on or off, is you.

We rarely judge any other activity in our life outside work by the length of time we spend doing it. You don't look at a pile of washing and think I'd better spend two hours doing that. You just do it. And then it's done. When you cook a meal, you don't really think about how long it will take to cook it. You cook it, and then you eat. Most people don't decide to spend a specific amount of time reading a book or newspaper. Why can't we think of work the same way? Parkinson's law is the old adage that work expands to fill the time allotted (and often more). But the moral philosophy that sees working time as a good in itself, is at least in part to blame when our working days stretch on and on. It's not just our inability to buckle down.

An eight-hour day is not a perfect working day. It does not represent the optimum amount of time a human can or should work. It is a by-product of the Industrial Revolution, an idea created by labour unions as a defense against the more common 10- to 14-hour days worked in factories. It was just the best those labour unions could hope for.

Today, even those sacrosanct eight hours are being eroded

and ignored – especially by solo workers, who have a tendency to work from 2–14 hours more per week than employed people, depending on sector (and whose data you're reading). In fact, one piece of research surveying 1,000 freelancers suggests that because self-employed people take fewer days of holiday and tend to consider themselves on duty for longer each day than employees do, we work up to 65 hours per week.[24] The average day starts at 8am with a first peek at our emails, and a last look at almost 9pm at night.

'There's this idea that if you work from home, then you can work whenever, and that you could slack off and do whatever you want,' says Heejung Chung. 'Watch TV all day. Empirically what I and colleagues have shown, using very sophisticated data analysis, is that people don't do that. Actually, what people working at home tend to do is end up working longer and longer, over time, even if it's unpaid. One reason is that for most of us, even in very good jobs, there's a lot of insecurity, a lot of competition. Alternatively, if you're employed and you're working from home, then what you may feel is that people are going to assume that you're not really doing your work, so you feel the need to overcompensate. Or you might work long hours as a self-employed person, because each hour can be more money for you and the viability of your business.'

There's a reason that the International Labour Organisation says we need limits on working hours, she adds. 'People need breaks: daily breaks, weekend breaks and breaks in-between work. There is a huge amount of literature about the negative impact on mental and physical well-being, and if you're having negative well-being outcomes you're gonna definitely have horrible outcomes for productivity and performance. We need to think about a smarter way of working.'

The Problem of Long Hours

Think about the derogatory terms we use for people who don't or can't work: slacker, shirker, loafer, drifter, idle, jobless. They're part of a dangerous set of phrases that hovers around the world of work. We talk about work as though it's a battle, that you've got to dominate, there's huge competition, it's a dog-eat-dog world, collateral damage, no-pain-no-gain. But there's no need to be heroic in most jobs. We are not soldiers. I'm not a doctor. Even if we are doing a job which is related to life-saving (consulting for a non-governmental organisation which responds to overseas emergencies, say), the idea that we have to be heroic is toxic, and can lead very quickly to overwork and exhaustion, and possibly even burnout. Crises happen on occasion, of course, but you shouldn't be lurching, heroically, from long-hours crisis to long-hours crisis. Whatever job you do, staying at your desk, in your car, kitchen, studio or workshop, for 50 to 60 hours a week because you have something to prove, is not heroic. (And what are we soloists proving, when no one but us is watching?)

You may say: but I LOVE my job. I love working all those hours. I'm ambitious. I wouldn't change it. And I would answer, sure, there are a very few outliers who can survive having built themselves a world where there is almost nothing but work. But I would still ask you to look at whether this is something you can sustain over the very long term, and if you really want to. Are you quite sure there's nothing you're missing out on? Are you quite sure, to nick the famous phrase by Harvard Business School's late, great, professor of Business Administration Clayton M. Christensen, that when you come to measure your life, at the end of it, you won't regret leaving so little space for anything but work?

I don't think the majority of people want to work

mind-bendingly hard, but things are getting poisonous. It should not be aspirational to be overworked. One positive: that Harvard study with the fake social media posts about being overworked? Its results have not yet been replicated outside America. When the same ruse was played on Italian subjects, they were having none of it. All is not completely lost.

For most of our history, this is not how humans have lived. We have been tricked, over the last 400 years or so, and certainly since the Industrial Revolution took us in its jaws, into thinking that work should be and is everything. We think that if we don't do it enough we should feel guilty, that we should be endlessly preoccupied by work, connected to work, engaged with work. That we should be continuously, diligently, morally, visibly, busily productive in a way which frankly only makes sense if you are a nineteenth-century factory owner hell-bent on squeezing a 14-hour day out of someone weaving cotton on a loom.

Overwork is a killer. There is no nobility, no divinity, in that.

We are not farming a hot and dusty hillside 7,000 years ago. We are not Victorian labourers. We can do what they were denied. More than any other group of workers, soloists have the opportunity to change things for the better.

6

Courage, Resilience and Doing Hard Things

The worst of times

When I started writing this book, life was normal. I worked four days a week, my soloist husband worked four days a week. My eldest went to primary school, my youngest went to nursery three days a week. My parents helped us out when we needed them. We shopped, ate out, saw friends, visited the park, the pool, the gym. We hugged.

Then, the novel coronavirus appeared (as it happens, I am writing this passage under coronavirus lockdown). The majority of my husband's photography work evaporated. We had to shut our photography studio. We had no childcare and could ask for no help; it was just us. My eldest daughter, five-year-old Isla, was very ill. It was bad for us, and much, much worse for millions of others. I have never before lived through such a fierce storm of worry – for my children's health, my husband's, my parents' (who were initially trapped in Australia, where they were staying with my sister and her new baby), my in-laws, mine and everyone else I care about; for the survival of my job, my business and my husband's business; about how we will manage with almost no income; how my sister is managing in Australia with a newborn and a toddler in a tiny flat with no outside space; for the global economy, the British economy, the economies and societies

95

in the developing world; for the friends whose businesses may collapse, and the friends who are already worn thin as they work to fight the virus on the front lines.

I am in this too deep to know much about what the answers are. This morning I visited our empty studio and the scent of a room freshener jolted me back a few months, to a chilly winter evening I spent trying to mend a toilet cistern, broken by a client who had hired the studio that day. While cursing and failing to mend it I spilled the entire bottle of air freshening oil down my coat and skirt and across the floor. It ended with a very late night, an emergency plumber and several hundred pounds to fix both toilet and coat. I thought it was one of the worst days at work I had had in a long while. It was not.

Today, the pressures on everyone are immense. Our routines have been torn to bits and our ideas about what 'normal' is have had to morph. The markers we had placed in the future, as rewards and as ways to help us navigate the passing of time – holidays, weddings, birthdays – are cancelled or uncertain. Half of us have been trying to educate our kids at home while attempting to do a passable impression of our jobs. Others have experienced fear and loneliness and social isolation or find themselves with no job at all, the identity they've held for their entire adult lives, ripped away in a day. We have lived shut away from others and from all the usual ways we would seek – and I would tell you to seek – support, steeped in fear, rumour, fake news and bad news.

My hope is that when this is over, however it ends, perhaps the smaller irritants, the breakages and spills of life, will grind us down less; and perhaps it will be easier to do the harder things. Perhaps we will find resilience we never knew we had, the ability to ride out the hardest of times – because we will have done so already – and the courage to try new things in ways that we never expected. After I had a caesarean section to give birth to my daughter, suddenly appearing on live television was nowhere near as terrifying (because there is little that can be more scary than being operated on, awake, while an actual human is removed from your body. And that stands despite all that coronavirus has brought so far). Will this experience be like that one, writ large? If we can, as individuals, as families, as communities, as societies, survive this savaging, harrowing time, might we thrive in its aftermath? It's the hope I'm holding on to.

Is it as simple as deciding that that is what we will do? In her *Harvard Business Review* article 'How Resilience Works', Diane L. Coutu wrote that resilient people staunchly accept reality. They believe that life is meaningful and have the capacity to improvise, when necessary. She says resilience isn't about cultivating an optimistic outlook but is instead about being able to stare down reality. And if you have a resilient outlook, you will be able to use that resilience when things get sticky.

Resilience isn't just about gritting your teeth and setting out into a wild and rainy head-wind with determination. It's also about having a mug of hot chocolate, wearing fluffy socks, afterwards. We need to allow our emotions to play out, to be heard, to be real. I am far from fearless. If I'm not coping, I need to accept that, ask for and be given help, and work around it, not truck on endlessly, regardless and disregarding my own needs.

It's a similar point to one Shawn Achor, a happiness researcher and former proctor at Harvard, makes, also in an article for the *Harvard Business Review*. The headline is: 'Resilience Is About How You Recharge, Not How You Endure'.[1]

The more you try and push yourself onwards, particularly in the face of hard things, the harder everything becomes. It becomes harder to work, to sleep, and just to be. You drain your reserves, leaving nothing left in the tank for the next round of work (or life). In the end, this pushes our brains into a fight or flight way of thinking and we become anxious and irritable, and can't think clearly.

Where normally our brain's frontal lobes would be in charge, and looking after executive functions, fight-or-flight lets the deeper parts of the brain gain more control over decisions than they would normally have – and they're not very good at it. This pushes the body into panic mode, which in turn reinforces the brain's under-threat position. The whole cycle increases in intensity until we are robbed of flexibility and creativity, flooded with impulsivity.

Recovery and recharging is more important now than it has perhaps ever been, and probably harder to achieve too. Our worlds have shrunk, but fortunately, the familiar is often what the brain needs for recovery, anyway.

I try and find pockets of recovery by growing herbs on a windowsill, and trying to coax some wildflowers into life from a packet of mouldy seeds I found in the shed; by watering my house plants; mending things which break (the lawnmower and my coffee machine most recently); tidying cupboards, sorting shelves; going for walks alone and without my phone, turning my face to the sky and not the grey pavements; I cook; I read stories to my kids; and I do this – I write, because although work is hard usually, this is the first time – only time, I hope – when life is harder than work.

There is endless data about how desperate our need for recovery is – and how little recovery time average workers get, and the price they pay for missing out (some of which was discussed in the previous chapter, on long hours). Some recent research in America suggested lack of recovery time as sleep was costing the American economy $62 billion a year in lowered productivity, or – more relevant for soloists – 11 days of work per year, per worker. Eleven days is a holiday we could be taking, but instead, we waste them being shattered, but trying to work anyway. Staying up late or all night to work is not a flag showing resilience. Pushing through is not resilient. You cannot roll with what the next day brings if you are exhausted. The harder you try to perform, the more you need to recover. (This is true for many things besides work – parenting and sports, in particular.)

As we already know, soloists are prone to overwork, to failing to take time off, rest or take holidays. By allowing yourself to recover from whatever hard thing (or day, or week) you've experienced, by giving yourself permission to need recovery and to then do things which enable it, you will make yourself more resilient.

Part of resilience is knowing you can and will survive the hard things, but another part is working out how to gain back the psychic and physical energy to get through and carry on. Whatever it is, it needs to be disconnected, truly, from your work. Margaret Heffernan recharges by singing in her local choir. 'I live kind of in the middle of nowhere,' she told me, 'and I do quite a lot within my local village because nobody really knows what I do and they have absolutely no interest, and I think that's quite fabulously humbling.'

There are two modes of recovery to engage in when it comes to resilience – Achor calls them internal and external. External recovery happens outside working hours, and obviously includes sleep. Think of it as unplugging your work brain. You probably already know what you need for your own recovery (even if you don't yet or regularly do it), but it could be anything from running, meditating, time with friends or family, to time outside in nature, to engaging in a completely separate activity like reading, playing a game, listening to a podcast, cooking or crafting.

TV and movies don't quite do the job – which I say reluctantly. A few evenings slumped in front of the television each week is probably fine – probably inevitable – but because watching doesn't require active mental engagement in the way that something slightly challenging like painting, sewing or cooking does, and involves complete physical inertia, passive watching can't do the same good things for our mental health as something which absorbs more of the senses. Humans thrive on stories, and we all need escapism, so I'm a long way from saying that we should throw out our TVs, but eating a bowl of pasta in front of Netflix every single night at 9pm won't refill our mental tanks. (Neither will getting drunk. Sorry. Occasionally fun, but a mildly dangerous way to unplug, and literally the opposite of recharging, because it depletes you.)

As we will see in chapter 10 about the spaces in which we work, getting outside is one of the most powerful ways in which we can help our brains and bodies recover from work (and life), so try to build outside time, even if it's brief, into your day, because it, too, will build up your resilience. We will talk more about communities and networks later, too, in chapter 15, but they also are critical to our resilience – it's an obvious point, but crises are easier to navigate with supportive friends, and a network of colleagues, whether personal or work-related. Find them, and talk to them about whatever is going on.

Internal recovery is about building short periods of

recovery into your working day, which effectively short-circuit the spiral of fight-or-flight panic and give the frontal lobes back some of their control. (Some academics call this intermittent recovery.) Like external recovery, it needs to be separate from work – a short walk outside, exercise, listening to music or a phone call with a friend. A few years ago, my work life involved a lot of time lost to vagueness, drifting around my house putting washing on, regular unnecessary phone calls with my mum, or just prowling aimlessly – I see now that it was my brain crying out for structured internal recovery periods (I thought it was procrastination). It could only slug on with work for so long before refusing to go any further.

Circadian rhythms control our sleep–wake cycles and are governed by hormones and our exposure to light and dark. But we are also subject to ultradian rhythms, 90- to 120-minute cycles of energy peaks to troughs, and we are almost completely unable to circumvent them. Many of us don't pause after 90 minutes of work because that doesn't fit the patterns by which we set our days: it isn't lunchtime; it's not coffee time; we think we haven't got enough done; or we have an urgent deadline we must force ourselves to meet. We don't listen to our bodies and push past the signs they give us when we need a break: yawning, fidgeting, feeling tired, hungry or restless. We need periods of intermittent recovery to help us regulate our emotions, as well as recharge our energy reserves. If we don't have these recovery periods then we get grouchy and irritable, or even end up in a panicky fight-or-flight mode.

Knowing this, I now build proper little breaks into the day – to make myself a drink, to walk in the garden or sit on the front porch if it's a sunny morning, to look at a recipe book and think about dinner, to do some stretches and twists every few hours, or chat to the people who work in neighbouring workshops and studios, as they pass by. Given what we know about recovery, it's no surprise that this means I get more done, in less time – my holy grail.

Resilience is a process, it's not a state of being. You can be more resilient one day than the next; you can increase your resilience. Also, it's not rare. We are all, to some extent, resilient, and soloists are both brave and resilient almost by definition – the way we work demands that we are and we can increase our resilience by remembering what we've survived in the past. When things go wrong – and they will – reflecting on how we navigated terrible things in our pasts helps us to know that we can and will do it again.

Solveiga Pakštaitė was just about to return to university for her final year, when her best friend, with whom she was about to move in, was killed in a plane crash. 'It was the hardest thing I'd ever been through,' she told me. Today, she is an inventor, entrepreneur and director of her own company, Mimica Touch. During her final year studying industrial design, grief-stricken, Pakštaitė invented her award-winning product: a food label which changes from smooth to bumpy in response to temperature changes and time passing, doing away with the need for conservative use-by dates, which are a major cause of edible food being thrown away in the home. Originally designed as part of an inclusive, people-centred design project to help blind people navigate impossible-to-read ordinary food labels, her product-specific labels are about to launch on fresh foods in supermarkets and will form a large part in the fight against unnecessary food waste.

'I would have never done such a risky project if I hadn't lost my friend,' she says. 'But I was in a state where I thought

"Fuck it, I don't care if I get a crap grade for my degree. I just want to do something interesting". Everyone warned me against doing this weird project, nobody thought I would get it to work. But I just didn't care any more. So I did go for it, somehow made it work, got a first class degree, and then somehow made it into a business.' Along the way, she won a James Dyson Award for her innovation – just after graduating – and was in so many newspapers that her surname featured as a crossword clue in *The Times*. Food companies contacted her, requesting that she launch the business and bring her invention to their market. 'For the first year or so I really struggled with the fact that I actually just wanted to finish this project and finish uni and just end the chapter. I really associated the time that I was creating the Mimica concept with grieving.' But the project refused to end.

'I wouldn't have ever described myself as a resilient person, but it taught me that I am,' she says. 'Whenever I'm in a really tough spot, I just think back to then, "Not only did you not drop out of uni, not only did you actually finish your degree, you graduated with a first and an award-winning concept". I try to find that in myself, and I always think that there's a way out of the problem, whatever it is, and some way of solving it. That's part of my insane optimism. Even in a really difficult situation I will think "This can't be the way it ends". She was going to go on and do great things that she never got a chance to do, so I now have to do it for her.'

There's evidence to show that people like Pakštaitė, who are resilient adults today, are often people who have gone through painful things in their pasts without being crushed by them. As the psychologist and resilience expert Megan Jay puts it, 'Coping with stress is a lot like exercise: We become stronger with practice.' Often such people are very good at accessing determination and see themselves as having a fighter mentality, another thing, that with practice, we can all adopt. Intriguingly, many of the people we see as high achievers in society (Oprah Winfrey, LeBron James, Howard Schultz) overcame extremely difficult childhoods.[2]

So, assume that you can access that bravery and resilience when you need it. We are brave when we first go solo and resilient when we carry on, despite the inevitable hurdles. And because we are tiny-organisations-of-one, we are nimble. If resilience is about adapting and then carrying on, then that's us, isn't it? Although I agree with Coutu that resilience isn't about blind optimism, it is about having a mindset which allows us to believe that change is possible, too.

Attitude and mindset

I happened to read an article on Medium.com by Drew Magary, an American journalist and author, about how to write 10,000 words a week – the headline was just the kind of clickbait I fall for. But the article wasn't about technical solutions to writers' block, nor anything practical. (Nor magic, damnit. And I could do with some magic.) Magary says he has chosen to love writing, and to see a life of writing as a crazy privilege and a joyful experience. How he thinks about writing when he's not writing. In the shower. When he's supposed to be having a meal. How he carries a notebook and stacks it with all the ideas his brain churns out. His attitude to writing is completely different to the better-known tropes about writing: that it's hard; that even the most lauded writers – especially the most lauded writers, like Philip Roth, or Jonathan Franzen – suffer through the process. 'I love writing. Every little goddamn bit of it. Writing is all I think about and all I wanna do,' he says.

'You'll flourish as a writer if you don't fear writing and don't force it, and if you know ... that there's no one way it should end up. If you treat your work like some impassable wall you have to scale (or if some dipshit boss of yours demands you treat it that way), you're gonna hate it. No tip I give you will prevent you from going on a snack hunt to procrastinate if your attitude is that every molehill is a mountain.'[3]

Perhaps you can't make yourself love something you truly hate, but I do believe our capacity to change how we think about things is limitless. Magary's basic principle can be applied to almost any task: if you view something that you have to do as almost impossible, as an impassable wall, of course it's going to seem scary. (Brick wall-type tasks which often come up when I talk with other soloists include picking up the phone to cold call a stranger, giving a presentation to a group, making a video, and presenting work at a pitch meeting or a conference.)

But if you can change your point of view, and choose to see it differently, you can change how you feel about it too. There's good evidence to show that merely perceiving something as a challenge leads to a very different – and more useful – neural response than seeing something as a threat, boosting energetic adrenaline, rather than the more stressy cortisol.[4]

When you have to do something you usually think of as either scary or hard, examine it. Is it really a brick wall? Or is there something else making you feel like it is? Have you been cultured or socialised into thinking it is more difficult than it really is? Could you shift your point of view and see it as a challenge to be enjoyed, rather than a horror to be endured? Can you figure out a way to learn how to do it? Could you ask for help? Can it be as easy as reframing the way you think about it?

If you've come across Carol Dweck's work on mindsets

before now, then what follows will be familiar. Over several decades of groundbreaking research in social and development psychology, she created her theory of growth and fixed mindsets – a theory so influential that it has even been adopted by the teaching profession across the UK, which is encouraged to use growth-mindset style language with kids. Essentially, if you have a growth mindset, you believe that ability and intelligence can change and improve, whereas if you have a fixed mindset you see intelligence and ability as things which don't and can't really change. You believe some abilities are natural or innate, and you ascribe limits to how much anyone can truly grow. To work out your own position, Dweck asks us to reflect on these statements:

- Your intelligence is something very basic about you that you can't change very much.
- You can learn new things, but you can't really change how intelligent you are.
- No matter how much intelligence you have, you can always change it quite a bit.
- You can always substantially change how intelligent you are.

The first two are fixed mindset statements, and the last two are growth mindset statements. Which ring truest for you? Dweck says you can substitute 'intelligence' for things like artistic ability or business acumen, and she also sets out similar questions which are about personal qualities, rather than intelligence – 'You are a certain kind of person and there is not much which can be done to really change that', versus 'No matter what kind of person you are, you can always change substantially'.

In her book, *Mindset*, Dweck sets out how very mutable we all are, both in terms of intelligence and ability, but also in terms of our personal qualities, and how worthwhile adopting and developing a growth mindset which accepts these truths can be. How it can help us to value effort – which is undervalued in the fixed mindset, because if you have to try, you aren't already good at something – and how it can help us to appreciate the process of trying to achieve something, rather than just fixating on the goal itself. She also notes that it is possible to have a fixed mindset about one thing, and a growth mindset about another – you might, for example, believe it is possible for people to become kinder, with practice, while simultaneously believing that intelligence is a fixed asset, and cannot be increased.

I grew up with a fixed mindset, and it was very damaging. By my second year at university I was miserable. I started having panic attacks, stopped sleeping, struggled with IBS and ultimately, lost the sensation in the ends of my fingers from hyperventilating for weeks without realising. A university GP fortunately referred me for counselling and I completed the first of – so far – five stints of therapy. (Which I thoroughly recommend.) I had sailed through the academic side of school, almost always the top student in almost every subject, and then landed at the London School of Economics, only just 18 years old, inexperienced and very young, a tiny fish in a gigantic pond full of other much, much more intelligent, successful, resilient fish, from all over the world and its best schools. Great things had been expected of me, and here I was, flailing about, failing for the first time in my life, entirely lost.

Although I had previously worked hard, I had always had a core belief that I was clever, which had been affirmed for years by my teachers. At the heart of who I was, was the 'fact' that everyone knew I was very bright and very successful. (That didn't make you popular at British comprehensive schools in the 1990s, incidentally.) But at LSE, I suddenly went from brilliant to stupid. Because I saw intelligence (and stupidity) as fixed, all I could think was that everyone had been wrong about me until now.

I hadn't been encouraged to really work on something I found difficult since I was seven and learning to do a handstand. (And even then, I was already considered naturally talented at gymnastics.) I worked, but only on things I was already good at, and avoided anything to do with music, team sports or ball games, ensuring I could never fail. I believed I was born clever, and would always be clever – and then that was taken away.

If you don't believe that things can change and improve, then it's really hard to be resilient. I had almost no resilience at university – just an almost unshakeable belief that my value as a human came from doing things perfectly and being clever, an attribute that I clearly no longer had. It was devastating for my mental health.

Over time, I have tried to cultivate an alternate set of beliefs. I can now, finally, at nearly 40, experience criticism and feedback as constructive, not as a personal attack. My self-worth no longer totally hangs on my achievements or measurements of intelligence. I know now that 'failing' isn't the revelation of stupidity, it just tells us that we haven't learned how to do something yet. I'm much better at appreciating the process rather than fixating on the results. (More on this later, in chapter 12, but I really think this is one of the great secrets to happiness: if you can be happy on the way somewhere, rather than assuming you will be happy once you get there, wherever 'there' is for you, you will have a profoundly better experience of life. Saying to yourself that you'll be happy when you graduate, or make partner, or get married, or have kids, or get a bigger house, or make more money, or win an award, has so many painful side effects. It allows you to accept unhappiness on the way to wherever you want to go – which could take years – and it means you expect happiness to magically arrive with you when you get there. And when it doesn't arrive, it can be agonising.)

Having a growth mindset unquestionably makes being a soloist easier. Mindset matters to soloists because people with growth mindsets are more resilient and much less afraid to try new or scary things – and for many soloists new and scary things are part of the territory. It makes you so much more likely to take a knock, shake it off, and carry on. It also makes us far more likely to think creatively about a problem, because the central belief is that things can improve, and that problems can be solved. Growth-mindset soloists are much less likely to give up on something because it seems complex and much more likely to approach the same issue from numerous angles, until they figure out a fix.

For a soloist within a fixed mindset, losing a client and having to find a new one might feel like failure, might even feel as though it reveals that you're in the wrong job and will never succeed. Those feelings can be incapacitating. From within a growth mindset, you're more likely to do whatever you can to learn from what happened.

Charlotte Scott is a soloist and chamber musician and performs with her violin all over the world, as well as guest-leading orchestras around the UK and Europe. Since 2015 she has been associate concert master of the Oxford Philharmonic. She got a first class degree from the Royal Academy of

Music; you've almost certainly heard her play on film scores and Grammy-winning albums as she spends a lot of time recording in Abbey Road studio. Her violin is an absurdly precious Antonio Stradivarius 1685 'Gagliano' violin. You don't need to know much about music to know she's very, very good. She also has a growth mindset. Six months ago, she auditioned for another concert-master job, and didn't get it.

'I played really well. And I didn't get it. My first thought was maybe I'm just not good enough to be going to these jobs,' she told me. 'I know that's not really true. But I thought people must think that, otherwise I would be doing better.' Her second thought was, 'I need to ask for feedback. But then I had a conversation with myself in my head. Are you sure? Because feedback is so subjective that it's not always helpful. In the end I decided, no, I really respect this orchestra, I think they're amazing, let's ask for feedback. I got the feedback and it was the best thing I've ever read in my life. Honestly, it was, because what it told me was that the thing I thought was my greatest error, I actually did really well. And the thing that I thought was not a problem was actually my biggest issue. And I just had no idea, but I'm so glad I had the gumption to ask, and I cared.'

I feel slightly heartbroken for my younger self. I spent years avoiding feedback. I buried my apparent failures very deeply and really believed that if I didn't think about them, they couldn't hurt me. I missed so many chances to ask 'How could I have done this better?' Instead I just said to myself, hands over my ears, 'It never happened. La la la.'

'But the things you bury will come knocking at some point,' says Scott. 'The thing that drives me is that I just *do not* want to make the same mistake twice. Sometimes, of course, feedback is just someone's point of view, and you can say "That's just their view. I can't win them all". Those will be obvious. But other times, you need to say to yourself "I really messed that up, that's my responsibility and what can I do about it?" I'm actually afraid of making the same mistake again.' And of course, by asking for feedback, you manage how you receive it and ensure you won't get it at the wrong moment, or in the wrong place (as I once got at an awards ceremony, when someone who didn't know I was the project manager gave a damning shakedown of a publication I had recently edited).

It is usually possible, at some point and sometimes with the right amount of distance, to gain something from even the most horrible of work (or life) experiences. We have to practise flexing our positive muscles and choosing to look for good things in among the awful. That said, during coronavirus lockdown, I constantly received press releases inviting me to use all my extra free time to learn patisserie skills online, or to try a new language or make sourdough, all of which made me want to reach through my computer screen and punch someone. Bad experiences don't *have* to be an opportunity for personal growth. It is enough to accept that they can be, if we want them to be. And only then.

Humans often default to fixed mindset behaviours, both in how we treat ourselves, and other people. None the less, it's still worth deciding to adopt a growth mindset, and then working on actually creating one. Like resilience, it's a process.

You are not your work

The weaker you can make the tie between you as a person and the work you do, the better you'll be able to survive the emotional or financial peaks and troughs that will inevitably come with being solo. Don't get me wrong: this can be incredibly hard for soloists because often we see ourselves as *being* our jobs, because many of us have a vocational drive to do our solo work – it's not only that we wanted to work for ourselves, but also that we wanted to create or share things, whether gardens, hats, wardrobes or websites. There's an interesting linguistic thing going on here too – many of us can't ever say 'I work for a distribution company,' or 'I work for a bank'. Most of us, when asked what we do, will reply 'I *am* a writer,' 'I *am* a designer,' 'I *am* a virtual assistant'.

Susan Ashford, professor of Management and Organization at the University of Michigan, studies the ways some soloists thrive. In a paper she wrote with Gianpiero Petriglieri and Amy Wrzesniewski, Ashford found that what she calls successful soloists – that is both financially successful and satisfied with their work – understood that they need to create what she calls 'holding environments'.[5] The original holding-environment idea dates back to the first half of the twentieth century, and theorises that our first experience of one is in childhood, via attentive caregivers, who create a safe environment and space for small children to experiment. Today, it's been adopted more broadly into theories of adult psychology, and has come to mean a place where people can grow and develop. Businesses, corporations and offices provide a kind of holding environment for the workers within them, as well as handing out a sense of identity which comes from being a member.

'I'm a professor even when I'm not teaching,' says Ashford. 'Even if I haven't been able to research for weeks, I still am a professor for the University of Michigan and I get all sorts of affirmations about that – I'm invited to meetings, I'm cc'ed on memos, I have my name on an office door. But if I was someone who works alone and for some reason, I'm not doing the job that I say I do, that identity can feel less legitimate and easy to claim. And so, therefore, I can start to wonder: "Am I really X? Should I stop kidding myself? I'm not really X. And if I'm not X, what am I doing, and who am I?"' She calls this experience identity precariousness, which sits right next to financial precariousness in the list of things-which-make-solo-work-weird.

The tighter the link between your identity as a person and the job that you do, the harder it is to navigate the darkest, scariest times. If your business isn't doing well, then the psychological implication is that *you* are not doing well, particularly when – in contrast to when we work within organisations – there really isn't anyone else to blame and the feedback all slaps back onto us. As Ute Stephan, professor of Entrepreneurship at King's Business School, put it to me, 'It feels like a judgment on you as a person, on your abilities, on your life choices.' There's a danger in identifying too closely with your work, because if circumstances change – whether via global pandemic, political change, advancing technology, or your own health – and you can't do it, or you can't earn from it, then that can have excruciating ramifications. 'You can't control when there is a crisis or there's political uncertainty, or when one of your major contracts doesn't come through,' says Stephan. 'In those instances, I think it's critical to reframe it, to de-couple and say, "It's my work that's not going well, and that's not a judgement on me as a person".'

Is it better to try and do this when things are going well, and you have the mental bandwidth to think about this kind of thing, rather than in the middle of a work-related crisis?

'I think it seems like a sensible suggestion,' she laughs. 'But ... I do think when things are going well, soloists get a lot of energy out of solo work. The ups are higher but the downs will be lower.' It's my turn to laugh. That's the nature of solo work as a whole, isn't it, high highs and low lows? In the good times, we might take quite a lot of pleasure in *being* our jobs. It's only in the bad times when that begins to hurt.

If de-coupling your sense of self from your work either before a crisis, or during one, proves difficult or impossible, then just being aware of how your identity may be bound up with your work might help soothe the situation. As with much of how we manage solo work's potential impact on our well-being, how tightly coupled you are in the first place depends somewhat on whether you have a decent amount of non-work stuff going on too, which also informs your sense of identity. Having kids is definitely not the only way to do this, but it was what helped me to begin the process. Before kids, I was emphatically *a writer.* After kids my personality had to split into different pieces, which took up a lot more of my bandwidth and chopped up the time and energy I could give to my work. The result? My job is no longer the most salient thing about me. Intriguingly I have much lower levels of anxiety and my lows are not so low ... my highs are not so high, either, but for me that's a tolerable pay off.

Does this mean we need to try and cultivate a sense of identity as solo workers, which is broader than just being about our work? 'In identity theory, you could imagine identity as a series of bubbles in your head,' says Professor Ashford. 'Most people have several bubbles – you're a soloist but you're also a daughter, a sister and so on. And the bubbles are of varying sizes depending on the importance of that identity. If you have a ginormous work bubble and some tiny little bubbles around it, there is a lot of pressure on that one identity to carry all of the psychological functions that humans need. If you have more bubbles you can spread that load.'

Holding on to your holding environment

Because we don't work within traditional business set-ups which provide them, we soloists have to build our own holding environments. If you can build a good one, you'll be less anxious and stressed and better able to tolerate the precariousness of solo life, better able to concentrate and think creatively. 'The things you need sound superficial, but actually they are profound,' Professor Ashford told me. In her study of independent workers, which was specifically looking for ways in which people who worked alone could thrive, she found the soloists 'who had a more vital work life were better able to maintain four kinds of connections. One is connections to people: they had as much contact as they need – regular or functionally sporadic – with people who provide some sustenance for their work life, who could say things like, "You're doing great, you ought to aspire to do more", or people who bring inspiration, affirmation or guidance.'[6]

Second is connection to place. 'These people were thoughtful about where they did their work and setting it up in a way that gives them what they need,' she told me, recalling a screenwriter in the study who does her earliest drafts in the dawn light in bed, before moving to a desk and computer for the rest of the process, and another writer who chose to work in a tiny shed in his garden, because he felt that it contained his thoughts. (See chapter 10 for more detail on your work space and why it's important.)

Third is routine (see below) and fourth is a sense of purpose in their work. Soloists who feel their work has purpose find it easier to get back on track when something knocks them off, whether a simple interruption or when they just don't feel into whatever they have to do. 'They are connected to the why of what they are doing,' she says. They also know better which bits of work to say yes or no to, and can more 'authentically portray what they do' to clients and future clients. Ashford was writing a book when we spoke, and for those moments when she feels lethargic or disconnected from it, she's written a three-page 'motivation document' about why she wanted to write the book in the first place, and the people she thinks it will help, as a way to retain connection to her own purpose.

'It's not like these people don't suffer some anxiety,' says Ashford. 'But they learn to deal with it; it becomes a tolerable precariousness. Sometimes the best of them really learn to make that precariousness work for them. It has a generative quality as well.'

Feeling the fear and doing it anyway

Being resilient is partly about being brave, but being brave is not the same as being fearless. Working alone can be frightening, and it's completely normal to feel fearful sometimes. It would probably be odd if you didn't. Solo work is by its very nature, uncertain. We can only build ourselves around that fact – we can't get rid of it. Oddly, when coronavirus made a lot of traditional employment suddenly unsteady, many soloists could shrug and say, 'This is how it always is for me. I never really know where the next payment is coming from.' We had had time to get used to the unpredictability of solo work already. (Soloists tend to be better prepared for rough economic patches than traditionally employed people – since many of us worry that our businesses are vulnerable, we often squirrel money away for safekeeping. If you don't, do. It's calming.)

Fear is a part of life, a natural response to unfamiliar situations and a useful way for our brains to alert us to threats. We can't talk or squash it of existence, but we can get to know our fears and how to live with them. Unarticulated fears are so much harder to deal with than fears we know and understand, and often lead to a feeling of generalised dread and anxiety. Soloists' fears often hover around whether our businesses will fail, and what would happen if they did, but we may have other fears specific to our own strengths, weaknesses and industries too, around things like writing, public speaking or professional networking.

There are a number of tools soloists can use to get around our fears. Margaret Heffernan batches tasks which feel scary to her. 'One way to get around intimidating tasks is just do a lot of them,' she told me, when I asked her what advice she had for people who find specific tasks hard to face. 'With things like cold calling or chasing up on unpaid invoices, I think batching it makes it easier. So if I have a lot of follow-ups to do, or a lot of article pitches to do, I try to do them all in a morning or an afternoon. I get in the mood, I'll be on a roll and then it gets easier and easier. If I have a whole bunch of stuff to do that I really don't want to do, I do it in one fell swoop and get it over with.' For Heffernan, just getting an unpleasant job done is a reward in itself, but paradoxically you can use work as a reward too – choose a bit of work you really enjoy. Do the nasty work, have a proper break, and then reward yourself with the work you like. I know that sounds weird, but it will leave you with a far greater, nicer sense of satisfaction than a biscuit ever could. It doesn't work the other way around, by the way – doing work you loathe after work you enjoy actually makes the nasty work feel even nastier.[7]

In her book, *The Gig Economy*, Diane Mulcahy sets out a fear mitigation strategy that she uses for fears both big – leaving a job, starting a business – or small, and that she has been teaching in her gig economy course (part of an MBA) for the last few years, and she's kindly allowed me to explain it here, too. 'The way that I approach it is to take a very concrete approach to addressing fears,' she told me. 'So if your fear is picking up that phone to make a sales call, then we need to figure out what is the worst thing that could happen. I take my students or clients through this exercise, starting with the worst-case scenario they can imagine and making it concrete by having them write it down. And then once it's on paper, we examine it. If that fear happened, what would be the outcome? How probable is that that it will happen? And is there a way that you can mitigate some of the risks that you're worried about so it doesn't happen?'

Mulcahy says although you can do her exercise alone, it's much better to do it with someone else, so the whole thing doesn't only exist in your own head. 'By getting them down on paper, you can minimise fears by seeing that they're not really that bad. In our heads they can seem a lot worse.' The other benefit of doing this with another person? 'Hearing somebody else say, "Are you kidding me? That's never gonna happen." Another person's perspective can help us see our fears more realistically.'

'Where fear becomes disabling is when it sits in your head in a vague, unexamined way. Articulating fear is really, really helpful. When you see, on paper: "I'm worried I'll never make any money and have no place to live", you can see it for what it is, a subconscious animal-brain sort of fear.'

My own fear was always that someone will discover I'm actually a terrible writer. It sits with me still, but now in the open. We know each other well, this fear and I, so it has very little power. It's just an unwanted companion, a bug trapped in my car, a blister on my foot. Irritating, but not disabling.

The next step is to examine what would need to take place for the thing you fear to happen. If the fear is that you won't make money and won't have anywhere to live, what series of events would have to unfold for that to occur? The case study Mulcahy uses in her book notes that all her friends and entire family would have to die for her to be left homeless. On the other hand, if the process reveals that some of your fears are well founded, or you can't get them out of your head just by talking about them, then you need to figure out a way to manage them. As Mulcahy points out, if you really don't have enough capital to go freelance without getting close to the point of losing your house, then you're going to need to wait until you have saved enough, or figure out a different, less risky approach like bringing in a renter, or starting to freelance while you're still working in a full-time job.

Mulcahy also advocates managing fear levels by mitigating real (rather than imagined or far-fetched) risks, perhaps by starting a business on the side of an existing job and gradually reducing your full-time hours until you can safely quit; insuring against risk (I have a sickness and unemployment insurance policy which would pay out if I ever became too unwell to work long term); and shifting your risk – which is similar to mitigating it – by doing things like taking on longer-term freelance gigs, to provide a level of security not found in shorter projects.

Again, this is about looking inwards and finding out what we really think and feel. By picking apart what our fears are, considering whether they are realistic and then how to contain them if they are, we can manage even very scary-seeming things.

Mulcahy also points out that sometimes avoidance is OK. 'You don't have to be a hero in every aspect of your life,' she says. 'If you are afraid of chasing people up for invoices, if you view that as an unpleasant task, then outsource it and get someone else to do it! Talent doesn't have to touch the money,' she laughs.

It's OK to avoid bigger things sometimes, too. It's easy to default to a position where we feel as though we have to say yes to every opportunity but sometimes there's a happier middle ground to sit on. Maybe speaking at a conference would be great for your business ... but if you spend three weeks leading up to it being sick with anxiety and not sleeping, perhaps that's too high a price? It's up to you to decide where the fine line is between being too cautious and being overwhelmed by risk, and it can mean consciously letting go of preconceived ideas of what you 'should' be doing, thinking or feeling. If the idea of saying no to something floods you with relief, not regret, then that's OK. If it feels like everyone else is smashing it and doing things that fill you with dread, remember: almost no one boasts or posts on social media about the things they didn't, couldn't or wouldn't do.

A lot of the general chatter about business is about growth or scaling, increasing reach or generating new leads, sales, clients or contracts. Of course, you can't let your business grind to a halt, but even the UK government was criticised recently, in a self-employment report called 'The Way to Well-being',[8] for focusing too much on growth. It pointed out that the vast majority of self-employed people neither need nor want their little businesses to grow. You don't *have* to grow your solo business. If you've got ten clients, and no desire to develop a team, and no time to take on more, then you don't need to grow. If you're a plumber, visiting your maximum number of properties per week, with no ache for a fleet of vans and a clutch of apprentices, you don't need to grow. Just because the language of growth and increase gets bandied around, you don't have to buy into it. You are, after all, *just one person*. Accepting that requires a particular kind of courage, but it also means you don't have to do a bunch of things you'd probably find scary. You can let yourself off the hook.

Throwing paint at the wall

'Throw paint at the wall' is written on a sticky note stuck to my computer. I took it from a conversation I had with Nicholas Hooper, the composer. You have almost certainly heard his music, because Hooper has written more than 250 film and television scores, won a couple of Baftas and been nominated for a Grammy. He is best known for the magical scores he wrote for *Harry Potter and the Order of the Phoenix* and *Harry Potter and the Half-Blood Prince*.

That quick precis doesn't do justice to the ebb and flow of his career – like all of us, he has had ups and downs, and found his theoretical career-high of scoring the Potter films extremely tough. 'My heart races just to think about that period,' he says. 'It was so scary. I did get stuck. I think just about everybody involved did at some point, because Potter was like a big mountain – with a big fan base, and massive expectations. And in my case, not masses of experience in Hollywood.' He recalls one Easter Day spent panic-working.

'I was writing the music for the dementors in the underpass in *Order of the Phoenix*.' If you haven't seen the film, the dementors are terrifying, soul-sucking floating shadowy creatures. The scene is grim and the music electrifyingly unpleasant. 'I hadn't been able to get it right so in the morning there I was, still writing it. Finally, it worked, and the neighbours still remember the horrible noises coming from the studio, the awful dementors' music.'

When Hooper gets stuck, he doesn't freeze up. 'It was like throwing paint at the wall,' he told me. 'I just chucked stuff around to see what happened. A lot of the music I composed was like that. But it does mean,' he laughs, 'that there are a further 12 hours of music sitting in Warner Bros vaults which won't be used for anything.' (He also, with a Britishness I identify with, likes regular breaks for a cup of tea and plenty of short walks.)

His perseverance is similar to something I heard the actor and entrepreneur Wendell Pierce say in a radio interview last year. Despite his TV roles in *The Wire*, *Treme* and *Suits*, and his stage performances in plays like *Death of a Salesman*, he was talking about how he deals with his own imposter syndrome. 'When in doubt, do the work,' he said. 'When in the deepest doubt, work even harder.'

That doesn't necessarily mean plough on regardless – we know that can lead to a spiral of panic and poor executive functions. But, if you feel the fear rising, you can cut it off by choosing an easy task to start on, perhaps even one which is not directly related to the thing you should be doing, the thing which is scaring you. Don't do this all the time, otherwise you will slide into procrastination, or busywork, but if panic is getting you by the throat, throw some paint at the wall by writing the title of your project on a blank document, or choosing how you will format it, or clean and arrange the tools you need to start a job. Break down what has to be done, then choose the very tiniest, most incremental way to start and then keep going. Write a paragraph plan. Decide on a colourway. Ignore the fact that you're starting something, and before you know it, you will have.

It's a technique the drinks writer Victoria Moore uses. She's so prolific, producing hundreds of thousands of words every year, that I find it hard to believe what she says about herself, but this is what she told me: 'It's about absolutely breaking everything down into contained tasks and mini-tasks. I'm fundamentally lazy and if I can put something off, I will. Writing a piece always feels very daunting, still, and I am apt to be lazy and not do it properly. So I break down every task – almost like they are boxes that can be coloured in – into things like research and then the actual writing ... Because if you have to research something without writing it, that's just fun! Then if you have to write something but you've already done the research, that's easy.'

Tim Herrara, who writes the *New York Times'* Smarter Living newsletter, calls this 'the magic of just getting started', and uses Newton's law of motion to illustrate the point – that is, something moving tends to keep moving.[9] Someone working tends to keep working.[10] He reckons that if you can just clear that first hurdle, starting, then you're likely to keep going (certainly much more likely than if you don't start, anyway). By using micro-goals, like Moore, you can also give your brain a micro-boost of feel-good dopamine, because it will reward every time you meet one, even if they seem tiny – just as we are rewarded with mildly addictive dopamine for social media likes. Another way to ensure that once started, we carry on.

Fear is so often the thing that stops us starting, or that stops us once we've started. By adopting these mantras and micro-practices, we can convince ourselves to start, and then keep on carrying on. By keeping Hooper's words in my head, when I get stuck, it is easier to take what I do less seriously, whenever it starts to feel so serious that I am intimidated. It doesn't matter – I'm just chucking paint at the wall. It's perfect for those moments when you're too frightened to get started, too overwhelmed, or too stuck. When a task seems too scarily big to even start, we can make it micro, and suck the fear right out of it.

Strike a pose

I was standing outside a TV studio, hoping that no one had noticed I was power posing – legs wide, arms wide, trying to take up as much space as I possibly could. The crew were passing to and fro, almost certainly assuming I'd finally lost my marbles, when in fact, I was just trying to play another trick on my brain. Live TV is one of the most fear-inducing things I do for work and came about unexpectedly – I was scouted via a magazine I used to edit, and innocently went along to the secretive audition not knowing I was trying out for a job as a regular guest on a weekly magazine show, *Sunday Brunch*, on Channel Four. I probably got the job because I blithely had no idea what I was getting into, and was only told what the gig was the Wednesday before my first Sunday show. It's live. And millions watch it. I was nearly sick on the set on my very first day.

Navigating the fear that came with this particular job took several years, and although I appeared 48 weeks a year for four years, anxiety about it still occasionally knocks me off course, although nowadays I only appear every few months. Power posing proved useful, and now I use it before interviews or anything which feels alarming, even ringing editors with pitches. However, the study which made power posing famous back in 2012 is controversial, with some over-the-top criticism levelled at one of the authors, Amy Cuddy, who quickly became famous for her books and TED talk. In 2018 she published new data refuting many of the criticisms and suggesting that power posing, or what she now calls 'postural feedback' really does make people feel more powerful. (She now plays down what she initially said about its positive hormonal effects.) Then, in 2019, another meta study pushed back, saying that power posing only appears effective in studies where it's compared with slouching, contracted poses (which make people feel much worse), and that it's never been compared with standing or sitting normally.[11] In my tiny, unscientific study of one all I can say is this: standing like a superhero, or with arms stretched in a V above my head, or making myself into a giant cross, makes me feel something close to invincible. It does make you look like a bit of a lunatic though.

Gratitude

When I was pregnant with my first child, after five harrowing years of infertility and IVF treatment, I was terrified. Fully, debilitatingly terrified. Terrified of losing the baby, terrified of having the baby, terrified of what all the hormones and drugs I had taken might do to me and the baby. Terrified of eating the wrong things, and not enough of the right things. My friend Marian Hodgkin, a global expert in education in emergencies and extremely good at knowing the right thing to say at all times, told me that I should try and feel grateful. 'Because it's very hard to feel scared and grateful at the same time.' While I was technically already grateful, I hadn't really accessed it as an emotion – it was more like something I knew I should feel. That was my first experience of the psychological power of gratitude. These days, it's a well-known phenomenon so I'll recap the evidence quickly: cultivating a grateful outlook helps us sleep better; increases positive emotions and decreases negative ones; encourages pro-social behaviour; increases creativity; curtails loneliness; lowers blood pressure; it might even help shorten episodes of depression.[12] It doesn't seem to have a downside.

You've probably already heard about gratitude journaling, the practice of writing down things for which you are grateful each day, which is probably the quickest, low-input high-impact way of developing your gratitude muscles. (I've always thought it's very closely related to saying an evening or a morning prayer, too.) I don't write anything down, but for the last five years, Steve and I have chosen three things to be grateful for each night. It sounds hokey – it is hokey – but it forces us to find something good to say about even the worst days. In fact, it's the irritating days when it's tricky to find three things to say – on those low days, we lie in bed grimly searching for something, anything, to say on a day when all our clients were nightmarish, our most expensive equipment broke, the internet went down and toddlers smeared a newly painted wall with hummus. But those are the days when being grateful has the greatest impact on our psyches. On the worst days, paradoxically, it's easier to find things to say thank you for, since those are the days when you're grateful for doctors, for somewhere to live, that we ever managed to have kids, or that everyone made it through the day at all. In general, the practice has tilted my mindset in the direction of generalised low-level gratitude. I've always known that I *should* be extremely grateful for where I happened to find my life taking place. Now, I actually am.

Help

I can't stress this enough: don't suffer alone. Whether you've got a fractious work issue that you can't unravel, or a deeper, longer sense of anxiety or sadness, help is available, and people want to help you. As I've said before, soloists tend to think we are more alone than we need to be, and we tend to think that other soloists are managing whatever we can't manage, by themselves. This is such a big mistake – all successful soloists have invisible teams behind them, and you deserve to have a team too. People love to feel useful – I get such a kick out of mentoring newer soloists who are struggling – but to get help, you have to ask for help. There's more on this in the chapter on networks (see page 244), but please, if life or work feels frightening, ask. (There's a list of resources specifically for solo workers on my website, which I update continually, at www.howtoworkalone.com.)

Caffeine

Caffeine is the world's most popular psychoactive drug. I would also wager that it is the world's primary – mostly unrealised – cause of persistent anxiety and panic attacks. The sweaty, shaking hands, racing heart and shortness of breath I used to experience most days at work were not because I was worried about anything specific, but because I drank three or four flat whites a day. Even if you have grown tolerant of its immediately stimulating effects, caffeine has a half-life of up to 24 hours in the body, so it messed up my sleep too – I rarely went to sleep before 1am in my twenties; now I find that too much caffeine means I wake at 3am for an hour or two, worrying or planning, with no memory of any of my thoughts in the morning.

I haven't given it up completely but I have cut down to one caffeinated coffee early in the morning, and nothing caffeinated at all – including tea and green tea – after midday. Annoyingly, it works like magic. I sleep better, earlier and longer, panic less and feel less like my mind is on the point of breaking. (Steve gave up caffeine completely; it fixed decades of persistent insomnia and he's much more evangelical about giving up than me.)

Society deifies caffeine, and we behave as though it's the only thing which allows us to function. I think it's the opposite way around: caffeine makes us lurch from high to low and back again in the daytime, and stops us recharging properly at night – if we manage to get to sleep, it affects the quality of it. For many of us, it gets in the way of our functions and accentuates our anxieties and fears. For soloists and office workers alike, it can become embedded in our daily rewards systems and break times, even though its costs can trickle well into the night.

7

Focus and Flow

Multitasking is a myth

Aza Raskin would like to say sorry. He is the inventor of the infinite scroll, the continuous way sites like Instagram, Twitter and Facebook allow us to use one finger to endlessly serve up content. 'I regret that I didn't think more about how this thing would be used,' he said at the launch of a campaign for better use of tech by the Centre for Humane Technology.[1] He says he still feels depressed about what he created, and how it contributed to smartphone addiction, distraction and perhaps even a mental health crisis.

I have done so much research for this chapter, but sometimes I feel like it could be summed up in a sentence. 'If you want to focus, put your phone in a drawer.' Maybe two. 'Log out of your email and social accounts and turn off all your notifications.'

Easier said than done, though right? I write as someone with a definite smartphone problem which I am only just beginning to grip on – my best days hover around three hours usage, but my worst tops out at seven hours. A day. That's an outrageous, horrifying amount of life to fritter away, scrolling – and the really hideous part of it, is that when I look at the screen time data my phone generates, although I do plenty of actual work on my phone, I almost always spend two to three hours on social media. I am not an influencer. I do not run an online business. *What am I doing?*

I also know the science. I know what smartphones do to our ability to concentrate and get our work done efficiently so that we can finish it, and go off and do something else (they derail it, and they lower IQ by 10 points).[2] I know that we interrupt ourselves as quickly as 40 seconds into a work task, or switch tasks as often as every three or four minutes. We check our email, on average, 74 times a day, but some of us do it more than 400 times.

I know that because we get interrupted, or interrupt ourselves with our devices, hundreds of times a day, we might never really focus, because it takes 23 minutes and 15 seconds to refocus properly on a task, after an interruption. Just 20 interruptions a day would mean we never get the chance to focus, on this basis. (I also know that self-interruptions are even more disruptive than external interruptions.)[3] I know that this floods our bodies with cortisol, leaving us feeling low-level, hard-to-explain stressed, all the time.

Linda Stone, the writer and consultant on technology and attention (who had a prior career at Apple and Microsoft) calls this 'continual partial attention ... an always-on, any-where, anytime, any place behavior that involves an artificial sense of constant crisis. We are always in high alert when we pay continuous partial attention.'[4]

So. If you want to get anything done, put your smart-phone in a drawer, log out of everything, and turn off your notifications.

Soloists love productivity. Professor Susan Ashford studies independent workers. She found that soloists have an 'obses-sion with being productive, staying productive and getting back to being productive on their "real" work, not back-office work ... the more they are drawn away from their "real" work or into procrastination, the more anxious they become.' When you're solo, no one is paying you for the hours you spend staring into space, or time gobbled up by pointless meetings, emails or calls. Staying focused, getting work done and getting it done on time, all really matter to us. A bad day's work on someone else's dollar is one thing. A bad day on our time is quite another.

And yet. The way the world is arranged today is *terrible* for productivity. Fortunately, soloists have more freedom than anyone else in the economy to wriggle free – not necessarily so that we can squeeze more out of each day, but so that we can get what needs to be done, done. And walk away.

Our brains are wired for novelty bias. We *love* beginnings. Novelty can feel, in the moment, a bit like being productive. It's not. It's hopping about like a fly stuck in front of a windowpane. Plus, the dopamine hit we get every time we move from one thing to another (let alone the added hit we get from likes or comments) is addictive.

Although we think we can manage multiple things, hopping from one to the next, multitasking doesn't really exist, at least not at work. Our brains just can't do it. The idea makes us feel like we should be able to do loads of things at once. In fact, all that happens is we flit from unfinished task to unfinished task (Instagram – work – Instagram – online banking – work – online shopping – Facebook – work – phone call – work), and every time we flit, or even swap between work tasks, leaving the first one unfinished, we leave a little more of our attention behind, spreading it more and more thinly.

The problem is called attention residue and was named by Dr Sophie Leroy, at the University of Washington. As we flit, nothing gets completed, or even done well, and our brains slowly run out of capacity to attend to any one thing, like the batteries in a toy running down. It's always been a feature of how our brains work – and probably had its plus points somewhere back in prehistory – but they really can't cope with today's multiple tabs, unread emails, unmet deadlines and dozens of competing bids for our attention. You can *sort-of* multitask if at least one of the things is so easy or habitual you can do it almost without thinking – having a conversation while cooking or ironing, listening to a podcast while putting away laundry, eating a meal while watching a film. Perhaps there are aspects of your work which fit this bill – digital retouching while listening to music, perhaps, or familiar manual tasks like sanding wood, or packaging products to send out. I listen to the radio when I'm cleaning the studio, or polishing glassware when it's been hired for a dinner. But notice that none of the lists include things like prepare an annual sales report while checking Instagram, writing a social media plan while cooking a meal, or proofreading while looking after children.

When you try to multitask, or start new tasks with earlier tasks un-finished and encroaching on your focus, you remember less accurately too.[5] Do you struggle to remember what you should be doing or were about to do? Or feel like you forget a lot? I routinely arrive at my desk, full of purpose, or pick up my phone to make a call or add a calendar entry and have no clue what I was about to do. It's because we ask our brains to attend to far more than they can manage. Remembering what we need to do at work is obviously useful, but not hampering our memory in general would also mean we would remember things in our non-work life too, things like birthdays or sending thank you notes, paying bills or family events.

Even if you think you have an exceptional brain, in practice you can only do one focused task at a time. You might
feel able to do several very easy habitual tasks at the same
time but most things are done better one at a time. It was
tricky to come up with the list of examples above because I
kept thinking of ways in which splitting our attention leads
to poor results: being deep in conversation means I've burned
whole meals; I've missed my stop on trains because I've been
emailing; I've put the washing machine on the wrong setting
because I've been talking on the phone.

It's not just that split focus is bad for productivity because
we get less done – we are also much more likely to make a
mistake. As Chris Bailey points out in his book, *Hyperfocus*,
our brains are bombarded with millions of bits of information (11 million a second, he says), but we can only process
about 40 at a time. Our capacity, relative to the complexity
of the world we are in, is quite limited.

Although we might run low on attention when we flit from
thing to thing, leaving stuff unfinished, and although doing so
sucks up our working memory, our brains still quietly keep
track of everything which has been interrupted. We may like
novelty, but our brains like conclusions too. This is what's
known as the Ziegarnik effect, which basically means stuff
lodges in our brains whenever we are interrupted (it's what
makes TV cliffhangers so effective – unfinished stories linger
with us). The Ziegarnik effect can contribute to our feelings of
overwhelm by adding to a general sense that there's a lot to do,
in a lot of places, and not enough time to do it. It whittles away
our remaining mental bandwidth, and is yet another argument
for doing one thing at a time and – where possible – finishing
it. (It's why giving yourself realistic to-do lists, and actually
doing the things on them, are so important. See page 151.)

My best days are the days when I remember this: humans are amazing, but we weren't terribly well equipped to deal with even the pre-digital age, from an information-management point of view.

Believing that we can take in, process, and handle everything the world throws at us is one of the things which lands us in trouble when it comes to trying to cope with the tidal waves of data that wash over us, every waking moment. As the writer of *Overwhelmed*, Brigid Schulte, put it to me, 'There are all sorts of strategies and life hacks and tips and tricks to be productive and get stuff done, but it really comes down to the very first and most critical step, which is setting yourself up with realistic expectations and priorities and learning to forgive yourself. You're not superhuman.'

For a long time, multitasking has been seen as aspirational: you were so busy and important, and you had so much to do, that you became skilled at a complicated juggling act. Except, no one is any good at the juggle. Expecting to be good at it makes us feel like screw-ups when things go wrong, whether little things – we forget an umbrella on the way to a meeting on a rainy day – or big things – we forget to bring the Powerpoint presentation for that same meeting. A better but less compelling image should instead be someone with just one ball at a time, throwing it up and catching it, throwing it up and catching it.

Productivity is not actually a virtue

Productivity is an end, not a virtue, as the organisational psychologist Adam Grant often points out. It's a way of getting us somewhere. Making whether you were productive or not the most valued thing in your day doesn't actually tell you much. You can productively sort your paperclips, or productively order stationery, but that doesn't make you effective at your job. Grant encourages us to be excited about the end that being productive might get us to, not productivity itself. He asks us to think about the people our work might help or bring joy to, about the people who might depend on us to do our work, or about the ways in which our work might improve the world, in ways however small. I am more motivated to get my work done when I think about the potential audience who may value or enjoy the results, which makes me more productive. It makes for a nicer day, too.

Jamelia Donaldson, founder of wildly successful Treasure Tress, a natural hair care subscription box for black women, put it this way to me. 'Remove the pressure to think you consistently have to create. You cannot pour from an empty cup. Days spent in silence with a notebook organizing thoughts can be much more productive and useful in the long term, than a solid and intense day spent answering emails. Don't let your to-do list fool you.'

Routine

'Having to invent yourself from scratch every single morning is much, much harder than people who haven't done it imagine,' Margaret Heffernan told me. 'What they see is freedom and what we see are overwhelming options: I could stay in bed, I could write a new book, I could book a holiday, I could phone my friends, I could do a million different things every morning because there's nobody to tell me no. Having that much freedom is actually really, really hard to manage.' At first, when you leave the confines of an organisation (if that's how your solo life started), it's fabulous, she says. 'And then it's a little ridiculous. I used not to be able to do *anything* I wanted, but now I can do *everything* I want. Where do I start? You tend to go for the stuff that feels urgent: "Yikes – I need to make some money" or "Yikes – I need to meet that deadline". On one level, that's okay because those things are important, but as time goes by trying to invent yourself every single morning is exhausting.' The result is that Heffernan is deeply committed to her routine and uses it to ensure she both starts her day, and finishes it. 'I'm somebody who tends to overwork rather than underwork, but routine, I-will-be-at-my-desk-by-9-o'colock, is also good for people who worry about being slackers.'

Having a routine provides structure, according to productivity coach Karen Eyre-White, who left her high-powered job as a chief executive in the UK civil service in order to help people get the right amount from their days. 'Most of my clients don't understand structure, and haven't quite understood that it's a problem for them. They just know there's something wrong – they feel really overwhelmed, can't focus or can't get started on things. But we are social animals, and I think there's a reason that lots of people go out and commute to work: it's because we like to do what other people do, and we like to have those structures and rhythms created for us; doing what everyone else is doing creates the idea of routine and normality. When people are at home, they don't have that.'

One recent client, newly solo after an office job, was in distress because she'd always seen herself as hard-working but couldn't focus at all. Eyre-White created a structure that simply involved not working at home, where – it turned out – the client felt terribly isolated and alone. Eyre-White encouraged her to leave her flat each morning at 7.30am and go to a co-working space or cafe. 'It turned out starting early was something that she associated with hard work,' she says. Working at home allowed her start point to drift, which stopped her from starting at all. 'Previously she hadn't realised this was a problem, but it's made a 100 per cent difference.'

Routine is crucial for focus because it helps focus become habitual. Habits require less willpower, and it seems that we have a limited amount of willpower each day. If you use up some of it bickering with yourself about when to get to your desk/work bench/laptop, then you will find it harder to access more willpower when you need it later on, for other things. Constantly arguing with yourself about when or if you'll start work is exhausting.

We need willpower to keep us at our desks when we need to be there, to stop us hitting social media or playing more computer games than we should, to help us make decent choices around what we eat or drink during our solo days, to remember to step away from our work for breaks. We need self-control to stop us staying at work far later than we should. We need it to help us separate ourselves from work when we take time off, and to help us exercise and get enough sleep. Willpower's finiteness is what makes it much harder to resist biscuits in the afternoon, and even though you said to yourself that you would go to the gym and wouldn't have a glass of wine tonight, much more difficult to hold to that decision at 7pm.

'Human beings are terrible, in the moment, at making decisions that will be good for them in the long term,' says Brigid Schulte. 'We tend to have what's called present bias. We think in the moment and make a decision in the moment.' But if you create a structure for your day in advance, you don't need to make ad hoc decisions all the time, based on what's immediately in front of you, meaning your choices can have better long-term consequences, whether that's because it gives you a framework to get more business, to see other people, or just meet your deadlines.

Having a routine makes all this much easier. If parts of your day or week are a given, you need far less willpower. The decision – that work starts at 9.30am and finishes at 5.30pm; that you only look at your emails after midday; that you won't buy biscuits; that you don't drink on weeknights; that you made a plan to go to the gym with a friend who you don't want to let down – was made in the past, and doesn't need to be made now.

Admittedly, you do need some willpower to follow through, but far less than if you have to invent your day, every day. Of course, there will be interruptions and distractions and unexpected events, but these can all be recovered from, as long as you know what you should have been doing when you were interrupted.

Even better, make a plan as you're interrupted for how you will get back to what you were originally doing. Sophie Leroy (inventor of the term 'attention residue') produced a paper which showed that people who were interrupted but who took a moment to note down where they were in their task and how to return to it were able to go straight back to it and do it just as well as before. People who were interrupted without making a plan took longer and fared less well at the task itself.[6]

In real life terms this is like sticking a bookmark in a novel you're reading – you can stop, safe in the knowledge that you know exactly where to pick it up from. In practice, it means making a note of what you are doing and where you will restart whenever the phone rings, or if you have to leave for a meeting.

This is related to setting communications boundaries too – if you're deep into a piece of work and it's going well, you don't have to answer the phone, or immediately respond to messages. We are wired – as discussed – to love newness as well as social contact. But at the wrong moment, these things can wreck a working day, forcing us to be at work for longer periods than we really need to be. Periods when we could be having real social contact with actual humans, at our leisure.

When it comes to finding the right style of routine for each of us, 'It's all about experimenting. Nobody ever figures it out from the very beginning,' Brigid Schulte told me. 'It's a process of adapting and changing. Be clear about your priorities: set your goals, intentions and values. Then, see if you can find systems that will help you realise them, your little experiments. Try something for one week and then stop and think "OK, did that work? How can I tweak things?" Or, "OK now I've got X sorted, I'm going to try Y."

'As a solo worker, could you have a day once a week where you go out to lunch with somebody new?' asks Schulte. 'Is Wednesday your networking day? Or is Thursday your day to drum up new business? Is Monday your writing day? Do you have in days and out days – in days for actually doing the work, and out days for making connections and getting ideas and new business? Creating systems that are going to help you make good decisions in the moment, decisions that are going to get you to your long-term goal, can go a long way to helping you feel a sense of ease.'

Levison Wood, the television presenter and explorer, spent his first three years after leaving the army completely routine free. 'It was hard because it included so much unpredictability and instability,' he told me. 'For those three years, while I was setting up a little expedition company called Secret

Compass, I was basically homeless. I went from having free clothes and free housing in the army, to sleeping on mates' floors between expeditions. I was working around the clock, answering emails at 3am and waking up at seven. I mean, everything was work, I didn't have a holiday for about five years.'

Today, his routines are firmly in place. Rather than a weekly routine, Wood has chosen to divide his work and non-work life into sets of days now that his career is more established and he can afford to do so. 'I forecast out up to 12 months and fraction off holiday time, as if I had a real job. I book time off with myself. It's important to have that for your own well-being but also your social life – if you go away the whole time or you're forever working, people will just stop inviting you to weddings, and you can't have any form of relationship that is going to ever work.' Now he works for blocks of days on things like book writing, and then rewards himself with chunks of time, ring-fenced to prevent work spilling into non-work times. 'I very much try and keep to work hours. And I will ignore things until the following day. You've got to be quite strict.'

'I need a routine!' says Dior Bediako, founder of Pepper Your Talk, a support and networking platform for young people entering the fashion industry. 'That is key. I work at a co-working space, and I'm one of those very rare people who actually likes getting the train in. I like dividing my day up into little chunks. I wake up, I get ready, I jump on the train, and I get to work.' At lunchtime she makes sure she leaves the building and she likes to do a bit fashion-based people watching. 'I like to see how other people have dressed for the day. I don't know if that's weird, I don't know if it's because I'm in fashion, but I like to see the different personas people have chosen. I get inspired by how people have chosen to show up for their day.' She doesn't fixate on her focus either. 'I think we can put too much pressure on ourselves to be super-focused all the time. When I'm not that focused I don't beat myself up about it. I'm human.'

Finding out how other people do what you do, or want to do, is a handy way to assess what kind of routine might work for you. The film score writer Nick Hooper told me he chose his (very methodical, very repeatable) routine after being inspired by composer Benjamin Britten, who worked to a very exact timetable: 9am until lunch, a walk, letters, then work until 8pm, dinner and an early bedtime. But maybe a nine-to-five routine makes you feel restricted. Maybe you're a night owl and like to work into the night, when the phone won't be ringing. You don't need to choose a traditional routine, and you don't need every day or week to look the same.

Some soloists might be better suited to creating a new routine each day, perhaps within fairly fixed parameters, like a start and end time. If so, it's usually easier to determine what the next day will look like at the end of the last one. Victoria Moore, the wine writer, always does her next-day planning, the night before. 'I break everything down into really small parts, lists and mini-deadlines – that's part of my time management and my energy management,' she told me. 'I sit down every single night before I go to bed and I write my to-do list for the next day. Sometimes I do it in the morning but it's never effective because I'm very sensitive to getting off to a good start in the day. If I spend a chunk of time faffing around with a to-do list, then it wears down some of that nice fresh energy. It's vital to do it the night before. I kind of pre-programme myself for the next day and if I haven't pre-programmed myself I get so much less out of my time.'

In her sessions, Karen Eyre-White uses a technique she calls Ideal Week, to help people create routines, using a blank week in a diary or online calendar to design what a dream working week could be.

'It forces you to confront how many hours you have,' she says. 'We all have ideas in our heads about how much time we've got and how long something's going to take. It also helps to get away from this idea that you have to work nine to five. It empowers people to think about their time differently, and to think: when do I want to work? And how can I use pockets of time that I might not think I could? And how can I have conversations about this with people that I live with?'

The first task is to allocate time each week to stuff which has to be done, fencing off household chores or shopping, which easily smuggle themselves into a solo day. Try to be realistic about what needs doing, how often and when – I, for example, would love to walk in after dropping my kids and get straight to work. But I struggle when our breakfast stuff hasn't been cleared away. I talked about this with Eyre-White (she must have been *fascinated*) and she suggested I leave it until an allotted break time. I tried, but turns out that for me, that particular untidiness interferes with my focus – it's an undone task, sucking up memory – and I work better knowing it's done, not waiting for me. Knowing this, it no longer fills me with rage every day.

'Once you've put the stuff that has to be done in to your week, and clearly identified what is work time and what isn't, then I recommend thinking through when you're at your most productive, focused best. When is the best time for you to be doing focused, head down work? This could be writing, strategic thinking, or responding to that really tricky client question. For many people it is first thing in the morning, so I talk to a lot of my clients about how they can protect those first hours of the day and push other work to later in the day. Others do their best thinking in the afternoon or evening. It's about parcelling your work time in to different types of work.'

In her own life Eyre-White, who has a small child who is only in childcare two days a week, noticed there was a pocket of time in the mornings she could be using, and gets 45 minutes work done between 7am and 7.45am, while her husband gets the breakfast.

The Ideal Week exercise is also a way to designate times when you are definitely in non-work mode, and by having them laid out in front of you, they are easier to stick to. Rather than a vague sense of 'it's the weekend, I shouldn't work', you can allocate a parcel of time, a Sunday night or a couple of hours on a Saturday morning, say, when essential over-hanging work can be dealt with, which can help your brain stop thinking about it. (I recommend getting it done sooner rather than later, so you're not carrying its weight in your downtime, but other time-management experts, like business writer Laura Vanderkam, reckon an hour or two on a Sunday night can set you up for a better week. Experiment.)

Once you've designed it, the next step is to try to implement a realistic version of it. 'That doesn't mean you'll keep to it exactly every week, and this isn't about planning out every minute of your life and then beating yourself up when you're ten minutes late to do something,' says Eyre-White. 'Stuff happens. But having a clear idea, in writing, of what an ideal week would look like makes it much more likely that you'll start to adapt your habits and routines towards that ideal, and make decisions which support it. For example, in my ideal week I see clients on specific days. When a client asks what sessions I have available, having done my ideal week reminds me not to offer them 2pm on any day. Instead, I only offer them the days that I would like to be seeing clients. If they can't make those days, and it's make or break for them, then I'll flex it, but I'm significantly increasing my chances of having a working pattern which works best for me by firstly offering them my preferred days.'

Like almost everything in this book, it's about knowing exactly what we, personally, need to get our work done effectively, and then aiming for it, while also being forgiving of ourselves. 'I talk to a lot of clients about what their plan B is if their intentions don't pan out. Maybe they've had a particularly bad night's sleep and when they sit down at their desk they get pulled in to their inbox rather than digging out that difficult client brief and getting started on it. When an hour later they realise what has happened, the instinct can be to think "I failed – I didn't do what I intended to do, so I may as well keep going on this track". Changing that mindset and developing kinder ways of talking to ourselves means we can get ourselves back on to our plan for the day even when it hasn't started well. That might be a specific ritual for when that happens, like going to make a cup of tea; when back at the desk, you can go back to the plan. Or it might be accepting that today hasn't worked but tomorrow will be a fresh start.'

Eyre-White also suggests creating transitional rituals for that moment when we shift from non-work to work, especially if we work from home. 'For some people it's getting dressed in the right clothes that signal to your brain that it's now in work mode. Another idea is burning a candle that you only have when you're working, which can itself feel almost like a treat, as well as being able to physically see the candle burn down as you're working.'

I have my own rituals, although I hadn't realised. For a long time, I viewed the slowness of my mornings very negatively – despite being awake at 6.30am, it's often 9.45am or 10am when I sit down to work, which drove me crazy. What was I doing for all that time? Why couldn't I shower and start work at 8am like my husband?

The truth is, what he does, who he is and how he works is very different to me, and I shouldn't and can't judge myself by his behaviour. What matters is only how I work, and the same is true of whatever it takes for you to get your work done effectively.

I could 'save' time by not doing my hair, not wearing make-up, not carefully choosing what I wear, and just throwing on jeans and a sweatshirt. But I wouldn't be transitioning myself into a working frame of mind. When for whatever reason I do skip my rituals, I don't get much work done in the time I would usually have been pottering – which is the time other people are using to travel to workplaces, pick up a coffee, greet co-workers and ease into their day. The start of the coronavirus crisis was difficult for people who were suddenly forced to work from home: stripped of their unconscious rituals, many struggled to create a boundary between work and non-work space *and* time, and as a direct result found it hard to focus or produce.

In some ways, my hair-and-make-up habit is shallow and a little vain – barely anyone sees me most days, so there's no real need to look smart. But it matters to me and contributes to my sense of self. It's part of my identity that I always wear a swoop of black eyeliner; if I let all the little things like that slip away, then who am I? And if I'm asking myself existential questions like that one, you can be damn sure I won't be getting much work done.

If you easily get drawn into home-related tasks when you work from home, then these rituals can be a powerful preventative. You're dressed for work, not doing laundry – and if you've allocated time for chores, as Eyre-White suggests, both will help avoid getting sucked in. (Of course, your rituals will be different – and probably less about eyeliner. There are plenty of people who would suggest yoga or mindfulness as a way to start a working day, and while those would be lovely, I also know how frenzied mornings are in many homes. Many morning ritual hacks call for creative visualisations, affirmations or journaling ... and all are good if they work for you. But they can be whatever you like – coffee in a particular mug standing in your porch watching the world walk by, going for a run, or like the digital strategist Vivian Nunez, watch the previous night's Stephen Colbert from *The Late Show* over breakfast. Once it's finished, she knows it's time to start work.)

The same is true in reverse – end-of-day rituals like writing tomorrow's to-do list, powering down your equipment, disabling your email or work-related apps like Slack on your phone, changing your clothes, having a shower, putting away your work so you can't see it or shutting an office door, all help transition us back into non-work life. And help us stay there, too.

Judging by results

Results Only Work Environments (ROWE) were invented in the mid 2000s by Cali Ressler and Jody Thompson at Best Buy in the US (they went on to write the best-selling *Why*

Work Sucks and How To Fix It and subsequently set up a consultancy which helps other companies become ROWEs). The premise is that if businesses do away with the requirement to be at work nine to five, and let staff be completely autonomous, then effectiveness and productivity goes through the roof. No more tug of war between the needs of home and work, freedom to work whenever and wherever and to take unlimited time off, as long as the work gets done. There's not a lot of data on the approach, but what there is suggests ROWE employees sleep on average almost an hour more on working nights and exercise more, and ROWE businesses have reduced employee turnover and improved morale. Ressler and Thompson reckon productivity on ROWE teams they worked with went up by 41 per cent.

I like the ethos for soloists because it can liberate us from the idea that a traditional routine is most effective. The only question is: did the work get done?

In a ROWE, arriving at your workplace at 2pm is not considered coming in late, just as leaving the workplace at 2pm is not considered leaving early. It is OK to shop on a Wednesday morning. You don't need to sit at your desk for eight solid hours. You can take unlimited time off, as long as the work gets done.

I adopted my old office's schedule when I started working on my own. While routine is a good thing, whenever my 9.30am to 5pm-ish routine gets disrupted because of life or if I want to take some time off, I feel guilty. (Thanks, Calvinist work ethic.) What am I feeling guilty for? I don't have an organisation, breathing down my neck. The only person who knows when I start work and when I finish is me. Hauling a big sack of guilt about, just because I made two cups of coffee, or was still in the shower at 9.42am, is a waste of time.

Whether the *work* gets done is not, in fact, the only thing which matters. I think we can apply whatever measure we want here. It could be: did the project get completed this week? Did I earn my target this month? Or it could be: did I manage to cut my hours enough that I saw my friends? Did I spend enough time with my family this month? Did I manage to take a week off work this month and still get everything done?

Know your time

Knowing what you currently do with your time is another part of building a new or improved routine. We already know how easy it is, when working alone and with no one to account to, to fill time with pseudo-work, prioritising easy jobs which can be ticked off your list and make a day feel full and productive, when actually you've spent most of your time ordering business cards, or responding to every single email just so that you can reach inbox zero. (Inbox zero is a topic of dissent in my house. My husband thinks my inbox is shockingly untidy. I think it's a waste of time when someone could be paying me, or I could be doing something which isn't work, to be wading through the 150 emails I get every day, even with filters and all the management systems I can find, in place. None the less, he literally cannot bear to look.)

There's a time and a place for some of this sort of work, but it shouldn't fill your days. In the long term, it's unsatisfying, but more to the point, when you work alone, it's unpaid. 'Sending emails feels like you've done work,' Tom Broughton, Cubbitts founder, told me. 'But I think this is one of the problems with email as a communication form. The more productive you are during the day, the more emails you send, the faster you're going to get more replies. Your productivity is just creating a relentless pile of more work to do.'

Business and time management expert Laura Vanderkam's trick to help incredibly busy workers – including high-level execs – is to get them to keep a time sheet of their entire life, in 30-minute chunks, day and night, for a couple of weeks (you can download a template from her website: lauravanderkam. com). For some of her subjects this was about working out where to fit an extra Latin class into an already packed week, or how to squeeze in marathon training. (Spoiler: sadly, the answer always seems to be watch less TV and/or get up earlier.) But for others – and me – it was just about getting a good look at what life actually looks like, and how we spend our 168 hours a week.

Doing it myself revealed something interesting, and not just that I spent an unnecessary seven hours a week travelling to meetings. I felt as though I worked about 60 hours a week and really believed that was true.

It was not. I worked 38 hours, spread over six days. Which is still a lot, but helped me twitch my mindset away from out of control and overwhelmed, and back to feeling like I was in charge of the way I worked, and doing a decent job of managing it. Vanderkam often shows her subjects the same results – people who talk about doing 75-hour weeks find they're doing 50 hours or less. As she says, 'If you think you're working 80 hours per week, you'll make different choices in your attempts to optimise, than if you know you usually work 55.'[7] In my experience, you feel very different about your work if you know it's not actually invading your entire life.

Time-sheeting your day gives a clear view of how you're using your time and whether it makes sense. Two hours on email? An hour on social media updates? Ten minutes for lunch? There are bound to be pockets of time which could be used better – not necessarily to be filled with more work – but without tracking them, they're impossible to see.

I imported another technique into my time sheets from the work expert Cal Newport, who is interested in the rhythms of our productivity, and started rating my productivity levels in each half hour, too. It quickly became clear that for me, mornings are the best time to do what I call grunt work – invoicing, ordering supplies and research. I only really get into my creative stride at about 2pm and ideally I would write until 8pm (which fits not-at-all with having small kids). Sometimes I have creative or knowledge work which has to be done first thing, and it helps enormously to know just why I find it so much harder to at that time of day. I'm more forgiving of myself and less likely to tip into despair. I also now try to leave my emails alone until that slow-brained period just after lunch, on the advice of Karen Eyre-White, who I moaned to about how my mornings are often whittled away by being sucked into emails. (By the way, she strongly disagrees with my inbox policy. It genuinely doesn't bother me to have thousands of unread emails because they represent a sort of database, a resource for me. None of them actually require any action. But I can see her point, which is that thousands of undone tasks, if that's what your inbox actually is, would have immense psychological heft.)

You may be the other way around – most people are at their creative peak very early in the day, and many get up extra early just to capture it. Novelist Haruki Murakami starts his day at 4am and Anthony Trollope wrote 63 books while holding down a full-time job at the UK post office by writing from 5.30am. The point is not which way up your day is, but instead that you find out what your personal rhythms are and build your days around the way your brain works, rather than forcing yourself to fit with rhythms set by nineteenth-century factory owners. Not soloists with the freedom to choose.

How (where and when) to write a to-do list

How much have you thought about your to-do list? Do you write it in a particular way? Does it have headings? Do you know what's most urgent? I suspect most of us just write lists of the things we have to do and leave it at that. That was me, until I interviewed Nat Rich, a personal responsibility coach with a refreshing approach (she rejects pursuing goals for herself and her workshops are called things '*Un-F#?k Your Life*' and '*Un-F#?k Your Money*'). I was at a lowish ebb at that moment, working on this book, plus a big investigative article for the *Guardian* newspaper, struggling to manage kids' drop-offs and pick-ups, failing to sort things like birthday presents and not exercising at all. I had two lists, next to each other – a work list and a personal list (which was jammed with things which never got done). Frankly, our conversation turned into a session, and I was nearly in tears by the end of it, which I wasn't prepared for at all. Because it turns out your to-do list can make you feel a lot of things, and mine was making me feel awful.

We counted, and I had 27 individual items on the two lists. 'The way that you've organised your to-do list is you've brain-dumped but you haven't sectioned them off,' she told me. 'So if you look at that to-do list you're like, "Holy fuck, I've got a million things to do".' Which is exactly how I felt. Rich's ideal was for me to choose three things a day from the list, three absolute priorities, and commit to doing them each day, with any other things completed being viewed as a bonus. Given that I had 27 things to do, that idea gave me something close to palpitations, but I think part of the problem was that I had written down every single tiny thing I needed to do, in a great flurry of scribbles. Prioritising three things is also known as the rule of three, and people who are far higher-powered than me run their lives using it, so it is effective. And once Rich tweaked my list's layout, it was easier to get on with.

The main problem was that my lists were arbitrary – important things were at the bottom, maybe circled or starred, but still hard to see, while basic things were at the top – there was no pattern. Equally, incredibly important and urgent things would be on the Personal list – examples from the time included coming up with a fortieth birthday present for my husband – but they'd be consistently left behind because they languished on the Personal, aka less important page.

With Rich, I designed a new format, dividing my page into three groups. Now, anything urgent gets put under 'Deadlines', regardless of whether it relates to work or not; anything financial goes under 'Money' whether it's invoicing or paying for a school trip; and anyone who I need to talk to or email goes into a section called 'Contact'. I now have a clear view of what needs to be done first and as things from the other sections become more urgent, they can transfer into 'Deadlines'.

Very often, I get a lot more than three things done, but the key is that the most important ones get done first because ultimately they are the ones which will yield the biggest pay-offs. (This is another version of the 80/20 rule or the Pareto principle – the idea that 80 per cent of the value comes from the top 20 per cent of your effort and time.) Note that most important doesn't mean most urgent. Sometimes it will, but sometimes tasks with no obvious deadline yield huge long-term benefits – like redesigning a website or creating a new portfolio.)

As a general rule, I think of myself as a segmentor – that is, someone who needs to fence work off from the rest of life – rather than an integrator – someone happy when the two merge and can swap back and forth. But clearly, when it came to list making, this wasn't working – I had segmented so sharply that nothing personal was getting done at all, which made me feel my own stuff counted for nothing. Now, because I can see what's most important and urgent across both, I can choose to get those done first.

This wasn't the bit that made me want to cry. That was when we realised how many of the things on the list were making me feel guilty. There were eight guilt-inducing things, many of which I was endlessly transferring from a previous list, another great way to make yourself feel inadequate. 'Guilt is heavy,' said Rich. 'That's going to weigh you down before anything else. Anything you feel guilty about needs to be gone. You need to fly through the guilty things on your list. You could set yourself the priority that anything that makes you feel guilty on the list, needs to be done by the end of the day.'

The reasons for the guilt varied – I felt guilty that I hadn't sorted that fast-approaching fortieth present, guilty I hadn't paid my sister back for my share of a holiday, guilty I hadn't planned social media posts for the studio, even though I'd promised that I would, guilty I was paying for two separate website providers, because I couldn't work out how to switch one over. The really strange thing, though, was that as soon as

I'd identified the feeling all the tasks became possible. That day, I did get rid of them all.

This is a more nuanced way of thinking about the eat-your-frogs mantra, a ten-year-old productivity hack from a book of the same name by Brian Tracy, which encouraged workers to do their worst or biggest task ('eating the frog') first, at the beginning of the day. Sometimes you do just need to get those things done or they hang over you, heavy with remorse, but whether eating them first thing works for you depends on your circadian and ultradian rhythms. I don't really get going creatively until the afternoon, so sitting down to work on a huge piece of writing at 10am just because it's the most important and scary thing on my list, wouldn't have readable results.

Rich's more emotional approach had a bigger impact on me. I needed to know *why* I didn't want to do the heavy things I was hauling from list to list. Some of my frogs were frightening me. What if I didn't have enough money to pay my sister back? (I did.) What if I had messed up the web provider thing and lost access to my business email account? I could tell myself over and again to just get the things done, but I was paralysed by how they made me feel. Once I knew it was guilt and fear, I was free to get them all done.

Feelings aren't bad, of course. Another interesting technique for making a to-do list more doable, is actually to feel more about what's on it. The theory is that if you can find meaning in each item – who will be helped, amused or served by you getting a thing done – then the list feels less overwhelming. It stops being a pile of stuff to churn through and getting it done has emotional resonance.

You could also experiment with a to-do list and a to-remember list. I tended to throw everything onto one sheet of paper, which made my lists look chaotic and daunting. But sometimes, my tasks aren't actually to-dos, they're to-remembers, like the article I have to write for National Geographic which isn't due for two months, or the fact that my passport expires in half a year. By loading them into the same list, the list looks ever more impossible. Both those items now go into my online calendar with an emailed reminder to put them in the real to-do list when they actually have to be done. The wine writer Victoria Moore also has two lists, a to-do list and then what she calls her 'fridge list', where she keeps a list of big things she'd like to achieve, which can be anything from books she'd like to write, to having a garden, and a few years back, a baby (which I'm happy to report, has happened).

It might even matter *where* you write your list. Although there are loads of apps for list-keeping and platforms to manage work-flow, it seems our recall is better with the written word, on an actual piece of paper with an actual pen.[8]

What you say matters too: 'finish website' might look impossible, but 'choose content for final page of website, upload, final checks' creates a series of doable, manageable tasks. 'Write report' is scarier than 'plan report structure'. There's good evidence to show that what you write effects whether you will do it or not. Being specific is powerful – this is true of goals, intentions and tasks. Saying 'exercise more' is as vague as 'finish project', much like 'earn more', 'spend less', or 'eat better'. In studies, results are far better when people are specific: 'go running on Mondays, Thursdays and Saturdays' and 'Add images to presentation, grammar check, print,' mean you stand much more chance of doing both.[9]

Yet another option – I know, I'm giving you a delicious smorgasbord of list-writing choices – is to create a schedule for each day, incorporating the things you need to do into the schedule. So if you have lots of people to contact, they could all be lumped into a block of time dedicated to emailing, and your inbox would then be left alone until the next scheduled block. The same could go for making calls, invoicing, packaging products to ship, social media, writing, making or preparing products and so on. Like Margaret Heffernan's task-batching technique, this allows you to burn through specific to-dos more quickly, and – theoretically at least – should help us cut back on interrupting ourselves, since it is clear what we should be doing.

When I do this, I sometimes set two timers – one which goes off at the end of a block of two hours, and another which goes off roughly every 45 minutes, during the block, to remind me to take little five-minute breaks (this is also known as pomodoro and is good not just for mental breaks, but physical ones). The downside of this is it needs a bit of discipline – you can't just ignore the timer, do something else, or carry on for longer than you should – but the upside is that like muscular strength, you can build it with practice. Start with short blocks of half an hour and slowly increase their length, just as you would increase weights incrementally at the gym, to make it less intimidating. (I gave up in a huff on my first try, being too ambitious and trying to do a three-hour block on day one.) Creating a deadline can stop a single task expanding to fill an entire day, too.

However, whatever mode of to-do-ing you choose, we also need to be hyperrealistic about what we can get done in a day, especially if you decide to create time blocks. 'There is a wonderful phenomenon called the Planning Fallacy,' Brigid Schulte told me. 'A number of behavioural science experiments over the years have revealed what we all already knew, which is that human beings are terrible at estimating how long something will take. We grossly underestimate the amount of time that something is going to take, so that we're always running and chasing our tails. It's a human quality to overpromise. Once I learned that, it gave me such a sense of relief! I was always thinking, "I can get this done by Thursday" and then Friday would come and I hadn't even started it and I would feel like such a failure. I was always late, late for pick-ups – I missed my daughter's Christmas concert once.'

A lot of this is down to the present bias problem. 'Whatever you're doing right now is so salient that it's really hard to change,' says Schulte. 'I think what I've come to realise is that I am like a gigantic two-year-old and transitions are difficult for me. I have to build in lots of transition time, as it is very hard for me to switch from one thing to another. It's not like I'm all-of-a-sudden always on time, but I'm better about it. I don't beat myself up quite as much. I try to create systems to ensure that I'll be able to switch tasks better, but simply recognising it and then not beating myself up has been really nice.'

At its beginning, a solo working day can look so long and plump with promise. How can we work around this? 'Expectations often drive your experiences,' says Schulte. 'And that is particularly true if you're working on your own because you're the one setting the expectations. One of the ways to counteract it is just to be aware that that happens. To be aware that we overpromise, and that we set ourselves up for under-delivery, which then creates more stress and panic. It's just part of being human.'

Slack

'I came across a really interesting study looking at a busy

hospital,' Schulte told me. 'The operating rooms were always booked and busy but emergencies would crop up. Patients were waiting long hours because emergencies would come up and operations would get bumped, so they had to redo the theatre schedule. Doctors were working long hours, everyone was getting totally stressed and it was just a mess. To sort it out, the hospital had consultants come in, who told them, "You need to keep one operating room empty to handle the emergencies. You need to create slack in your system." Everybody fought it. "How could we possibly do that, there's no way, we're always so busy, there's no way we can create slack." But the consultants said, "Just try it." So they did, keeping one operating room unscheduled to handle the emergencies. What they found over time is that it made *everything* work better. Because there was a place for the emergencies to go, all the other operations that were scheduled didn't get bumped, doctors were not working crazy hours any more and the paperwork was getting done. It made the entire system more efficient.'

From then on, Schulte treated her own calendar the same way, scheduling blocks of slack time every week, where she can catch up or finish the unfinished. 'I give myself two hours where I can catch up on the things I feel behind on, or where I can think big about something, or finish a project I thought I would have finished by now. I still miscalculate time all the time, so on a Friday from 2–4pm, I'll put it on my calendar, block it out and call it slack.' She encourages all of us to allow ourselves the same. 'Get in the habit of creating and keeping that space to counteract that breathless tunnelling. Slack is important because in the long run it's going to make what you do better.'

Procrastination

Procrastination is rarely about true laziness. It's usually about fear: of the task you need to do and whether you're competent to do it, of whether it's about to reveal you're an imposter, of asking for help or support, even of success. I know you might think you procrastinate because you like playing games online, but really, they're displacement activities. What are they displacing?

When it's not about fear, it's about not having taken enough breaks. We know, by now, how important it is to take breaks in a working day and between working days. When you find you can't get down to work – especially if you're doing something else, just not the thing you're supposed to be doing – it's not usually because you're a lazy bastard who just can't be bothered. (Unless you're a student, who self-report procrastination levels of around 80 per cent.) Hardly anyone works too little – the trope of the freelancer in their pyjamas at midday watching television is no longer true. Sometimes we work on the wrong things, pretending to ourselves that we are hard at it, when we are putting something else off. Sometimes we're exhausted by the work that's gone before, and truly can't get going, because our tank is empty. But we very rarely sit about in our underwear doing nothing.

Occasionally we all have tasks which are boring or off-putting – some stuff, we just don't like. Mine include painting any kind of wall, fence or woodwork (so, so dull), sorting through my magazine back issue collection (copy of *Vanity Fair* from 2005 anyone? It's moved house with me four times, so far) and dealing with my various cloud storage accounts. They're big, unwieldy jobs and will give low-value results for the amount of time they will consume. I'll probably get round to them when I've got something really terrifying due the following day.

The majority of tasks which we put off doing have emotional weight – I haven't transferred my website to a new provider, even though I've finished its redesign, because I can't work out how to do it and I'm scared to really try because I think it might reveal that I've done a load of pointless work for no purpose.

Often a task makes us feel bad right now, and we put it off because we believe that in the future, our future self will feel differently about it. We get away with this in the present moment because we think of our future self – who will pay the price of you not doing the thing right now – is not really us at all. It's like we are shunting it onto someone else entirely.[10]

To prevent the future you paying that price, think about the real reason you don't want to do something. It's probably not simply (or only) that it's boring. What weight is it adding to your day? Soloists have to fulfil so many different roles in our little businesses that there are bound to be jobs that fill us with fear and dread, as well as occasional boredom. Hating yourself for not being able to start something is not the key to productivity.

(Want to know a funny thing? After writing the above, I took a break and transferred my domain to my new site. It took three minutes to initiate the process. There were no problems. Twenty-four hours later the site was live. I had to do a five-minute thing to make my emails work. This is an item which has been sitting heavily, mocking me, on my to-do list for well over a year.)

Incidentally, if you really can't get started, look out of the window. If the weather is amazing, that could have something to do with it. Studies have shown that we are most productive when the weather is bad.[11] If it's glorious, we're screwed.

The creative power of procrastination

When you fall into a procrastination hole – and you will, we all do sometimes – remind yourself of this: it turns out procrastination boosts creativity. If you are given a task, or give yourself one, and then go and do something unrelated (the very first studies of this effect had people play Minesweeper or Solitaire for a few minutes), you are likely to be 16 per cent more creative when you do start the task, than you would if you started straight away.[12] (Great minds have used this to their advantage, including Steve Jobs, Margaret Atwood and Truman Capote, who all knowingly procrastinated.)

It's not about getting so close to a deadline that you're kick-started into action. It seems as though left to its own devices, the brain quietly chews over the task, in the same way that it can't forget other unfinished work.

Unfortunately, the same studies have shown that leaving a task until the last possible moment doesn't result in better ideas – presumably because by then we are in a panic. The key is engaging in a little controlled procrastination without letting it run riot, rather than pulling all-nighters in the hope of a flash of genius. Even if you are an all-night type of person, it's a good idea to get familiar with the task as soon as it hits your desk, even if you know you won't start it for ages, since it gives your brain time to get to work, while you're playing Minesweeper.

In fact, even if you're not a procrastinator and the very idea of not getting straight down to work gives you sweaty palms, then you can still use this idea, not by playing Minesweeper, but by trying what philosopher John Perry called 'structured procrastination'. Rather than by doing something you really shouldn't be doing, you can get on with something else on your to-do list, turning procrastination into productivity, harnessing our innate rebelliousness to actually get stuff done.

The creative power of mind-wandering

Mind-wandering is the less active cousin of procrastination. With procrastination, we tend to engage with something we shouldn't be doing at that exact moment – Minesweeper, or Instagram, or the Modern Love section of the *New York Times* website. In contrast, mind-wandering is often more physically passive, or the physical and mental are not connected – you're washing the dishes and thinking about which shoes to wear to your cousin's wedding. Many studies suggest our minds wander almost half the time, about 47 per cent of every day. That figure does date back to a 2010 study, though, and so I do question if we mind-wander that much today, in a world of constant stimulation and scrolling. Even as far back as 2012, an American time-use survey reckoned over 80 per cent of American adults hadn't done any 'relaxing or thinking' in the previous 24 hours; and things are far, far worse in terms of smartphone use now.

The thing is, we need to let our minds wander, ideally with a little gentle corralling at the same time. In recent years, there have been a few studies which suggest mind-wandering has some negative effects and it's true that our thoughts can spiral into dark places quite quickly, if left unchecked. (This might have been because mind-wandering and rumination were conflated; it also has to do with the original mood of the wanderer). Whatever the general effects or emotions related to mind-wandering are – and they're not all that clear, as yet – we can't stop ourselves doing it and nor should we try, because in the right circumstances, like procrastination, it can help us be creative and productive, as well as plan for the future. Creative mind-wandering actually isn't mentally passive and it's not quite the same as running on auto-pilot, like those blank, terrifying moments when you arrive at the supermarket without any memory of the drive there.

In his book *Hyperfocus*, Chris Bailey says there are three modes to mind-wandering:

1. Capture mode – just let your mind trundle off and see where it goes, but capture what comes up.
2. Problem-crunching – having a problem 'loosely' in mind, and seeing what your mind comes up with.
3. Habitual mode – doing something habitual, repetitive and unrelated, and seeing what ideas or plans come up while you're doing it.

Bailey deliberately practises with all three: the first by sitting with a coffee and a notebook, to capture whatever bubbles up. Second by letting a problem unspool in his head over quite long periods of time, but always with a notebook to hand to grab any solutions as they float in. And third, by doing something easy, habitual and pleasurable – like walking to a cafe in the sunshine – and then letting the brain ramble off on its own. He says that this mode is the one most often shown in research to have creative results, especially in problem-solving, even compared to taking a simple rest. It's yet another reason why breaking from work makes us work better. It's probably why you have eureka moments in the shower, when out for a run, or while baking a cake. (I once asked a behavioural scientist whether anyone had studied shower thinking; she replied that sadly it had never been ruled as ethical, but that she'd love to try it, one day.)

There's an obvious difference between intentional mind-wandering like this and the anxious places our minds try to drag us into late in the night. The value of practised mind-wandering is pretty clear from research. But I do worry that we don't give ourselves much of a chance to do it. So much of the productivity literature is about squeezing every last drop of work out of ourselves (not Bailey – he, like me, wants us to work better so that we can work less); it challenges us to focus, more, more, more. Then the tech that we are surrounded by steals away many of the chances our minds would once have had to amble freely – on the loo, on the bus, waiting in a shop, waiting for a friend, having a drink by ourselves, going for a walk ... when was the last time you did any of those things without looking at your phone?

Accountability

Working with a coach is an obvious way to bring accountability into an otherwise solo life, but Victoria Moore has my favourite method. She has paired up with another writer and whenever they are on deadline they set each other arbitrary word-count deadlines throughout the day. They message each other: 'I want 458 words by 11.37am', 'I want 632 words by 2pm', until the real deadline has been hit.

Some soloists find they need to recreate some parts of the office experience in order to get their heads down and get things done – the colleague we don't want to let down, the social expectations we need to meet.

You could even try 'body doubling' which is when you virtually connect with someone else who is also working, and their mere presence acts as a catalyst for getting started and for extended focus (it was originally a tool to help people with ADHD to focus, but has become more widespread). It is simultaneously soothing, knowing someone else is sort-of with you, but also creates a virtual sense of accountability.

Flow

Flow is one of those things which pops up quite often in conversation about some kinds of solo work – especially industries specifically thought of as creative, like music or the arts. It's rather casually used for such a complex and rare experience. Flow was first recognised by psychologist and happiness researcher Professor Mihaly Csikszentmihalyi in 1990, in his famous book of the same name. Flow is a highly focused mental state, when you're so absorbed in what you are doing that almost nothing else seems to matter. You are, as he has put it, 'Completely involved in an activity for its own sake. The ego falls away. Time flies. Every action, movement, and thought follows inevitably from the previous one ... Your whole being is involved, and you're using your skills to the utmost.'[13] You have a clear, reachable goal, and you feel in control of pursuing it. You are fully aware that you're doing whatever you are doing to the best of your abilities and you receive a positive feedback loop from yourself – you just know what you're doing is going well. It is, he says, also when we are at our happiest.

It's such a compelling idea, and has received a lot of academic and popular attention. For soloists, achieving flow at work sounds incredibly desirable. There's a lot of literature out there about how to cultivate flow, but it's led me to think two things. One: in work terms at least, creating a context where you can experience flow can be quite a challenge; and two: by attempting to find it or advocating it, are we just putting another layer of pressure on ourselves? Not only do we have to navigate this really challenging way of working, but we are also meant to have transcendentally satisfying experiences while doing so.

So. I am conflicted about flow. I'm not against it, at all, and my feelings may be down to my personality. I'm not sure I have ever experienced true flow at work, or ever will. People who struggle with anxiety seem less likely to experience flow – we are more prone to interrupting ourselves with anxious brain chatter and less likely to be able, consciously or unconsciously, to let go of ordinary self-oriented concerns. It seems as though it might be easier for conscientious people and people who are very motivated by intrinsic (internal) rather extrinsic rewards (cash or status) to experience flow. And although I am one of those people (I've yet to meet a rich freelance writer), I'm also anxious.

Getting anywhere near flow is partly about working out how to pay attention and how not to get distracted. You won't experience flow with a stream of notifications waving at you from a phone. But it also depends on finding the right kind of activity – flow just can't happen if you're doing something you find really difficult, nor can it happen when things are too easy. Easy things are not engaging enough, and can even be boring. (It's why the calming meditative state some people get from adult colouring books isn't really flow – flow is about doing something brilliant, brilliantly. It's stimulating, not soothing.)

Angela Duckworth takes the idea of flow on a stage in her

book *Grit*. Duckworth studies what makes people gritty – that is resilient, tenacious and likely to carry on in the face of setbacks or challenges, often to the extent that they achieve great things – and wanted to understand more about where flow sits in all of that.

Her elegant theory of grittiness is this:

$$talent + effort = skill$$
$$skill + effort = achievement[14]$$

You can have talent but put in no effort, and your skill level will at some point flatline. But gritty people use their initial talent (which could be a talent for anything – it doesn't have to be painting or running or algebra) and add effort, which leads them to improve their skill. The grittiest take their skill onwards with yet more effort. It is this which leads to achievement. She calls this 'effort counting twice'. Duckworth wondered where flow fitted in with all this effort. She often uses competitive swimmers in her analysis and saw them slogging away at practices, clearly not experiencing flow nor even much enjoyment, but carrying on. Then, occasionally they'd hit a state of flow in competitions and smash a world record or two at the same time. What was the connection?

Duckworth believes that these individuals, who have the grit to get up at 4am and jump in a pool every day, are able to cultivate flow in the longest run, despite rarely, if ever, experiencing it while putting in the effort. Practice, as she puts it, rarely seems intrinsically pleasurable and the higher the level of the practiser, the less pleasure still they report. But, through the hours of hard work and practice they put in, they make it more likely that at the crucial moment, they'll experience flow. This mirrors a lot of what people who say they've experienced flow say – they tend to be people like musicians or orchestral conductors, who have worked extremely hard at perfecting a skill, and only then, at the top of their game, do they enter a state of flow.

We can't just expect flow to come out of nowhere, nor think of it as the same state you get into doing something pleasurably repetitive (I know a writer who finds washing up meditative and a playwright who is calmed by hanging out washing. Neither are experiencing flow). Getting to a point where you have a skill level just right for flow takes time, and effort, plus, perhaps, a little original talent. Given that flow has been reported when listening to music, playing computer games, competing in sports, dancing and during many hobbies, we might have more success finding flow outside work. (Personally, I've only ever experienced it when making a quilt. A clear goal, a level of skill I just about had, constant positive feedback as it grew in size, no associated anxiety, only intrinsic rewards.)

That said, we can encourage flow. Notice, if you do experience it, what you are doing when you do (and it may well not be work) and what circumstances allowed it. As well as activities which require focus from the brain, activities which absorb the body can also lead to flow. New and unpredictable environments can also trigger flow states, which may be related to why great ideas can bubble up when we take a holiday. It seems meditation can also help train the brain towards flow.

Mindfulness or meditation

So much has been written about the power of mindfulness

and meditation that I'll just leave this here: because there is so much evidence about its benefits, and because it makes me feel, live and work better, I'm one of those annoying bastards who meditates. My practice is pretty erratic – I use an app (Calm) a couple of times a week, and I use a body-scan meditation track if I can't get to or stay asleep.

Being able to focus at work is not the most interesting thing about mindfulness, because the positives it can generate for mental health are more profound, but that it helps us pay attention is a pleasant and valuable side effect. Mindfulness training and meditation have been shown to increase working memory in general and, most usefully, when the brain is under stress, a time when it usually loses capacity, rather than gains it. In a number of studies, students taking tests score higher if they've been taught mindfulness techniques in the weeks before. It even seems to help if you have a tendency to procrastinate. Although it's often celebrated as an anxiety management tool, because mindfulness trains your brain to attend to the present moment, it's not really surprising that it helps us pay attention as well.

8

Be Your Own CEO

When you work alone, you have to be everything and everyone to the business, at least at the beginning. You're head of marketing, social media manager, bookkeeper, accountant and, often, the person who cleans the loos, buys printer ink and provides IT support. It's tough having to do all of these roles at once – and hard to do them all well.

If you were told you were going to be given the job of heading up an organisation tomorrow, would you feel qualified to do it? If it were me, I'd immediately go and look for books, find a mentor or a coach, ask for help. But when we start being the untitled CEO of our own businesses, most often, we just crash straight into it. When I interviewed Brigid Schulte, she recalled a conversation with a very successful journalist friend who had gone freelance a few years earlier, with the aim of creating a more flexible life for herself. 'She worked at the *New York Times* for many years and then went to work for herself,' Schulte told me. 'She looked at me and said, "I've realised I work for the biggest bitch in the world." She was really hard on herself, really driven, never felt like she was doing enough. She was working all the time. She had gone out on her own to try to give herself more flexibility and control over her time, but ended up working more. While on the one hand she certainly had freedom, on the other, she had set up unrealistic expectations for herself in a way that made it very difficult to live day to day.' Her friend had been far more brutal on herself than any real-life boss had ever been.

We sometimes forget that we are the head of our own little organisations-of-one, and what a big job that is. We are the MD, CEO, CFO, COO. We are in charge of making sure the workers get job satisfaction, don't burn out, have good working conditions, enough time off, a decent space in which to work, and all the tools we need to do whatever our job is. We are also the Human Resources director. It's up to us to make sure the workers – us – take time off, finish work at a sensible time, have a feasible amount of work to complete and are not set unrealistic deadlines or widely optimistic targets.

It's a horrible thing to say – I enjoy hearing it even less than writing it – but if you're continually drowning under the weight of your work ... it's kind of your fault. You *are* the boss. (I know how unpopular this will make me with you, because I've had the same conversations. Usually with my mother. Fun.)

'I have to say yes to all the work that comes my way because otherwise I'll lose the client/I don't have enough money to say no to work when it comes along/I'd rather be busy and stressed than have no work at all/Having lots of work makes me successful.'

All these things may be true, if we only take account of the current moment we are in. But – as I've learned but will probably never tell my mother – it's damaging in so many ways when we overwork. The quality of the work we do degrades, it becomes joyless and more and more stressful; and, as we will discuss in chapter 12, if you try and define what success looks like on paper, no one ever writes down 'I want to work all the hours there are, and have no life.'

Gallup recently looked into what causes burnout, surveying 7,500 employees. It reported that the key causes were: unfair treatment at work; unmanageable workload; lack of role clarity; lack of communication and support from managers; and unreasonable time pressures.[1] Obviously the people surveyed were in organisations – but we can create the same problems in our organisations-of-one. We are just as capable of unfairly giving ourselves too much to do in too little time, with only a sketchy sense of what we're expecting of ourselves (often it's just A LOT. AND NOW). And when we do, *we* are the problem. It's our fault.

Certainly, at the beginning of freelancing or running a new business, there's value in working extra hard, and all of us have patches when there seems to be more work than there is time. That's normal and navigable, and you can probably just about bear it, as long as it's finite and happens for the shortest possible period, a few months at the most. But it's easy to slip into really quite dangerous long-term habits.

Solving this particular problem means learning to say no (along with learning to use time well) or at the very least, learning to ask for more time. Many deadlines are created arbitrarily, or with a lot of flexibility built in. Once you've proved you are someone who delivers whatever it is your client needs from you, on time, try asking for a longer lead time right at the beginning of the next project, if you can.

Deadline extensions aren't going to work if you're an emergency plumber; but even an emergency plumber could create a system in which you refer clients on to another, trusted plumber on days when you are off or fully booked, on the basis that she will do the same for you on your days off.

The aim is to dial back the pressure on your working hours, whatever those hours usually include.

We are also the business development manager, and as such should outsource anything we can, as soon as we can, to give us time to get on with that part of the job. As Diane Mulcahy, who teaches an MBA course on the gig economy at Babson College in Boston, Massachusetts, put it to me: 'When you work independently, it's very difficult to take on all of the roles of running a business yourself. It's time-consuming and generally people have tasks they don't like, or they're not good at, which they would rather outsource.' Hiring help creates a team around you, even if it's virtual or occasional, and gives you the space to focus on the things you're best at. Building a team might sound initially daunting and potentially expensive, but doesn't have to be either. 'To make it less daunting, you can hire somebody in your own network or community, ask for referrals, or use a platform like Upwork to find the skills you need. And you don't have to spend a lot of money: a social media person could cost under $20 an hour, and at two hours a week, that's not going to break the bank. As you grow your business, get more work, and raise your rates, it becomes even more reasonable to make that time–money trade off.' Plus, research on happiness and money suggests that outsourcing – whether chores or work – improves well-being to a greater extent than keeping the money would have done. (Time–money researcher Ashley Whillans thinks it's possible to spend $5,000 a year on outsourcing and gain a well-being boost equivalent to over $18,000 in earnings, which are pretty compelling numbers.)

What if the thought of paying someone to do something we consider horrible feels unpleasant? 'People think, "But I can do it myself, so I should." They feel reluctant to hire help. People from middle-class backgrounds grow up not used to having people do things for them, so they feel slightly uncomfortable. So what I say is, "Let's not frame it as though you're hiring somebody to do your social media or clean your house or run your errands. Why don't you look at that person as an independent business, and you're helping them grow their business, because you're a client? Think about how you feel when you win a client and how happy you feel. That's how that person feels – they're running a business too."'

(Mulcahy is really firm about outsourcing, and takes it even further: 'This is something I talk about with other women entrepreneurs all the time. How do you deal with shopping [for work clothing]? Do you go online and buy all the same brand? Do you have a uniform? Do you work with a stylist? What do you do about your hair? Do you get it blow-dried twice a week while you're reading work stuff? I mean, these are productivity hacks.')

And then, there is the role which almost all of us ignore: business coach. If you've got the cash (or can do a really good skills swap – see page 263) then you might have thought about hiring a real business coach to help you think about your business, its aims, practices, policies, mission statement and goals, but most of us feel like we haven't got the time or money, especially when newly solo.

Strategising is really valuable, though, and if you can't afford a professional, you can still adopt the main principles of business coaching, whether on your own or with a team of your own creation. Margaret Heffernan told me that she knows soloists who assemble a 'personal board of directors. It's not a formal thing but they have colleagues or friends that they talk to about professional, financial, social and family development. It's a way to stay on track and check in to make sure they aren't losing themselves. Whatever you call them (I just call them friends!) I think it's important to have such figures in your life – to avoid drowning in work, to help with panic or overload, to maintain some kind of humanity. Success and failure are both gigantic challenges and sometimes I think success is a bigger test than failure. I've seen more people derailed by huge, sudden success, but both it and failure are hideous tests of identity.'

At some point, a good coach is a good investment for any soloist – many of the soloists in this book sing the praises of the people they have worked with, over short or very long terms, including Victoria Moore and Charlotte Scott.

Even if you can't afford a coach, try using some of the principles of coaching on yourself:

- Create a mission statement for your job. What are your values? What is the aim of your business? Who are you helping, or entertaining, or feeding, or fixing? What do you contribute, or want to contribute? This doesn't have to be lofty stuff, although it can be. As Brigid Schulte puts it, 'Being really clear on why you went solo and keeping that uppermost in mind is important to keep coming back to, especially as you work on figuring out what systems work for you. Then, when the shit hits the fan – and it will – this is what's going to keep you going. Even on the worst day you are still moving toward and honouring whatever your goal or intention was in the first place.'
- What are your personal, professional and financial goals? For this year? For five years' time? For ten years' time? (This can be anything from what you'd like your romantic or family life to look like, to

where you'd like to live, to how much money you need or want to make each year. The personal and professional are tightly linked together; by planning for both at the same time we can at least try to avoid overemphasising one side at a cost to the other.)

- What do you need to do to meet those goals? Break any big and nebulous goal down into micro-goals, which are easier to achieve and to keep track of. So rather than saying, 'I want to make more money,' instead say, 'I will find two more higher-paying clients this quarter,' or 'I will increase my hourly rate by 3 per cent,' or 'I will keep on top of my expenses so that I don't miss out on reclaiming money I'm owed.' Instead of saying, 'I want being freelance to mean I can travel more', say, 'I'm going to book a trip for the second half of June' (and then actually do it).

- How can you plan for the future – including for the possibility of things going wrong? Do you need to set money aside, or build up some savings? Do you need to think about ways you can diversify your income streams? Could you take out sickness insurance so that your bills would be covered if you were put on long-term sick leave for some reason?

- Is there anyone who could help hold you accountable? It's not impossible to hold ourselves to account, but it's definitely easier if you can assemble a team of people (ideally outside your direct family or co-habitees, otherwise things can get a bit ... fraught) or join an existing group, who will periodically check to see if you've done what you've said you'll do.

There are two really important things about this kind

of planning to keep in mind, though. One is that although you can emerge from it with a really fantastic list of goals, and even a fairly clear plan about how to reach them, the best way to achieve them is to tackle them one at a time. If you try and change or do too much at once you will overload yourself with tasks, feel overwhelmed and dump the lot. It's like New Year's resolutions: 'I will lose weight, join a gym, be a better parent, and learn the ukulele'. After just a few exhausting days being the New Us, our willpower flatlines, and we go back to exactly where we were before, but a little more defeated and deflated.

Be ambitious in your planning, but conservative in your day-to-day execution. Nail one thing, and then move on to the next.

Given that you are the CEO, HR manager and sustainability director of your company, you do have to be both realistic and gentle, on your business and yourself, though. The sociologist and solo work expert Heejung Chung says, 'You can't just take on the role of the CFO and be like, "You know what, we're going to double our profits in the next year," without thinking about what that will do to the rest of your company (you). Because then as HR manager you could respond, "Well we're not expanding any staff members to meet that goal, so what you're going to do is exploit my current one staff member that we have here. Is that sustainable, is that something that you want?"' Instead, she says, 'What you need to do is weigh different things across the scale: if I want to aim for a goal, what does that imply for the rest of what I do? What does it imply for my family, for my leisure and health?'

9

Other People

Without other people, your solo work wouldn't exist, and how we interact with and react to, or even manage other people will determine how well or badly work goes. Although solo work can be very inward looking, it's time to look out at the rest of the world. Here are a few of the principles I try to use:

Manners

I wrote for one client every week for five years, and can count the times I got a thank you back on the fingers of one hand. It stung every single time.

Let's be kind. Let's be nice. It's not a weakness. Let's remember that almost everyone, any time, has a thing going on in their life. Say please, say thanks. Be a human. Don't reply to briefs or pitches with 'going to pass'. Help people you can help. Pass people you can't help onto people who can. Don't ask too much of people.

Listen. Don't think of your next comment while someone else is talking. Take a moment of silence when they finish speaking – often that is the moment they say something even they didn't expect to say. Or ask for more from them. We treat conversations like a game of tennis – my go, your go, my go, your go – but that's not actually how we learn the most about people, or have the best ideas with them.

Relationships

It's self-evident that the relationships we build around our work are crucial to its success, but the leadership expert Tom Morin gave me a novel perspective on it. He – a fellow soloist – thinks that when it comes to getting people to do what we want or need, soloists lack what's known as legitimate power, the power to take someone's livelihood away and the kind of power held at senior levels in a non-solo business. 'I have to be an organisational leader and in the organisation that I run [his solo business] I don't have legitimate power over my cohort,' he told me. Our organisations are hard to pin down, changeable and free-form, and generally we work with people who are not our direct employees. Often, we aren't the ones paying them – the designer who works on my books, for example, is chosen by the publisher. I don't pay her, but I do have to try and get her to do things I want.

Because his relationships are not based on his hiring-and-firing powers, Morin says, 'I have to influence them. I have to inspire them. I have to build these trusting relationships. The wonderful thing is if you're really good at it, you're able to get things done through other people, and they'll do it for less money or do more of it than the money you paid them, because you've done such a good job of inspiring them, showing them their value, that they just want to be a part of what you do. You can really inspire people to do a lot. I have a lot of people that work for me who have said, "I'll just do that for you, you don't have to pay me." Whereas, if I was in an organisation, it would be completely transactional.'

Think of it as like soft power in diplomacy – and as just as important. 'I hope that one of the first things people learn when they're working on their own is how much they need other people,' Morin says. 'We become very quickly aware of how dependent we're going to be, interdependent hopefully, on other people. The moment that soloists want to change or become more so-called successful at what they do, I think the necessity to be dependent on other people will come to the surface rather quickly.'

Collaborators and teams

In recent years, I've started trying very hard – and often failing, then trying again – to see the people I work with as they really are. It's tricky, because sometimes I never even meet them. For the first five or six years of my solo life, I spent so much time feeling frustrated that people didn't know what I do, or what goes into what I do, or how to work on the kinds of projects that I do. I completely forgot that I've been doing this, and learning this, since I was 23. I forgot that I'm still learning, and that my way is so emphatically not the only way. I probably made people feel small, and sad and belittled. And I'm so sorry.

I've collaborated with people who haven't got the first clue about how to do what we have to do, and I've tried to teach them as though *they were me*. And when they've messed up, I've been as angry, as if *they were me*. I didn't look for their specific strengths. I didn't try to find out who they were, or what they wanted, or why they were doing what they were doing. It was my way, or not at all. (This is why I'm freelance, and not in management, I suspect.)

I really hope I've changed. In the same way that I've had

to learn to be forgiving of myself and know myself better, I really hope I'm at a point where I can do it for other people too.

It's a step on from being kind. It is, somehow, trying to know who people are and what their version of working looks like. Not trying to force them into a mould they cannot fit.

Communications

It's harder to pick up subtleties and nuance in an email, and it's tougher to quickly capture and correct mistakes than it is in spoken conversation. Once sent, an email is there forever – if you can, enable a delay-send action in your email client. Using my delay-send function, I have 25 seconds to realise I've sent something to the wrong person, or used cc when I should have bcc'ed and I use it to stop an email going out most weeks. If you're the kind of person who worries about emails once they've been sent and chews over the phrasing you've used, then batch the times when you send them. Write them whenever you fancy, but save the drafts and send them all out at 4pm, say, so that you can mull over what you want to say and check it back with a clear head, rather than dashing something off, pressing send and regretting it for the next few days.

With the writing itself, shoot for clarity, rather than brevity, which can come across as curt, cold, rude or dictatorial. Don't write an essay, obviously, but I don't mind taking an extra couple of minutes of people's attention if it means they really understand what I am trying to say.

Accept that conversations may take longer than you'd like when you're not working in the same place as other people in a team or on a project. If you possibly can, set parameters for when those conversations happen. My friend, the crime journalist and podcast host Alex Hannaford, admits he drove a collaborator crazy with all-hours messages until they set up a Google Doc into which he can brain-dump over the weekend. His collaborator checks it when he sits down to work on a Monday morning.

On the other hand I have a client who likes to Whats-App me on Friday nights and Saturday afternoons; she's a senior executive and intensely busy during the normal working week, and over the years I've simply had to accept this. I had an editor who thought nothing of texting me feedback on a Sunday. If possible – and as with my exec, it's not, always – try and have a conversation about this and the effect that their lack of boundaries might be having on both of you. Encourage work contacts who use instant messaging to your phone to switch back to email, and then don't check your email until a designated work time. If I absolutely have to send emails at the weekend, I head them 'not urgent, for next week', or 'a question for when you're back in the office'. By continuing to accept and perpetuate the softening of the boundaries between work time and not-work time, we maintain a situation which – as we know by now – is harmful to all of us, as well as the quality of the work we do.

Video calls

Do you find Zoom, Teams or Houseparty calls exhausting? Such services are more popular than ever, and they can be a brilliant time-saver for the remote worker or freelancer – no travel time needed. But they aren't without their downsides, and it's worth knowing what these are in order to understand why some people on your calls might seem off or strange, and why others will do anything to get out of taking part.

Although some socially anxious people have stated that they find video calling far more relaxing than real-life encounters, when you think about it, it's obvious that video calling would be unbelievably hard for most of our poor little brains to handle. Halfway between a voice-only phone call and a real-life meet up, our brains don't quite know what to do with the deluge of information they are being given, none of which quite adds up. Sometimes there's a delay, or a blur to the image. You can't see, or can't see clearly enough, the parts of the body that we rely on for non-verbal cues, like hands or posture. Normal meetings allow us to make judgements about other people's states of mind, via their body language or even their dress, that a video call rob us of. When else do you look at four or five faces at once? In a normal conversation, we only look at one person at a time, turning our heads to read each face in turn. Equally, in a normal conversation we can't see our own faces, either, contorting or grimacing ... or just looking distractingly much older and more tired than we expected.

Frequently, calls commence with little in the way of ritual – no one offers drinks; no hierarchy is established; no chit-chat smooths the rough edges of the group; it can be hard to tell who is in charge of the conversation. Other people cut out if more than one person talks at once, which can stifle debate and creativity – people hold back and are less involved than they would be if everyone was in the same room. Silences, a normal part of a real conversation, make everyone else think the screen has frozen, tensely rushing in to check or fill the pause. Some people treat calls infor-mally, revolting others by eating noisily, or dressed for the beach, which can make it hard to divine what our expectations should be of the conversation.

Most discussed are the bloopers – people thinking they're muted when they're not; accidentally sending a snide comment about the boss to the whole meeting; naked children (or partners) running into the room or mundane domestic life encroaching on a serious agenda. But these are the least of it, really. Video calls are performative and intense, which is why you (and the people on your calls) may find them shattering. So give yourself (and others) a break; acknowledge that they are a challenging medium, and take a beat to mentally prepare before, and decompress after each call.

Gender

Most heteronormative families still uphold relatively traditional gender roles, and this can have an impact on the solo workers within them. As sociologist and solo work expert Heejung Chung explained to me, 'Approximately 50 per cent of all households in the US have a female breadwinner. Yet in Europe, the UK and US, it's still considered – especially in dual-earner, heterosexual families – that it's the man's role to bring home the bacon, and the woman's role to take care of the household as well as doing the majority of child-care or elderly care.' In this set-up, often, nobody wins. 'I see so many women who work from home and have flex-ible working hours, meaning they'll drop the kids off, work, pick the kids up at 3, do the tea, homework, bath, bed, pick work up at 8 o'clock and work until about midnight to make up their hours. But Dad goes into the home office, shuts the door, doesn't come out, maybe he goes for a walk in between,

but at 5 or 6 o'clock, he's still there working.' In her experience, men tend to work longer and longer – or at least more
obvious – hours. (They also tend to win career premiums for
doing so.)

'They're able to work from home and maintain their
boundaries,' says Chung, but they also feel more societal
pressure, especially to work visibly long hours. Depressingly,
employers of women who work at home *don't* expect those
women to work longer hours – they actually expect them to
blend work with household responsibilities.

'One of the things women [working from home] need to
be careful about is whether they are perpetuating the gender
norm by carrying out both household tasks and work tasks.
Having said that, a lot of mothers do appreciate flexible work
– often it's one of the reasons that they work from home. But
there is a question of whether you're adapting your work patterns, your workload, to meet both work and family demands
and you're not questioning the unequal distribution of
work and power within your relationship. Essentially you're
exploiting yourself, is how I see it. Rather than pushing your
partner to do their share, you adjust your work so you can do
everything, stretching the day to fit it all in. But this leaves
you pressured and exhausted and can lead to all sorts of other
very negative outcomes.'

This absolutely isn't true for all families, but anyone
familiar with the mental load idea might recognise part of
the picture Chung draws. Mental load is the idea that women
tend to do more of the emotional labour in a heterosexual
relationship – which can involve anything from keeping
household supplies topped up, to buying children's clothing,
arranging birthday parties, sending cards or presents, lots of
lists, shopping ...

It's a sad picture, but the research supports it and I raise it here so can we all examine our own set-ups – heterosexual or not. Is one person – doesn't matter who or what gender – carrying a heavier household burden just because they work at home or flexibly and outside a traditional set-up? Is that fair?

What does it do to their ability to do their work and the status that it has?

The people closest to us

Most people who haven't worked alone have no idea what working alone is like. Hopefully, they will have slightly more of a clue if they live with someone who does it. Most often, people say a version of the following to me: 'You must be so disciplined. I would just watch television all day and get no work done.' I think that if they thought for a minute or two they'd realise this is insane. You might loll around for a day, or even a week, but our cultural work ethic, plus the fear of falling behind with the rent or house payments, gets most people moving pretty briskly. Innate discipline is helpful, but it's rare.

So here's a little guide (which you can also download from my website – www.howtoworkalone.com – and casually leave lying around your home), for anyone who is in a relationship with or living with a solo worker. Below it is a similar one for anyone you know who employs or uses soloists – probably not one to give your actual boss, though.

If you have a solo worker in your life ...
- Don't behave as though their work is less important

than your work, because it takes place out of a
traditional setting or during non-traditional hours.

- Do not assume they are enjoying the sunshine if it's
sunny. We are working, just like you.
- Do not assume they can take in that parcel, drop off
that dry cleaning, pick up that thing, that child, those
groceries.
- Don't assume that because they work flexibly, they
can also bend those hours around you. Chances are,
they are already struggling to put their own work
first, to give it the weight it deserves.
- Don't assume they should be the ones to do any school
holiday childcare or to deal with elderly relatives,
dinner reservations, other people's doctors/dentists/
hair appointments, or parent-teacher meetings.
- (Maybe) don't buy biscuits for the house in which
they live.
- If they consistently work crazy hours, challenge them.
- Celebrate their successes. Mark the things they've
achieved – you don't have to buy them presents, but
show pride in what they've done, because many solo
workers won't get it from anyone else.
- Let them talk. Even if you've just come in from a busy
day at the office, understand that it is vital for them,
perhaps alone all day, to shore up their mental health
by talking to you, even if you feel like you need it
to be quiet. (Don't make them feel silly for needing
this.)
- Take them out occasionally, even if you don't really
want to go out because you've been out all day.
They've been in, and alone, all day.
- Don't assume that they have no boss. Most likely,

they feel like they have dozens – maybe hundreds – of bosses.

If you employ a solo worker …

- Pay them. Fairly. And on time.
- Pay them.
- Oh my god. Just pay them.
- Don't ignore them when they contact you. Thank them for their work. Give them feedback. Reply to their questions or pitches. Acknowledge their existence.
- Know that they are almost certainly juggling a number of projects, desperate to do each one brilliantly.
- Don't ask if they're enjoying the sunshine.
- Assume they are working very long hours; never assume that because they are freelance, they are slacking off.
- Reply to their emails. If you possibly can, set fair deadlines. Let them have a couple more days if they ask, and you can.
- If you have regular soloists, take them for lunch now and then. Especially at Christmas. If you can't, then buy them a beer. Send them a card. Send them flowers when they complete a big project, or on their birthday. Anything to show that you know there's a human on the other end of their email account, not a piece of AI software.
- Just so we are clear: pay them. On time.

Part 2

Where We Work

10

Inside and Outside

Inside

Grey carpet. Black chairs. White desks. White walls. Tinted windows. Artificial light. Synthetic materials. Shiny chrome. Screens and machines and phones. It is almost as though someone sat down to write a list of all the things which mess up our circadian rhythms, mangle our ability to sleep, lower our productivity and generally makes us more distractible and miserable, and then used it to decorate office buildings the world over. It's baffling. The way that almost all offices are decked out is literally the opposite of what the human brain needs to thrive at work. Offices often lack any of the stimuli that we do need, and are stuffed with things that make it harder to work, while also trying to squeeze the maximum number of workers into the space. (Cubicle offices are even worse, since they enclose workers in tiny segments, preventing them from seeing much beyond the synthetic partition stuck between them and the rest of the world.)

Globally, 47 per cent of offices have no natural light.[1] And it's not just offices – think about what hospitals look like, or factories, or workshops, many shops and supermarkets, the staff room behind your favourite restaurant, and even public buildings, like libraries or gyms. All too often these spaces have minimal daylight and maximum bright electric light, and are full of synthetic or metallic, hard-edged and monochromatic furniture and fittings. There is now buckets of data to show that not only do the people working in such spaces not thrive, but neither do the customers (or patients) using them. In theory, all this is to minimise distractions in pursuit of efficiency; the results are anything but.

For soloists, the danger is that this visual language filters into where we choose to work and how we make our own spaces look. If you've spent years either working in, or being exposed to ideas of an office which is cold, hard and grey, it might not to occur to you that you don't have to replicate that in your own workspace. In fact, it's startlingly important that you don't replicate it, for your own well-being and mental health, as much as your ability to work and focus. All of those co-working spaces with huge windows and so many pot plants they look like garden centres? They're not just doing it to be trendy – it's because they know what the human brain needs to get its work done; they know our brains need spaces which don't torture us with their unnaturalness.

How much thought have you given to the place where you work? In the same way that it can be hard to remember to give attention to *how* we work, it can be hard to think about *where*, too. Sometimes, it will feel as if there's almost no choice – I spent a couple of years with nowhere to work but the kitchen table, sitting on a rock-hard dining chair – but even when your choices are extremely limited, there are still things you can do to upgrade your set-up and your surroundings, whether that's by improving the environment in which you work and how it makes you feel, or by making it possible to shut work away at the end of each day. Both of which serve to feed your brain when you are working, and allow it to recover and recharge, when you are not. And if you really can't improve the space where you spend your time – because it's the driving seat of a car or van, say – then getting outside into a natural environment during breaks is even more important for you than it is for the rest of us (and it's really, really important for the rest of us, too).

Emma Morley has designed more than 80 offices since founding her commercial interior design agency, trifle* in 2008. Her project list includes big workplaces for companies like the business card provider Moo.com, but you won't find grey carpet tiles and strip lighting in her portfolio. Instead, she and her team use their knowledge of how workplaces can contribute to well-being (or damage it) to create really beautiful spaces in which people actually want to work. The principles that she has developed can be used anywhere, including your kitchen table, because for a long time, Morley worked at home herself, so she knows exactly what soloists need.

'When you're working on your own, the nice thing is that you can check in with yourself and ask, what is it that I need, what are the things that make my day better?' she says. When we speak, she's working on a project which involves designing for a client whose team members have varying requirements – some are highly introverted, others are autistic, and still others are extroverts, so she's navigating the fact that some people want a pared-back, simple space because for them, colour is distracting, while others want something more vibrant. It has reinforced, for her, that everyone's workspace needs will be different. 'And, since we have different needs, we need to know what ours are, and how to tune into them. If we monitor our reactions to different environments and spaces and what they mean to us, we can start to find out,' she says.

Despite our differences, there are some things which are true for all of us: highly artificial environments stress us all out. 'We know now how important daylight, fresh air and nature are to us as human beings,' says Morley. 'They are fundamental to how we think, how we feel and how productive we are.'

Access to daylight is often restricted in office buildings and senior staff are rewarded with it as a perk, says Ingrid Fetell Lee on the phone to me from New York. She is an industrial designer, founder of The Aesthetics of Joy website and author of *Joyful: The surprising power of ordinary things to create extraordinary happiness*; her TED talk has been viewed more than 17 million times. Her aim is to help us all design joy into our daily lives, through making what are often quite small changes. As it happens, when we speak she is also in the middle of renovating her apartment and designing her own home office, for the first time. 'Research on natural light, or good artificial light, well-being and mood is so well established now, and yet I think a lot of us aren't really aware of it,' she says, echoing Morley. 'Studies of workers show that people who sit near sunnier windows or near daylight have fewer sleep disturbances at night, they sleep 46 minutes more per night, and are more physically active during the day than their counterparts who sit in windowless spaces.' The take away for solo workers? 'Get yourself a space near a window. And if you can't, then get lighting that makes your space feel vibrant and alive. Because that's what's going to make the difference in helping to regulate your circadian rhythms and making you feel more alert during the day, and help you sleep better at night. It's a basic but fundamental thing that will make any workday better,' she says. If she's not working at home, she always chooses a window seat. 'I know that is what's going to make me feel best over the course of the day and that I am going to need less caffeine, too.' Even better, find yourself a window seat from which you can see trees, or water – studies across the world have shown that they have a calming effect on things like our cortisol levels, and generally seem to improve creativity.[2]

But what if you live or work in a basement, and you can't sit near a window? 'Give yourself a daylight bulb,' Emma Morley says. 'It's really nice to have cosy lighting, and I love cosy lamps in my home, but we recently realised that we had cosy lamb bulbs in our desk lights at the office, which is not a good idea! I changed them for daylight bulbs. It's a quick win, and it's not expensive.'

Access to daylight isn't just about circadian rhythms and having enough energy during the day. Our circadian rhythms are involved in so much more than just sleep, that it is vital we don't disturb them. Recent research has shown that our sleep–wake cycle is critical to the maintenance of a healthy immune system, mood regulation via hormones like dopamine, serotonin, cortisol and melatonin, our blood pressure, and how well or badly we absorb nutrients, energy and fat from food. The vitamin D that we get from sunshine is also part of this sensitive, fragile web of reactions. Hospital studies looking at patients exposed to different light levels have shown that inadequate amounts can even effect how quickly or if we recover at all from things like heart attacks and effect rates of discharge from hospital. Some studies have even suggested that rising levels of short-sightedness in children are due to the amount of time they now spend indoors.

And yet. Both traditional workers and soloists regularly underexpose themselves to natural light in the daytime, and overexpose themselves to hyper-stimulating blue light from screens at night. Almost all soloists have done it: we work late into the evening, our faces ghostly in the white glow of a computer screen or phone, and then find it impossible to sleep for hours into the night. It's because our brains cannot cope with the abrupt change from day to night that we expect them to make – it's not just that the work itself is hard to switch off from, but also that the brain needs the gradual shift in light levels historically given to us by sunset and dusk, which we wreck by switching on brilliant lights as soon as it gets dark, and cranking up the brightness on our televisions and phones. To make it worse, if we've spent the day holed up in a gloomy office or at a desk shoved into a dark corner of the room, our eyes won't take in enough bright light to prime the brain for night-time, which leads to even more sleeplessness. The US Center for Disease Control has declared sleep disorders to be a public health epidemic because the consequences are so grave: car crashes, medical errors and increasing rates of diabetes and obesity. We throw our body clocks out still further by failing to eat or drink regularly – there's a reason why it's hard to sleep after a large, late evening meal, and it's not just that we feel full.

Fortunately, the fixes are easy, perhaps even easier for those soloists who can choose their own routine: get outside during daylight hours, several times if you can, and let natural light work its endorphin-releasing, mood-regulating, disease-preventing magic. This is particularly vital if you work somewhere with low light levels. Since you don't have a boss who has nabbed the corner office, work near a window with plenty of natural light, if you can. If you can't, fit daylight bulbs into your office lights, but switch them off at dusk and change to warmer-toned, lower lighting throughout your home, which unlike blue or white light, won't confuse your brain into thinking it's trapped in a never-ending day. (And avoid screens of any kind for an hour or two before bed.)

Sense and sensibility

Sticking a plant on your desk is surprisingly powerful too. One study found that house plants can lower both mental and physical stress levels.[3] Another, at the University of Technology in Sydney, showed a 37 per cent fall in tension and anxiety and a 38 per cent reduction in fatigue after plants were dotted around workplaces. A further study suggested that plants increase feelings of generosity (no one seems quite clear how or why, though), and still more point to higher levels of productivity and creativity in offices where workers can see a plant.[4] One house plant per metre (which is, OK, a lot) improves memory retention, according to a study by the University of Exeter. The famous NASA Clean Air study also suggested that many common house plants remove toxins from the air – exactly the kind that office appliances like printers leach out. Plenty of succulents and house plants prefer low light, so it's possible to have greenery even if your office is gloomy.

I have four plants in my home office, but had to decamp to various alternative desks to write this book whenever my kids were home. I'm sure my neighbours think I'm quite mad as I routinely leave the house with a laptop bag in one hand and a peace lily tucked under my arm, but I work better, longer, and more happily when it's next to my screen, its big green leaves shimmying gently in time to my typing. (I don't take it to cafes, though.)

Whether it's the plants specifically which help, or whether it's the colour and subtle movement they lend to an environment which gets to work on our brains isn't yet known, but one thing is clear. 'Compared to people working in what are known as "lean work environments" – basically the standard office, that has nothing on the walls, is very minimalist and beige – people working in enriched environments, with art and plants and texture, are 15 per cent more productive,' says Ingrid Fetell Lee. 'And when people are given control over those objects [can choose their own], the productivity boost rises to 32 per cent. The way we always thought about workspace design was that we were trying to keep you focused on your work and not distracted. And the problem with that is that's not how the mind works. The mind needs to take little detours and wanders. While our minds are focused on work, our unconscious minds are assessing our surroundings and asking, "Am I safe? Am I comfortable? Is this space healthy?" And if all it sees is just bare walls and nothing else, then the unconscious mind starts to get antsy. It starts to worry.'

Both Fetell-Lee and Morley agree that bringing natural textures into our workspaces play a neat trick on our antsy brains. 'The textures around you certainly have an impact,' says Morley. 'Avoid having a white plasticky desk and get a wooden one. If you can't afford a wooden desk buy something vintage (but cheap), or go for one with an oak or beech veneer. Have something green as well, whether a throw, an armchair, or a cushion.' Morley is British, and fascinatingly there seems to be cultural specificity to the colours and textures people like: Australians, Danes and Spaniards are more productive when their offices contain the colour blue, but Australians also like wood; French people are more productive when surrounded by the colour orange; Germans like stone textures, and Indian workers like green.[5]

Another way in which we can soothe an anxious sub-conscious is to bring imagery of the outside world inside. 'Anything that makes you see the sky or see the outdoors is a really good idea,' says Morley, which is the moment I look up and realise I've decorated my own office with three big photographs of skies – they're what I look both through and at when I'm working on a problem, or stuck for a word.

We know, by now, how important recovery is for both our working brains and bodies, and I think these little outside-in tricks represent mini recoveries. 'The idea of mini recoveries makes a lot of sense,' says Fetell Lee. 'You're a whole person when you show up to your desk, but if all you do is sit and type into a computer and you're sitting in a blank box, then you've left parts of yourself in the dust. You've basically told those parts of yourself to be on pause. So many [of our] senses are just not stimulated over the course of a day. Most of us probably don't use most of our senses at work – we don't use our smell, we might not use our sense of hearing much, we don't really touch. If you can find ways to stimulate those other senses by bringing tactility into our space, by bringing scent into our space, that will keep the unconscious mind feeling engaged and at ease. As opposed to it thinking, "I'm bored. I need to go to the fridge and find a snack." There's something about low-level pleasing sensorial stimulation that really helps.' There's no research that says it enhances focus, she says. 'But I think that's what it is doing: giving the unconscious mind something to engage it, while we focus on the task in hand. Bringing these pleasures into the day, these little joys, I think can give you a feeling that work is not a slog, that work is a joyful place. I'm excited to sit down at my desk in the morning because I get to be surrounded by things that make me feel good, instead of viewing work as this thing that we're so afraid we're going to get distracted from. If you chose to work on your own, then why not celebrate that and say, "I'm going to make my work life, my day, joyful". Because there's absolutely nothing stopping you from doing that.'

As it happens I keep a lambswool fleece on the back of my office chair for similar reasons – I thought it was because I like feeling snug and warm, but perhaps I've subconsciously been softening the edges of a potentially angular space? The fleece is partly about comfort, of course, and I know other soloists who go so far as to have a weighted blanket over their legs to help them keep both warm and calm.

Warmth is critical – especially in Britain, and especially if you work in a draughty old house, as I do – but many soloists don't allow themselves to be warm enough at work. I asked a group of solo workers what they would like me to cover in this book, and one of the most common issues was that they feel cold all day, because they don't want to turn on the heating for an entire flat or house when it's only them working. This is understandable from an environmental and financial point of view, but it's a miserable way to spend our days. There are a number of relatively eco portable or plug in heaters on the market now, so that's one option. If that doesn't work, re-imagine what you wear – I have fingerless (cashmere!) wrist-warmers which help stop my mouse hand, which is nearest to a chilly external wall, getting cold and stiff, along with a thick, soft (if shabby) cardigan which can go on top of whatever else I'm wearing, plus a scarf on really cold days.

Being warm enough is more important than we might think – the studies so far on office temperatures are smallish in scale but striking in results: one review study showed that productivity in offices increased as the temperature rose to 22 degrees Celsius, but then started to fall is it got hotter.[6] Another showed that people in colder offices consumed more calories at lunchtime than those in a warmer office.[7] One more showed that people are more creative when it's warm.[8] In fact, it looks as though 22 degrees Celsius is the optimum temperature for getting good work done, which is warmer than many houses, workshops, garden offices and studios ever get, and explains why being chilly can be so distracting.

Sitting

Do you mostly sit to do your work? 'One of the first things I say to anybody starting their own business or getting their first office: where are you going to sit?' says Morley. 'Really think about this. I know there are all sorts of office chairs, and some of them are absolutely hideous and you would not want them in your home. But I found an office chair online this morning for £50, which got really good reviews. You may think you can't invest that, but every time you see a chiropractor, masseuse or physiotherapist, because you haven't been sitting in a proper chair, it is going to cost you more than £50. Even if £50 feels huge, it's a very good investment. A more robust, top-of-the-range chair would be £500; equivalent to ten appointments.'

Things like a keyboard which suits your typing style (I have a very flat one, which suits my wrists) and a comfortable mouse (I use a flat bluetooth trackpad because the round grippy ones give me repetitive strain injury) also represent good investments. You wouldn't expect anyone working for you to carry on in pain or discomfort; we should extend the same respect to ourselves.

Our sitting habit really bothers Morley, whose concerns about workplace design go well beyond what colour to paint the walls. 'Sitting is the new smoking,' she tells me. 'Sitting is slowly killing us all. We all sit way too much.' There are a number of studies which show that sitting for long periods every day increases our risk of early death,[9] via things like heart disease,[10] including one study of 92,000 women which showed a linear relationship between being more sedentary, and early death. 'Over 80 per cent of us sit for four to nine hours a day. Even just standing up and stretching on the hour every hour helps – if you move your body for three minutes every hour you reduce that risk of premature death by 33 per cent.'[11] Her personal trick is to set a timer to remind herself to stand up and move around – when she designs large offices she refuses to give everyone a waste paper bin so that they are forced to move, and deliberately sets things like water coolers at a distance, so that people have to take a walk.

Not everyone will sit to do their work; if you don't have to, it's probably no bad thing, although any repeated movement or posture can cause strain in the end (when I work in kitchens, which I do a lot, I have a terrible habit of resting my pelvis against the worktop in front of me and arching my spine backwards). Equally, some rare people somehow manage to work on computers from their bed, armchairs or sofa – and genuinely love it. If you're one of them, and you think it works for you, then nothing I can say here will (or should) talk you out of it. I know some writers who manage their complex mental health needs or physical illnesses by working from their bed surrounded by papers and books, or with a tray table propped on their knees in a cosy chair. The critical thing, if you use a computer but don't arrange yourself in an ergonomically advisable way, is to listen to your body and – just as with those who sit on office chairs – take regular breaks and move as much as you can. Getting help with any postural or repetitive strain-type injuries quickly is also key, because the longer they are aggravated, the harder they are to treat. You are your tools: don't let your tools wear out.

The 'correct' way to sit in front of a computer is like this: arrange your chair so your feet are flat on the floor with your thighs more or less parallel to the floor; your forearms should also be parallel to the floor, gently resting on the desk or table, and your hands should easily reach your keyboard and mouse; your eyes should be level with the top of your computer screen, which should be about an arm's length away. Your back should be supported in a naturally straight position by your chair, and you shouldn't feel hunched, or stretched – your mouse and keyboard should be in easy reach.

If any of this is impossible then you might need a foot-rest and an adjustable chair – I'm quite short, so I can't rest my feet on the floor and have my arms at 90 degrees. I currently have a very ordinary office chair made from a piece of curved beech plywood, from IKEA, having journeyed through super-expensive but very uncomfortable apparently ergonomic chairs, a kneeling stool which gave me a rash on my kneecaps, excruciating dining chairs and even, for a full year, a pink Pilates ball.

Storage

If you don't or can't have a separate room to work in – and for 10 of the 11 years I've worked alone, I have not had my own space – you can still make room for yourself. 'Carving out a little space, even if it's just a desk that has a roll top, or that shuts, is worth doing. Just having a psychological boundary around it is valuable,' says Fetell-Lee. Morley agrees. 'If you're working on the kitchen table, then the most simple thing is to have a lovely big box. Shove everything in it at the end of the day and then you get it all out the next day,' she says. I did something similar during my year at the kitchen table – I had a shelf in a kitchen cupboard. Everything went into boxes and onto the shelf, allowing me to shut the door on it all.

Apologies to Morley, but my boxes were quite dull and pla-sticky. She avoids ugly or ordinary office stuff – which makes sense given what we now know about lean environments and how our brains respond to them. 'It's your home, so if you've got to have these things then make them nice,' she laughs. 'What are the tools that you need around you? Make them beautiful – obviously that's from a designer, and not every-body will give a damn about what their pen or ruler looks like. But I think plenty of people do. If you've got a beautiful little pen pot, say, right by you, which has gorgeous things in it, it's like having a little treat.' She suggests seeking out stationery and other office gear from suppliers who specialise in making lovely rather than just-functional products, and using things like good-looking glass jars to hold things like tape or bulldog clips, rather than standard issue office products.

Morley also advocates careful and tidy storage of all the paper stuff which comes with work. 'Make it really easy to be organised and tidy, whether it's having a small box for each project you're working on, if that's a system you like, or look for a system which works the way your brain works,' she says. By which she doesn't mean put it all in a big heap in the corner and hope you can forget about it for the evening (which is how I thought my brain worked until relatively recently).

Boundaries

Ingrid Fetell Lee is creating two office spaces during the renovation of her New York apartment. They don't have a huge amount of room to use, so her husband – who is also solo – suggested perhaps he didn't actually need an office. 'I said no, no, no, we both need offices – they can be very small! They are going to be like little phone booths, basically. When there's no place to put work, it bleeds into everything and all sorts of subtle things happen, in your relationship or in your family. I need a space where the work goes at the end of the day, where my notes go, my books go, where I can shut the door. Our previous workspace was on a wall in our living area but I was always taking over the dining table. It felt like work and home were bleeding together. It can get very displacing when you have two partners who work from home – for example he'll need to take a phone call, and I need to change and get ready for something, but he's taking a video call in the bedroom, which means I can't go in there, and I need to shower. It's so easy for work to displace the activities of the home and I really wanted home to feel like a home. Soon, it will no longer be this thing where work is with us all the time. I'm excited to try a different scenario where we have a little bit of just a delineation around it.'

Sociologist Heejung Chung backs up our need for a line between work and home, even if work is *in* the home. 'If work is everywhere and anywhere, all the time, is that going to lead to productivity? It is useful and beneficial to have not just emotional, but also physical detachment from work. Some people want everything blended and want to dip in and out of work and family life all the time, so as to kind of manage everything. It works fine and that's how they like to do it. But for others, you need those spaces in between.'

She argues that most people do better if they can create a barrier between work and the rest of their life – even if that barrier is a box – and that even people who think blending works for them should keep an eye on life over the long term. If work sits visibly in the corner of your kitchen, sitting room or bedroom, and isn't symbolically shut away when your non-work time begins, then it will continue to take up space in your head as well as in the room, much like the emails on our phones allow work to leach into places like the breakfast table or gym, where previously it never could have reached. Both have an unavoidable impact on your mental bandwidth for everything else – family, relationships and downtime – and serve to lengthen the number of hours per day that your brain is engaged with your work.

Co-working

I don't often use co-working space these days, although before I had children I did most weeks. I don't live close enough to a venue, and as my time is pretty tight, travel to a co-working space would cut an hour or so from my already shortened day. So, I went to talk to a man who really knows co-working. Robert Kropp left his home in Tampa, Florida in 2016, after his marriage ended. During this awful period, he had been so bolstered by the friends he made in a co-working space he used, that he decided he wanted to find out more about what makes a good co-working space, as well as having what amounts to an adult gap year (several, in the end). First he travelled around the US using different co-working venues to run his computing business, and reviewing them, then he went overseas. His website (robertkropp.com) has reviews of co-working spaces from Dubai to Los Angeles, as well as a series of articles about everything from co-work space etiquette, to why they are more than worth the money.

'A workspace can definitely impact how you work,' he tells me on the phone from Barcelona, where he is now remarried and has slowed to moving once or twice a year. 'Because in general, one thing you do lose, if you're a remote worker or freelancer, is a workplace with colleagues. Remote work is important and it's going to keep growing, but nothing replaces handshaking and talking to somebody face to face.'

That's not to say you need the people you work near to be your actual colleagues, and in fact, there are advantages if they're not. 'You're not competing against the person next to you [in a co-work space]. Even if the culture of an office-based organisation is collaborative, it's still rare to not feel like you're competing, sort of, or that there's office politics to deal with.' That allows relationships to develop a little more easily in a co-work space (if you want), rather than the often slightly fraught relationships which can exist within an organisation. There's data to back this up, too, which suggests this lack of direct competition allows co-work members to be more themselves at work than office workers – there's less obfuscation and politicking, and more chance to simply be you.[12]

You also get a certain amount of accountability. 'I tried working from home a couple of times,' he laughs. 'I told myself I gotta save a little bit, but it's worth every penny for me. Because at home I'll end up on YouTube for hours! I need a little bit of pressure – not somebody looking over my shoulder, but somebody in the vicinity who would probably judge me if they noticed I was just watching YouTube.' Like many of us, Kropp also thrives on routine, which is something an out-of-home space gives him. 'I need to walk out the door and go to work. The way my mind works is that I need to compartmentalise my workspace, and I need stability in a workspace – home internet goes down a lot more than business internet, for example.' Like Fetell Lee, he too likes a window, and has learned over the years to be choosy about his spot, especially when arriving at a new co-work venue, rather than doing what I have often done, which is plonk myself down at the first available table, disregarding light levels and ambient noise, usually in pursuit of nothing more interesting than a plug socket.

What makes a good workspace? For Kropp, the precise answer will always require each of us to reflect on what exactly we need in order to work effectively, and happily, and he emphasises how important, if difficult, it is to have those conversations with ourselves. But in general terms? 'What makes a bad workspace is the same as what makes a bad company. It comes down to, do the people in charge care, and if there's a change that needs to happen, does it? Even if it's as simple as the coffee's out and somebody refills it.'

You can, of course, get some of the benefits without paying a membership fee – if you happen to have a nice library nearby, for example. But many co-working space founders are already aware of the power of positive design on our brains and productivity, and will have gone out of their way to choose the right kind of chairs, helpful lighting, and natural textures, which can be harder to find in public buildings and cafes.

For Diane Mulcahy, the value of co-working spaces lies in the creation of communities. 'They are places where independent workers who don't want to work from home can actually be part of a community of like-minded individuals, pursuing a similar work life,' she tells me. 'And I think one of the reasons they have become so popular is because they do represent a community. There are lots of places that people could choose to work – a coffee shop, a library, you can desk-surf at friends' offices – but I think the reason people are willing to pay for co-working spaces is in large part due to the community element.'

Looking back, I think one of the reasons I don't feel attached to the idea of co-working is that my experiences weren't rich in a sense of community. In the venue where I worked, I don't think there was ever a sense that you could ask anyone for help, and the people who ran the space were more interested in cultivating an atmosphere of exclusivity and trendiness, than in inclusion or support. Looking back, I can see that as much as I got stuff done, I always came away feeling slightly like I didn't belong. We should probably add that to Kropp's list. There's no point paying to belong, and feeling like you don't.

Get outside

When I interviewed explorer Anna Blackwell, I didn't know she was now at Exeter University, completing a master's degree in the effect of nature on well-being. I only planned to talk to her about her treks in the Arctic, coping with sol-itude and the public speaking she does about her time in wildernesses. 'There has been so much research in the last few years about the benefits of nature on your mental health and general well-being,' she told me, explaining why she'd taken a year off trekking to study. 'For example, chemicals are released by trees, plants and flowers, cut grass and leaves. If you spend 15 minutes walking through the woods or in a field where the grass has just been cut, smelling those natural smells, these chemicals, it triggers a response in your brain that lowers your cortisol, which is a stress hormone, and lowers your blood pressure and heart rate. There are very physiological reactions to spending time in nature.'

We already know that spending all our time inside – as much as 90 per cent of our entire lives, and most of the 3,500 or so days we work, inside too – is bad for our brains, bodies and circadian rhythms. Interestingly, you only need to spend a total of two hours a week outside to counter much of this. 'One of my lecturers, Dr Mat White, was lead researcher on a study this year which was about how spending 120 minutes a week in nature is the optimum amount of time,' says Blackwell. 'It doesn't matter whether it's time in green spaces or blue spaces – so by the sea, a lake or a river – or if you spend your 120 minutes in little pockets of time, going out for a 20-minute walk in your lunch breaks, or if you have a whole two-hour chunk in one go. Your overall sense of well-being and your positive mood will increase and any depressive symptoms and anxiety will be lower.[13] I find it really interesting because I have spent so much time in nature, and I really value it personally, so now I'm really enjoying learning that there is actual evidence and I haven't just been banging on about this unnecessarily,' she laughs.

Even before she knew the science, Blackwell was putting it into practice – and her habits are ones we can all adopt. 'I worked for a law firm for a year and a half and I felt the effects of a nine-to-five office job on my mental health, but I made some changes which were really successful. Rather than getting the bus to work, I started leaving the house about an hour earlier. I would walk through a couple of parks and along a river. So I would start my day with nature but also with exercise, which has a whole host of extra benefits as well. I walked home too, even if I was walking in the dark, and in my lunch breaks I would go and find the nearest park or little green patch that I could. Just sitting on a bench and having my lunch outside and watching the birds or leaves falling from the trees really helped me a lot. This applies to working at home as well. If I feel I'm struggling to focus, getting a bit fed up and bored or losing my motivation, I put my shoes on and go for a little walk, just to get some fresh air – slightly polluted air, but air, anyway.'

On the day of our interview, I happened to be working on the edge of Oxford, where it's much easier than my bit of south London to find green spaces. And as soon as we finished talking I put on my trainers and walked up the large hill behind my parents' house. On the way up, I grumbled to myself about how impossible it is to find parks close to my house and how I hardly have any time at the beginning and end of the day, anyway, and how I'm not going to go out at lunchtime when I've got so much to do in a day. And so on.

As I came down off the hill, I started to think a bit more laterally, more creatively perhaps. One of my kids has a dance class right by a massive park and it doesn't start for an hour after school finishes. If I remember wellies and raincoats and trainers, then we could fit in half an hour of time near trees. On another day, we have swimming, also next to an enormous green space. Perhaps rather than sitting, steaming, inside the sports centre, waiting around in the strip-lit cafe, we could run around outside. Kick leaves. Look at squirrels, visit the pond. It's going to take some organising. But if it's better for them, and better for me, and better for my work, then maybe that's a compromise worth making.

But why does being outside help us work better when we go back inside? 'We can only focus for a certain amount of time,' explains Ingrid Fetell Lee. 'Our ability to concentrate wears down over time. But one of the things that is very, very successful at restoring our attention is nature. It seems to do it better than anything else: just spending a few minutes in nature, taking a walk in nature, going outside, has a tremendous capacity to restore our ability to concentrate and focus.' The idea even has a name – attention restoration theory. Although bringing natural elements into your workspace can help, nothing beats getting outside.

Even if you live in a busy city and don't have a garden, you will still be able to seek out nature somewhere. 'Nature is the sort of thing that is good in any dose, but great in a bigger dose,' says Fetell Lee. Is it worth it even if all you can see are a few trees planted along a pavement? 'Studies show that in neighbourhoods with more trees in them, people have fewer mental health problems – it is as simple as more trees in a suburban area can influence your mental health.' It's even been shown that access to nature reduces irritability and social tensions – a study of public housing in the US showed that tower blocks surrounded by green space and trees had lower incidents of aggression and violence as well as lower reported levels of general mental fatigue than identical blocks without trees.[14]

Of course, it's always worth looking for more than just a tree, if you can. 'Wide open spaces have benefits because they provide this sense of freedom and spaciousness and they allow the eye to focus in the distance, as opposed to in the foreground, which is something we don't get a lot of in cities, where there may be very few opportunities to extend our gaze. That's really helpful because eye muscles that are staring at computers all day need some time to zoom out.'

There are all sorts of other aspects to nature, she says.

'Like the fact that there are hidden fractal patterns in nature. Look at natural scenes and you'll see that many of them have a certain fractal dimension. The idea is that there are patterns that our brains, our unconscious minds, are reading in nature.' Fractals are repeating patterns that occur throughout nature – in clouds, leaves, rock formations, trees, ocean waves, galaxies, and perhaps most recognisably, in the spiralling of a Romanesco broccoli. Jackson Pollock's paintings are full of fractal patterns, despite their apparent randomness. Viewing fractals has been shown to have a similar effect on the brain as listening to music, and looking at them even briefly helps us recover from stress.[15]

Ever since I learned all this, I've been using nature as a recovery tool, and I've been amazed by its power. Even if all I can manage some days is looking up at the trees on my street, I really do look at them. Leafless black branches spread against a dusky sky. Fluffy with cherry blossom in early spring. Dropping fat berries wetly onto the road. Silver birches shedding coils of paper-thin white bark.

11

Food and Drink

How many of us eat well when we are working alone? Who among us hasn't eaten a packet of biscuits for lunch? Eaten cereal for lunch? Eaten cereal for dinner? (Eaten novelty cereal for dinner?) Eaten a whole tub of hummus and a box of breadsticks, *before* dinner? Eaten a bag of chocolate chips meant for baking? Not eaten anything all day? Eaten mainly toast? Absentmindedly eaten half a block of Cheddar? Been so desperate for chocolate mid-afternoon that you walk all the way to the petrol station even though it's raining? (Not me. Nope.)

You, and your work, deserve to be fed well. You deserve a lunch break (or dinner or breakfast, depending on your particular schedule), but solo workers seem very hard to convince of this. I think that often, when we tell ourselves there's no time for food, or we eat something crappy like cereal or toast, (or, um the cooking chocolate) or tell ourselves we're so in the zone that we can't afford to stop, what we are actually saying is, I don't deserve a decent lunch. I don't deserve the break. I haven't done enough. I could do more. I need to do more. I shouldn't have a break. Or, I can have a break but only one that's short, functional and almost meaningless, one which shovels in enough calories to stop the hunger, but that's it.

I think this behaviour also says something about where

we place our own work and its importance in our lives. When you don't pause and refuel your working brain properly, you're essentially saying, to yourself and of your work: this isn't important. We think that we're saying: my work is so important that I can't even stop to eat. But we are actually failing to place our own well-being and our ability to work – as well as function in the rest of our lives – in the centre of our day, where it should be.

I crowd-sourced some questions for this book in a couple of solo-working Facebook groups. 'What would you like me to try and answer?' I posted. I was really startled when dozens of people responded with a version of 'Please help me stop eating the fridge', or 'What can I eat for lunch that is incredibly fast, but isn't cereal or toast?' Once I started to scratch away, I found it was a real problem: what to eat that is fast and satisfying, when we feel like our time is quite literally our money.

Navigating what and how you eat when you're alone can be complex. The stress hormone cortisol increases appetite, especially for sugar or fat. If you're alone there's less accountability, less oversight. There's no canteen to socialise in, and often no one to wander down the road and grab a sandwich with. There are advantages to this of course – five £6 lunches costs £1,560 over a year, and you can make something nicer than an over-chilled salad in a plastic pot. But a lot of us don't (my solo-working mother drove me mad insisting a slice of ham between two pieces of dry bread was a decent lunch). I think that reveals something quite profound about how many of us solo workers feel about our work, and its place in our lives.

Of course, there will be days when there's no good food nearby, a massive project deadline, or you're travelling somewhere remote. There will be days when food falls off the radar. But not adequately feeding your body and brain on a regular basis has really profound long-term health implications, not just for things like weight gain but also the way our bodies become habituated into dealing with blood sugar and insulin, whether our brains and hearts get enough of the right kinds of healthy fats and whether our gut biomes (which we are only just beginning to understand) are well-populated with good bacteria, which help support our immune systems and even bolster our mental health. Not eating enough, or eating empty calories, will make it harder to do your job well: your body and brain (and soul as well) won't thrive on carb-heavy, nutrient-light meals like cereal or toast.

It might feel difficult to think of lunch as an issue worth giving serious attention to, but food is one of those tricky, tangled things which can make us feel anything from joyful to despair. Sometimes, it feels like there's no time to make something decent to eat, that the day is whizzing past and feeding ourselves is the last thing on a long and scary to-do list. But from the time poverty research back in chapter 5, we know that feeling time is scarce can make us do all sorts of weird things, and one of those is to eat unhealthy, fast or convenience foods, cook less, and eat less sociably. All of which have been shown to increase our risks of obesity and other chronic health problems.[1]

If you were employed in the UK, you'd be legally entitled to a break of 20 minutes if you work more than six hours in a day (many employers give far more than this); some states in America have no mandatory break times but many, including California, give a 30-minute meal break if you work more than five hours, with others, like Nebraska, requiring workers to have a 30-minute off-site break during an eight-hour shift. We really need to grant ourselves the minimum our employed colleagues usually get. Imagine an employer telling you that you aren't entitled to a meal break at work. You'd be incensed. We shouldn't do that to ourselves.

Sometimes it feels indulgent to prepare something fancier than cornflakes, when it's only us. Things like toast and cereal are usually fairly high in refined carbs (even cereals which claim to be high fibre or made with wholegrains), which can cause our blood sugar to spike, followed by a crash in both our blood sugar and our feel-good brain hormones, which leads to lowered energy levels, and then more carb cravings ... setting a cycle of toast for lunch and biscuits at 3pm. Refined carbs turn into glucose in the bloodstream, and our pancreas generates insulin which converts the glucose into energy to be used right away, or stores it in small quantities in muscles or larger quantities as fat, for future famine periods. In the long run, the body can struggle to deal with this rollercoaster. If you're unlucky and especially if the carb-loading has caused serious weight gain, then you might find you start to become insulin-resistant and really struggle to process sugar at all. (This can lead to pre-diabetes illnesses or diabetes itself, in the very long term.)

I have no interest in what size trousers you're wearing. We all process the food we take in differently, and we are all different shapes. I have zero interest in fat-shaming anyone. I love good food and I am hardly skinny myself. But the food we eat can alter the way our brains and bodies function, as well as limiting our capacity to work efficiently and well, which I think many of us – including me, until fairly recently – are unaware of. After years of feeling crushingly tired at 3pm, I finally realised that it was my chocolate bar habit which was undoing my afternoons. As soon as I stopped eating super-sweet milk chocolate bars after lunch, I also stopped feeling like I needed a sugar injection an hour later. I no longer needed a mid-afternoon caffeine shot. Which in turn stopped me being awake, wide-eyed and watching crime dramas, at 1am.

The carbs aren't the only problem though. Our brains and our gut biomes need a range of nutrients to function well, many of which need to come from vegetables and fruits, some of which need to be raw. Eating a wide range of different things for our solo meals, and keeping the carbs low or lowish (a cupped handful is a useful way to measure carb portion sizes) helps to give our brains what they need to do good work for the rest of the day, while mellowing out the blood sugar peaks and crashes that can smash anyone's afternoon to pieces.

If you do a weekly shop, habit-hack yourself in advance: stop buying the things you can't help eating but know you shouldn't. It sounds self-evident, but if you don't have the unhealthy stuff, it's just much harder to eat it. By all means snack, but make it easy for yourself by getting stuff in which is good for you – nuts, fruit or hummus, even proper dark chocolate. I never have biscuits to offer anyone if they visit my house, because if I have biscuits I eat biscuits. *All the biscuits*. I don't even like biscuits that much, but we are so well programmed to like sweet, fatty, carby foods, which have only been readily available for a fraction of human history, that I find them irresistible. (My husband keeps a stash of biscuits at his studio for clients; annoyingly, he can resist them. I am writing this at 11.53am in the studio and have already eaten four of the little bastards.) The same goes for chocolate; I can't have it in the house, or I find myself, midway through writing an article, in the kitchen, face full of it, and no memory of leaving my desk.

If you have to have biscuits, for guests or your kids, freeze them. If you can create a lag between the point you absent-mindedly reach for a biscuit and the moment you think, 'What am I doing? I don't even want a biscuit', then biscuit consumption drops. (Biscuits are horrible straight from the freezer.) If you know you're having guests, defrost some beforehand. Do whatever you can to limit the amount of willpower needed to resist the irresistible. The easiest way is to just not have the stuff in the house, but if we have cake leftover from weekend guests or a birthday, I slice it up and freeze the pieces – anything to stop me being able to graze on them.

I find meal planning boring but helpful. I don't plan each lunch but I shop so that I've got a range of things to hand which can be made into quick, nutritious and, crucially, tasty meals. There's something very grounding and centring about the process of chopping, slicing and assembling and it's a great way to give yourself the kind of break where your body and brain are absorbed in something else. But I think it also demonstrates a level of respect for yourself that slamming something in a plastic tray into the microwave doesn't quite reach.

I don't prepare everything from scratch. Instead, I add fresh ingredients to things which are ready-made: I'm not above a fish finger sandwich, for example, but I use really nice bread (which I keep in the freezer, sliced up), cucumber for crunch, plus salad leaves if we have any, or sliced fennel or radishes, and I make a tablespoonful of tartare sauce with chopped capers and gherkins, mixed with mayo from a jar.

I keep lots of long-lasting vegetables in my fridge: like fennel, sweetheart cabbage, cucumber, carrots, endive or chicory, green beans, broccoli. Then I can add a little hit of fresh, raw or very lightly cooked veg to my meals, even if the bulk of the meal is coming from a tin or jar. If that's not possible, I chuck in a handful of frozen vegetables – I like peas in a bowl of pasta with pesto, or cooked frozen whole-leaf spinach, with lemon juice and a little butter, and piled on toast under a poached egg. Whether fresh, cooked or frozen, they raise the nutritional profile of the meal and add fibre, which helps steady blood sugar for the next few hours. And it feels good to know I'm eating well.

Where possible, I use big flavours – chillies, capers, strong cheese, anchovies, more chillies, garlic, ginger – to make the meal as tasty as possible, with minimal effort. Sometimes I can add extra ingredients which ramp up the nutrient levels – a pinch of ground almonds into pasta sauces; peanuts, sesame seeds or eggs into Asian-style noodles; crunchy toasted pumpkin seeds or nuts into salads. I have a whole fridge shelf dedicated to jars: curry pastes, chutneys, chipotle paste, olives, roasted sweet red peppers in oil, pickled chilli peppers, fish sauce, sriracha, hot sauce, mustards of all kinds ... anything which adds oomph with no more effort than twisting off the lid.

I make sure the cupboard is well stocked with dry stuff for the days when sandwiches won't cut it: plenty of pasta and dried noodles, but also lots of nice tinned soups (they do exist). Cooked pulses in jars or tins are useful too: little nutty Puy lentils, chickpeas and cannellini beans are all brilliant in salads.

I started batch-cooking when my kids joined a nursery and I needed something I could make them in the 15 minutes after evening pick-up before they were too exhausted to eat at all. It was so useful that now I make double quantities of much of what I cook, and not just for them: lasagna, mac 'n' cheese, carrot and cumin soup, squash soup, black bean soup, lentil curries, bolognese sauce, fish cakes ... I even batch-cook piles of baked potatoes, so there's always something for those lunches when you really do need to stick something in the microwave and forget about it.

There are a few foods which are touted as being good for brain health. The reality is that the science of nutrition is far from simple, and just eating more blueberries isn't going to give you a better memory. But making sure you get the right balance of omega 3 and 6 fatty acids is worthwhile. Most commonly found in oily fish like salmon and mackerel, a slightly less easy-to-access form is also available through flaxseeds/linseeds, avocados and walnuts (take a supplement if you really think you aren't getting enough). Other foods which won't do your brain or gut any harm include green leafy vegetables like kale and broccoli, dark (but not milk) chocolate, red or purple-coloured berries, whole grains like bulghur wheat, freekeh and pearl barley, which between them give our good gut bacteria plenty to consume and us a range of vitamins and antioxidants, all thought to help keep our brains healthy and perhaps even slow long-term cognitive decline.

If you're stuck in a solo-eating rut, and all this feels like an unmanageable level of change (plus too much shopping), try adding just one or two new meals to your weekly routine, and choose something which feels easy and achievable. If cooking really doesn't appeal, what foods could you buy that would make your meals more joyful? Are there ingredients you can add to ready-meals which would improve them? A salad on the side of a shop-bought fish pie? Feta and avocado crumbled on top of tinned spicy bean soup? If you don't think you can move on from sandwiches, could you use better bread, nicer cheese or mackerel pate, plus some raw veg and a posh pickle?

For solo lunch ideas visit www.howtoworkalone.com.

*

We should talk about solo working and alcohol. There isn't data on whether self-employed people are more likely to abuse alcohol than employees, but we do know that being young and being male can make it more likely, and there are certain professions where alcohol abuse and drug taking are more common and perhaps more acceptable. They include the legal profession, arts and entertainment, food and drink, construction, finance, and admin and support services – categories many soloists will be part of. People who feel lonely or isolated may be more at risk of developing a troubled relationship with alcohol.[2]

I have had periods of quite heavy drinking, especially when working on a newspaper, and then later when working as a drinks expert every week on national television, after going solo. It never got really out of hand, but it's not a recipe for long-term happiness, nor is it a way to do particularly good work. A lot of work events back then were boozy affairs; because everyone at them drank a lot too, getting smashed was normal. When you're in that kind of environment, it's hard to step back and be objective about whether you're consuming too much, on your own terms.

The way I manage alcohol is by having rules about when and where I drink. The problem is not just about the alcohol, but what it signifies. When I pour a glass of wine, a very clear marker has been set down – perhaps clearer than any other in my life: I do not drink and work (when I'm writing about drinks, I spit). Therefore, if I am drinking, I am not working. (Nor, most likely, am I parenting!) Alcohol is about socialising, relaxation, de-stressing – all of which are, of course, chemically enhanced by alcohol itself. While alcohol in itself can be addictive, the social and cultural aspects are perhaps just as alluring. Solo workers can be so vulnerable to this – without a team of people physically around you to celebrate or commiserate, an easy way through an emotional logjam is a drink.

I write about wine, beer, spirits and cocktails. Alcohol has a fascinating place in society and I love the rituals around it, and the way we use it to signal and celebrate. But ... it's not a good idea to use things you can eat or drink as a reward for working, and alcohol is probably the worst. Two years ago, Steve and I decided we needed to cut down, and that we wouldn't drink Monday to Friday at home. Once a month we are allowed to let ourselves off for a single weeknight, if we have a good reason, like a birthday or something major to celebrate. It works because – like all the best rules – there's a little bit of managed flexibility to it. It would be harder to stick to if the rule was simply: no booze, Monday-Friday. But because we might get a pass on nights when we are out or with friends, it doesn't feel draconian.

Being accountable to each other is useful too. I went away for a week to work on this book, and all my rules went out of the window. It was interesting to use my behaviour as a way to try and understand the way that rewards, especially ones which are intrinsically relaxing and also delicious, like booze, can become problematic when we are working hard, or are out of our normal routines or settings, or when we are more alone than normal. You also don't need me to tell you that hungover work is rarely creative or productive. Hangovers are when you are most likely to find me archiving emails or rearranging paperwork – not writing books.

Part 3

What's the Point?

12

What Does Success Look Like?

It's 1996. The 57-year-old comic book publisher Marvel is on the point of collapse. Comic books no longer sell like they used to, the market has contracted, digital technology is eclipsing traditional publishers and it looks as though the company will go bankrupt.

It's 2008. The first of Marvel's wildly lucrative self-made movies comes out, *Iron Man*, and takes $585 million at the box office. Subsequent Marvel films make at least $100 million each, with the first Avengers film and the third Iron Man film taking over a $1 billion each at the box office. Over a 12-year period, Marvel went through a sometimes agonising reinvention – not into a wholly new creation, but instead into a company which capitalised on its existing assets (familiar, deeply loved comic book characters) in a new way: making spectacular movies, exploiting the latest digital technologies to do so. In 2009, Disney bought Marvel Entertainment for just over $4 billion.

Success and failure are not helpful words. Real life is not as binary as they are. Failure is viewed, culturally, as a negative, but then we see businesses teetering on the clifftop of failure turn things around. Think of Apple when Steve Jobs left in the 1980s, and how it pulled back from the point of death when he returned in 1997. Think of FedEx, which in its first few years of life in the early 1970s, came so close to running out of cash to buy fuel for its planes that founder Fred Smith took the company's last $5,000 to Vegas, winning enough on the blackjack table to keep the company afloat for one more crucial week. (FYI this is not a recommended financing tactic.)

Sometimes our biggest apparent failures pay out with unexpected rewards further down the line, not just at work, but in life in general. I only had time to write the proposal for this book, which netted a publishing deal, because I had no other paid work for months after I returned from maternity leave. Not exactly a 'successful' phase in my career. I 'failed' to get a job at the UN. I 'failed' to get a job at the *Telegraph* newspaper, which ultimately led to my getting a much better job at the *Observer*. I spent my twenties 'failing' to have relationships with any hope of a future. I spent my early thirties 'failing' to get pregnant. And sometimes, what looked like success, when aiming for it from far away, doesn't feel like success at all when you get there.

Many of us are tormented by the success we think we 'should' have had by now – we should be this, we should be that, we 'should' own that other thing. But success and failure are (like meaningfulness), just constructs. They aren't objective things. With different perspectives they ripple and change. There is no 'should'.

Why attaching happiness to success makes both less likely

When you unwittingly create a framework in your head that says, 'I'll only be happy when I'm successful', especially if you don't know what success looks like, the chances are that both happiness and success will always appear as though they are just over the next hill. We think: 'If I just work a bit harder, and a bit longer, and make a few more personal sacrifices along the way, I'll reach it'. But if success is still a vague idea, the summit will always appear further away, and the sacrifices that may be needed for your version of success might weigh even heavier. It sounds like an Instagram-worthy aphorism (it is), but annoyingly it's true: you have to make the journey towards success to do with your happiness in itself, otherwise you're going to be so miserable on that journey.

It's akin to those apocryphal executives who work like demons for 30 years so they can retire filthy rich, but find that either their lives are hollow and empty, or who even, tragically, die before they can enjoy their retirement. This is even more critical for those of us who work alone, for all the reasons we've already discussed: the toll solitude can take on your well-being and the ease with which solo workers can slip into a life of endless, formless slog.

Success can make you happy of course – and it should! – but it shouldn't be the thing on which we pin our hopes of happiness. If you catch yourself thinking 'It will be better when ...' too often, then ask if you are doing this? Perversely, one way round this is to celebrate your smaller successes, as a way to bring joy to the journey – you won a new client, you were asked to submit a brief, something you wrote was published, you had a good month financially, you were invited to join a prestigious business network, you got great feedback from someone.

What does your version of success look like?

Without having a sense of what success means to you, it's

going to be hard to know what you need to do to achieve it, and it will be even harder to tell when you've reached it.

As best we can, we need to remove other people's expectations from our thinking. It doesn't matter if your mother thinks you should own a house by now, or if everyone you graduated with makes twice as much money. For Dior Bediako, for example, success is about being able to send her future (as yet unborn) children to university – which is a long game for a 27-year-old to be engaged in, and wasn't the answer I expected her to give me (I really should know to expect the unexpected by now).

What matters is what your own success would look like to you. Even more important is that you don't make it solely about your work. We get the best results from thinking about our whole lives as one big picture – which, given the amount of blurring there is in solo work-life, makes sense. Work is not a discrete, set-aside section of life – it both *is* our life, and affects the rest of it.

As Diane Mulcahy says, 'It's very easy to default into what everybody else is doing, and then you're sort of following everybody else's version of success.' She often helps her clients and students work out their own personalised version of success. 'What kind of lifestyle do you want to live? Name the things that really matter to you, so that we can decide how much they cost, and then figure out how much you really need to earn to live the lifestyle that matters to you. Because you don't have to live the lifestyle that everyone else is living – you don't have to have a suburban house. Maybe an apartment in the city is perfect for you. Maybe a cottage in the country is amazing. Those things have very different cost structures. This blank slate exercise often reveals that if people were living a life that was completely aligned with their priorities and their values, in many cases, it would be cheaper than the one they're living. Because the one they're living is all about what everybody else is doing.'

Remember Levison Wood's struggles with success at the beginning of this book? He felt swallowed up by all the things that swirled around his work – events and engagements particularly, which he felt immense pressure to attend, often every day, in support of his actual work. He struggled to detach two very separate things. One was the thing he was succeeding at – going on expeditions, making television programmes and writing books about them. The other was stuff that came with success, but wasn't part of it. It left him questioning the point of 'success', until he realised that he could say no to some or all of the stuff which was leaving him no time to live his life. He had – temporarily – lost sight of what his definition of success was, it certainly wasn't having no life of his own.

A vision of success

To work out what success is for you, go big. Rather than a set of career goals, think of it as a vision for what you want from the whole of your life. What would life look like for you in five or ten years, if you got to design it yourself? Do you want to have more time for life outside work? Do you have a specific goal – speaking at a big industry conference, working on a particular kind of project? Do you wish you could employ a team? Do you want to have enough clients that you're able to rent an office so you don't need to work at home? Perhaps there's a particular account you want to land. Or do you want to sell enough of your product that you can live off the proceeds? Do you want to launch your service online? Do you want to have your business operating in multiple venues, cities, or even countries? Do you just want to keep on doing what you love?

And what about the rest of your life? Where do you want to live? In what? Do you want a family or a partner? Do you want to be fitter or healthier? Do you want to have learned any new things? Is there something you want to achieve, like a new level in your sport, or to finish making, renovating or refurbishing something? Make the picture as detailed as you like (remembering, equally, that you don't have to change or grow anything, unless you truly want to). By allowing work and non-work to sit together, we are more likely to make choices and plans which allow both sides to co-exist effectively, or to see where a compromise might be required.

When we're figuring out what our definition of success is we need to be both imaginative and precise. You need to be imaginative because you have to consider a life you don't already have. You need to be precise because in order to be reached, a goal has to be concrete and it needs to have an end point – otherwise the bottom of the rainbow moves further away: 'I want to pay off my student loans.' 'I want my business to have 10,000 followers on social media.' 'I want to save a deposit for a flat.' Hell, even 'I want to buy nothing but designer handbags,' is OK, as long as you are clear about what you're setting out to do and what the end point looks like.

Write the answers down, if you like, or just mull them over, but make it clear to yourself what your work is aiming at. (I have a notebook solely dedicated to this kind of thinking. Others love a vision board. You could just as easily use a Pinterest board, or brain-dump on a big sheet of paper. Frankly, whatever feels least ridiculous is the way to go, as long as you do it.)

What Does Success Look Like?

Whatever success is for you, it won't look the same for anyone else.

Present tense journal

I want to preface this by saying the following paragraphs are not the kind of thing I ever expected to write. But I have taken the vision-setting idea one step further. This is a version of a technique taught by the motivational speaker Rachel Hollis – she calls it (and sells) the Start Today Journal. I call it a present tense journal and do it in any old notebook.

The process starts as above – you write down what you want your life to look like in ten years, on a big sheet of paper. You cover everything – ambition, health, fitness, work, appearance, achievements, family, home, money, the lot. My 'best version of my life in ten years' sheet of paper included big stuff like 'joyful and able to appreciate the present' and 'financially stable' and 'is an empathetic partner and parent' to 'has great hair' (that vanity, again). Then you distil all those things down into ten statements, which if they were all to come true, would give you the life you've just imagined. Next you write them down in the present tense.

For me, statement one became 'I am a runner'. I was not, at the time, a runner. But I knew that running regularly would move me in the direction of the life on that sheet of paper – I would be healthy, I would be toned and strong, I would be less anxious, I would be more joyful, I would be more focused and would feel less time-poor.

Another in the present tense list became: I am not addicted to my phone. Others included: I have a great marriage (I do already and I want to keep it that way); I am organised with money; I am kind and patient with myself and others; I have staff who support my businesses and so on.

The trick is to rewrite the list every day, always ten things, and always in the present tense. At the bottom you write down one thing which you are actually going to act on. The idea is not to try and achieve everything on the list – instead, you choose just one, and get to work on that. My first was running. So after writing the whole list out again, under it I would write: 'The goal I made happen is I run three times a week'.

The first weird thing was that I started running three times a week straight away and kept at it. (I got a glute injury about six months later and can't run quite as much; now, instead of writing 'I am a runner', I write, 'I look after my body'. And at the bottom of the list I write: I exercise three times a week. And I do.)

The next weird thing was that the second item of the very first list was 'I write books which were my idea and they sell very well.' Until this book, I've generally worked on books which were either other people's ideas, or I've been a co-author. I have loved this, but I had a yearning to do something that was completely mine.

I dutifully wrote this out for several weeks, while concentrating only on the running. And then my agent rang. He'd had lunch with a publisher who was starting a new list for books like this one and liked the sound of the idea – an idea by then five years old. Within days I'd met her, written sample material and got a contract. I do not believe in the universe manifesting things. I do not believe the universe gives much of a toss about me. I do not believe in self-actualisation. I find this whole thing hard to explain (apart from as a big and delightful coincidence).

I find it especially weird because Hollis says that this will happen. She says that by working on single things on the list, other things on it will start to fall into place, too. And that has been my experience. Since writing 'I am organised with money,' I have completely reordered my finances and started some long-term and retirement investments. Since writing 'I have staff who support my business,' I have found a VA and started using freelancers. I didn't particularly plan to do these things – they just happened, apparently quite naturally and definitely easily.

Why would it work? There's clearly something which is simply about accountability. Writing down 'I am a runner' every day, and not going running at all, feels pretty ridiculous, but it's also a positive and motivating statement. There's clearly some kind of trickle effect, where ideas get drummed into your brain and quietly affect your actions day-to-day. Writing in the present tense helps make it about now, rather than putting it onto your future, distant, slightly other self. It has the benefit of setting clear intentions for the day ahead. (Sorry, I know I sound like a wellness guru.) I can't entirely explain the whole thing. But I like it.

13

The Power of Planning

Are you a planner or a winger? Planning – short- or long-term – is a newish thing for me. For a long time, winging it seemed like the best option. I'm not sure why – it's stressful, lowers the likelihood of good outcomes and makes me anxious. I suspect it was about unspoken fears. If I started thinking too hard about what I was about to have to do, I was afraid I'd realise I couldn't do it. Sometimes, I believed I didn't have time to plan, but mostly I think I was metaphorically sticking my fingers in my ears and pretending whatever was about to happen, wasn't.

That's not a great way to navigate a career.

Today, I take planning seriously, whether for an article, a video, an event, or the next five years of my career. I think I once felt that there was no point in planning since life is unpredictable. It felt like planning would make me inflexible. Maybe it even felt sort of cool to be so ... free. But it's not that binary. Planning is only problematic if you're rigid. It's so much easier, in the face of unexpected chaos, to alter an existing plan, than it is to cope with no plan at all.

Emma Morley, from trifle* creative, is a fan of the business plan, and often says so when she's giving talks about starting a business. 'No matter how small you are, no matter whether you need investment or not, create a business plan,' she says.

'Every single year since I started working for myself, I've created a business plan, and updated it every year,' she says. 'That process of pausing and thinking, and having a strategy for the year ahead, I personally have found really important, even when it was just me, I didn't need any investment and I wasn't going to the bank or anything. When you start a business there is no manual to tell you what to do. There are so many things that you're going to learn about organically, but giving yourself a bit of strategy and structure, is a really positive thing. And it stops you feeling like you don't know what you're doing.'

Margaret Heffernan does the same. 'I sit down every year and think about the past year,' she told me. 'What went well and what went badly and what do I want to accomplish this year. I write up my conclusions and often won't look at it again but I generally find when I go to review it the next year, that I've done most of it. Some psychological research suggests that just saying you'll do something to yourself makes it more likely that you'll do it. I think through what I would like from a financial perspective or personal perspective, from a physical health perspective, from a professional perspective, what I would like next year to look and feel like. So do I want to be busier or less busy? Do I want to have more time to socialise or am I doing too much? Do I want slightly to change direction? I also do a financial plan which is, "What does it cost me to be alive and how much work, if any, do I have booked for next year, or will there be any kind of recurring revenue like royalties? And as a consequence, how much money do I need to make this year to be okay?" And, you know, initially, that's extremely frightening.'

She plans her time, loosely, too. 'I do a time budget: I analyse how much time I spend away from home. Let's say I was away 150 nights this year, which is sadly not implausible – if that were the case obviously I'm not going to cut that back to zero but clearly 85 would be a lot better. I'll keep track of it for the next year and see if it's getting better or worse. Because I can't really write anywhere except home, so if I'm on the road a lot, I'm just not going to be writing very much; the way to write more is to stay home more.'

Violinist Charlotte Scott plans even more deeply. She visualises her way through most of the challenging situations her career throws at her, before she experiences them, a technique she was taught by a sports psychologist at the performing arts school Julliard, in New York. 'Let's take an audition,' she tells me. 'An audition is up there as one of the most stressful things you can do. It's a completely false environment, and people are there to give you a yes or no answer. The thing about visualisation is that it gives you the capacity to go into the situation as though you've done it so many times before, as though it's not a new thing. On top of that, you are projecting what you are wishing to play like.' Scott's a musician, but the same would hold true for a speaking event, a pitch meeting, a conference. 'What it does is create another level of focus. Let's say I've got an audition coming up: two weeks before, I start visualising.' And what do you visualise? 'Everything. Waking up that morning. What I'm wearing, going into the building, the whole day. Walking in, who I'm going to see, do I go to the bathroom, washing my hands. Do I know the room? If I don't know the room, I will look online to try and get the best possible idea of what it is all going to look like. Is the pianist going to be OK? I'll imagine them being OK, and not being OK. I'll do so many scenarios. How do I feel? What am I doing with my breath? Most importantly, you have an intention for what you are about to do. Imagine it going the best it can. Imagine how that feels once it's over, what has happened while you've been doing it. You're teaching yourself on all levels what it could be like.' It's not that she troubleshoots – the experience is always set in a positive light. It means that, as much as it's possible to be, she's in control – in the best kind of way.

Being a proactive and agile freelancer has been shown (in a survey involving freelancers in both the US and Europe) to lead to higher billable hours, and greater satisfaction with work.[1] It's also just less frightening – planning doesn't mean you always know what's coming but having a clear sense of what you were aiming for and how you planned to get it, makes re-routing a shattered plan so much more likely than creating one out of the dust.

14

The Curse of Comparison (and Why Social Media Sucks)

I explored why it's important to build your own idea of success without reference to other people's version of it in chapter 12. But we need to talk more about comparing ourselves to others, especially in the age of hyper-curated, heavily filtered social media. Yes, social media offers lone workers access to free marketing and publicity. Yes, it can make soloists feel more connected and offers a valuable way to find and learn from other people working in the same way, or field as you. But it also allows us to consciously or unconsciously compare other people's lives with our own. A few years ago, an editor I work with but rarely see commented that she'd been look-ing at my posts and that it looked as though I was having a really happy life. She was being kind, but I also thought she sounded wistful, and I knew she felt a bit stuck in her office job. I pointed out that I didn't post pictures of myself at mid-night typing rewrites or chasing invoices, that it wasn't all perfect. What I didn't say was that I was also in the middle of a harrowing infertility diagnosis which threatened to break my relationship, and quite possibly, my mind. My online life looked absolutely nothing like my real life. It was a fiction.

You almost certainly can't escape social media. But soloists need to mitigate its harmful effects, which are particularly pernicious when we are alone or outside formal working structures.

There's a really interesting passage in Angela Duckworth's book *Grit*. In it, she talks to Dan Chambliss, a sociologist who wrote a study called 'The Mundanity of Excellence', which argued that excellence in any field is nothing more than the accrual of hundreds, if not thousands, of tiny mundane acts, often done repeatedly.[1] Excellence doesn't appear from nowhere. Most often, success doesn't come from anywhere dazzling. It comes from getting up, getting on with the work – whatever it may be – and more often than not, doing something pretty much the same today, as yesterday.

The reason this is important to us soloists is that every time you compare yourself to someone apparently more 'successful' in your field, you don't see all the mundanity that preceded, bolstero or maintains that success. Who posts that stuff on Instagram? Like my editor, we don't see the thousands of small repetitions, rejections and second, third, fourth attempts, the boredom, the effort, the grit, it takes to succeed in almost anything. Culturally – and *Grit* shows this in dozens of vivid ways – we are inclined to look for genius and celebrate talent as though almost no effort is required. Chambliss points Duckworth in the direction of Nietzsche to explain this. Nietzsche says: 'With everything perfect, we do not ask how it came to be ... we rejoice in the present fact as though it came out of the ground like magic.' And we all love a bit of magic.

The flipside of Nietzsche's point is that we also use this perspective on excellence to insulate ourselves from having to make the effort. If genius or talent are everything, we can reserve the idea of extreme success for people with exceptional gifts and let ourselves off the hook. If we compare ourselves to someone and ruefully think, 'They are so talented, I could never be like them,' even if that makes us sad, we don't have to do anything about it. They have the talent and that's that. We don't. Ho hum.

So, that's one thing to remember: when we see achievement online – and this goes for personal stuff like physical transformations, as much as it does for work – we don't see what was necessary to get there. If you want it, you'll have to slog too. Whether you want to slog or not is up to you, but let's be honest about what glittering 'success' requires – even if almost no one on social media is.

The second thing is that being on social media seems to have an effect on mental health. We already know that high levels of social media use seems to correlate with higher levels of loneliness. But social comparison also adds to the pain – we can't help but judge our own lives negatively against the (curated, hyperreal/semi-fake) lives we see on our feeds.[2] Indeed, the effect on our self-esteem may be even worse when we follow people who seem admirable. One study looked at what happens to us when we look at people with profiles indicating a 'high-activity social network' and 'healthy habits'. No prizes for guessing the punishing effects on our self-esteem when we do: it falls through the floor.[3] The bitter irony, of course, is that we may well seek out exactly that kind of person to follow online – health and fitness influencers, motivational speakers, business leaders in our fields – because we think we will find them inspirational or educational.

Social media is not all bad, of course, and in recent years there's been a huge upswing in greater honesty online, as well as accounts providing mental health support and guidance, along with the new body positivity. It's not like I'm suggesting we all go on a social media strike. At the risk of sounding like a stuck record, it's about knowing what the possible effects are and how they make us feel – then we can make a choice about what and who we engage with.

15

Freelance Networks and How to Build Them

Whether you choose to create a real or online community, or both, you need to have a support network if you're going to thrive at freelancing. If you're naturally solitary, then you might need less frequent contact, or perhaps your group will be a small one – but even introverts need people. If the idea of attending a networking event makes you want to hide in a cupboard, that's understandable. They can, in fact, be quite lovely, if you choose one that suits you – they are no longer stuffy, formal affairs. The photographer Carmel King started a group called Hive, which operates in north London, and its events are close to perfect, with wine (in glasses, not paper cups), chocolate brownies and talks from diverse solo businesses – the last I went to involved a wallpaper and fabric designer who gave a talk on his career, and a panel discussion including a stand-up comedian.

There's plenty of evidence that we need networks – especially if our friends and family don't work in similar ways to us. As Brigid Schulte told me, 'Human beings are social creatures who do so much better when connected to larger networks. Look at health research and longitudinal studies that have looked at which people live long, happy, fulfilled and healthy lives: it is the people who have strong social networks. It actually increases resilience. Connections with other people help you stay sane but also might lead to a collaboration or an idea or a way to further your business.' They can also give us solutions to our own very particular problems.

She says we need to make space in our calendars for this. 'Whether you join a business association or a networking group or some kind of affiliation, connect with others who are in the same boat so you don't feel so alone,' she says. 'I was talking with a freelance writer yesterday and she's part of a number of different groups, some of them virtual, and she says that not only do they share resources, which helps her from a business standpoint, but they able to tell each other things like, "This is just the way the business goes, it isn't just you". Networks can give you perspective.'

Granted, you might not want to network. Jamelia Donaldson, founder of Treasure Tress, is the kind of person who seems like she could own the room in seconds. 'I absolutely hated it at first,' she told me. 'I had to force myself out of my comfort zone to do it. Building connections with people I have some form of pre-existing relationship with, like friends of friends, friends of colleagues, that comes pretty naturally to me; leaving my house alone, to attend an event alone, knowing that I do not know anyone who is attending – that was a challenge.' How did she get over it? 'Putting on a brave face and remembering that nothing great ever comes from your comfort zone. I learned how to translate the fear into excitement about who I could meet, and what I could learn. Confidence compounds. Once you've done it a few times, you start to recognise faces and those are the first few strings of your new network – not just for business partnerships, but for the human aspect of business. Finding people who truly care for and about you, your work, the community you serve and the mission you're committed to.'

Whatever you do, there's probably an organisation designed to support you. If there isn't one for your trade, then join a freelance collective – look at Perspectivity.org in Holland, Enspiral.com in New Zealand, Belgium-based Smart (Smarteu.org) or Dutch-based Broodfonds, or the UK-based Hoxby Collective, and there are many, many others. Some only exist within Facebook – I am part of a 5,000-strong female freelance creatives group on Facebook – while others only exist in the real world. Alex Hannaford helped found Deadline in Austin, Texas, a group for freelance journalists which meets up every few months – they have 500 members on Facebook, and the face-to-face events usually involve a maximum of 60 people. Recently a lot of networks developed what they could offer online, with virtual networking, webinars and Zoom calls as ways of offering support as well as training.

If structured networking really isn't for you, then do it informally. Start by asking questions of everyone you meet who even vaguely works in a similar way to you. How do they make time for themselves? What changes have they made recently which are really working for them? What do they wish they'd been told by someone at the beginning of their own solo-working journey? What do they feel stressed about right now? Very few people dislike talking about themselves. Most people love it, and this is a way you could get quite tailor-made hacks for your own work life. You might find an informal mentor this way, too – I don't mean that you should be disingenuous about it, but most people like being looked up to, and the sense that they're able to help someone else.

I don't want to fall into clichés, but men often find this stuff trickier, and can be less used to this kind of communication than women. If that's true for you, take heart from

Alex Hannaford's approach. 'I think that a conversation over a cup of tea or a pint of beer is really important because that's where men can talk about stuff,' he told me. 'I've always thought a problem shared is a problem halved, or whatever the saying is. Me and my friends have always been really open about stuff about work and family life or whatever.' As a result, when he's needed help, he's found it relatively easy to ask, partly because he did a fellowship which involved working with other journalists who cover traumatic stories, as he does, through which he maintains a wide-ranging informal network. Hannaford's beat includes violent crime and the death penalty, and as such sometimes needs more than even his incredibly supportive wife can offer. 'I covered an execution a few years back for the *Guardian*, and I wasn't sure how I would deal with that,' he told me. 'So after I came out of the prison, I had a two-hour drive back, and I got in the car. I had five or six people I'd set up calls with, all connected with this sort of loose world of trauma journalism, and one person who was a psychiatrist. Not because I needed a shrink, but just because I knew that he'd be a good person to talk to about what I'd just seen. I talked for two hours, listened to what they had to say. It was really good talking. And actually, I was fine.'

Other solo experiences will not be as harrowing, but that doesn't mean we don't all need similar support – and sometimes it will be support that our friends and families, however willing, aren't the best people to give. By cultivating a professional network, formally or informally, we provide ourselves with a sort of pressure-release valve, tailored to what we do.

16

The Problem with Money (Psychological)

Money is an extrinsic motivator, and it's very good at driving us to work hard in the short term, but in the long term a number of studies have suggested that money saps workers' enthusiasm. Which is weird, because that's not the message we are generally given about work and being rewarded for it. The usual frame through which we view financial reward is that being paid more makes you feel more valued, and so able to work harder. Being underpaid is definitely demotivating, but it turns out that we need more than just cash to motivate us to work, and that money on its own – without any other warmer, deeper motivating factors – can make work feel like drudgery and can even lower performance.[1] (This has been shown to be true even for non-financial rewards, like those given to children for good behaviour. Rewards seem to mean we automatically reframe whatever we've been rewarded for as a negative activity, unless there are other very powerful intrinsic motivators at play at the same time.) There doesn't seem to be much of a relationship between pay, whether high or low, and job satisfaction.[2] The majority of the research on this subject looks at workers within organisations, and there's still a lot of debate around exactly what the findings tell us, but I'm fascinated by what we can extrapolate for solo workers.

The Problem with Money (Psychological)

If you're going to work alone, you've got to have or find some intrinsic motivation. Being paid for what I do is incredibly important and money matters to me (especially when I don't have any; especially when a client is dithering over an invoice; especially when someone tries to pay me way below the going rate). But the other big reason why I get out of bed in the morning and do my job is that I love it. I like finding out interesting stuff and then telling other people. That's my intrinsic motivation. Would I do it even if I wasn't paid for it? That's a more complex question. I would certainly write if I wasn't paid to do it ... but I'd have to be rich enough not to need another job, or have one which didn't suck up much of my time and mental or physical energy. You can't entirely untangle intrinsic and extrinsic motivations – I love being a journalist in itself, but I also love the status and access it gives me, for example – and soloists can't survive with one but not the other.

You may already be intrinsically motivated to do what you do, but you might not realise it yet. Being aware of our intrinsic motivations helps prevent thoughts about money or status (respect, accolades, awards) taking up too much space in our heads and squashing the warmer, fuzzier intrinsic stuff.

This is part of what's known as the self-determination theory of motivation. It suggests motivation comes from three things. To be intrinsically motivated at work, we need competence, or the chance to achieve it. Second, we want to be connected with others through and in our work. Third, we need autonomy – we like feeling in control, and able to set our own terms.

This mirrors a lot of what we've talked about already – all three are connected to ideas about meaningful work, to resilience and courage, to mitigating loneliness and finding ways to focus. And it turns out that they affect our relationship with money too. If we have those three things, and are intrinsically motivated to work, money can become less of an obsession. It's still a need itself, but it can take a back seat.

This matters, because when you are solo, sometimes it feels like our income is the only assessment tool we can apply to our businesses. It's a measure of whether things are going in the right direction, especially if it's hard to get external feedback or gratitude from doing it. Not having enough money can make it hard to think about anything else at all, and money is deeply tangled up in our sense of self, too. There have been a number times in my working life when money has been tight, and when I was very young there were occasions when my credit card reliance got out of hand. Much later, after I was technically well established as a writer, after my second maternity leave, I hit a terrifyingly lengthy quiet patch, during which I learned again just how much I use my income to prove my worth to myself, both as a worker and as a functioning adult, one I can consider worthy of respect. Not having money is a much more intense experience than having money. When money feels scarce it uses up a lot of our mental energy.

Money has other unhelpful side effects. Research about being paid an hourly rate found that once people were encouraged to think about their work time as having an hourly monetary value, they wanted to work longer hours, in order to earn more money (even if there was an option to work less); other research showed it made it harder to enjoy unpaid time off, too.[3]

This explains many freelancers' inability to turn down paid work, even if it means their hours grow ever longer and more unmanageable. As soon as you start pricing your time by the hour (or by the day, or even by the job) rather than a set annual salary which hits your bank account regardless of the number of hours you work, two things may happen: first, you want to use more of your finite time resources to earn money (because you can, in a way you usually can't when you're on a salary). Second, monetising your time, and dividing it into billable nuggets has the odd effect of making it seem more scarce.[4] And scarcity makes us behave less rationally, and to make worse decisions. Separate research suggests getting paid more makes the situation worse – the more we get paid, the more highly we value time, and it feels even more scarce. Rich people in the developed world feel more time-poor than anyone else.

It's hardly a crime to want to use your potentially valuable time to earn more money, when you can. But we need to be aware of these unexpected effects, so that we can moderate them. As we know, feelings of scarcity can generate feelings of anxiety, which are unpleasant and potentially counter-productive when it comes to getting any work done at all. As well as by overcommitting to what can be done in a day, we can also make ourselves feel stressed just by applying a high monetary value to our time because of this trick our brains play on us. That doesn't mean soloists shouldn't value their time highly – but if a big money job makes your palms sweaty, or if you just can't say no to another project even when your calendar is full, that trick is part of the reason. Just knowing that our brains are responding in this way can help put a lid on the sensation.

On the other hand, happiness expert Shawn Achor's research has suggested that nine out of ten people will – in theory anyway – take a pay cut for the duration of their careers in order to do work they consider meaningful.[5] So all is not lost for humanity.

What does this mean for us in our real lives? Finding intrinsic motivation means things like actively looking for ways to increase our competence at work, through learning, feedback and new skills. It means making sure we establish relationships through our work, or that our work has positive effects on other people. And it means ring-fencing, valuing and protecting our autonomy as soloists, rather than feeling pulled apart by our multiple potential bosses and clients.

The other thing that the data shows? We consistently look at money the wrong way up. We spend our time to get money. But the thing that actually leads to a long and happy life? Spending *money to get time*. (Although you do have to hit a certain level of affluence to make this possible.) We believe that money makes us happy, but correlational, longitudinal and experimental research of over 100,000 adults by Ashley Whillans and her team at Harvard shows the same thing over and over again: 'People who are willing to give up money to gain more free time – by, say, working fewer hours or paying to outsource disliked tasks – experience more fulfilling social relationships, more satisfying careers, and more joy, and overall, live happier lives.'[6]

We say we want more time, but her research has shown we are absolutely rubbish at acting on it.

Can money buy happiness at all? Not necessarily. Some scholars contend that if you spend it right, on things like experiences, rather than stuff, then money can generate, rather than buy, happiness. It is true that a shift from poverty to having enough money unsurprisingly leads to a pretty sharp uptick in well-being, which continues as income rises. But at around £48,000 to £60,000 ($60,000 to

75,000) of annual income, well-being starts to flatline, and doesn't improve, regardless of how much more money you make. The actual figure varies from country to country, with lower income countries having a lower well-being ceiling, but it's repeated globally. The ceiling figures are well above national average incomes – the UK average is about £30,000 – but around 4 million British taxpayers earn over £50,000 a year, so it's a level low enough to be relatively attainable.[7] By which I mean, you do not need to be among the rare super-rich to be more than satisfied with what you earn. It's thought that the flatlining may have something to do with the additional stresses and worries that can come with the kinds of jobs where you earn a very high income, although it's been shown among lottery winners (who sometimes have tragic outcomes), so there's obviously more at play – some have suggested it's also about guilt and responsibility that might come with having a lot of money.

Seeing time as valuable has unexpected side effects too. Another study by Whillans showed that students who said they value their own time over their earning power ultimately went on to report significantly higher levels of happiness at work a year after graduating than their money-valuing counterparts. The mindset shift alone can give the same well-being boost as if you were to receive a salary bump of £1,770 ($2,200) a year.[8] Family life in recent years has forced me to see time differently too. Steve and I rarely buy each other birthday presents, instead, we give each other time – a day off on our own, doing things like seeing friends, having a massage, which are much more psychologically valuable than a pair of earrings.

We need to start seeing our time in the same way we view our earning power. In fact, no, we need to start seeing our time as more valuable than our earning power – and our earning power as only being valuable because it can buy us time.

Time can't buy happiness – it can give it to you.

17

The Problem with Money (Practical)

Even soloists who make a decent-to-very-decent amount of money will almost certainly have periods with little work, and even with savings, these periods can be scary and destabilising. All of which can make planning for big financial decisions like where to live, holidays or time off, challenging. But it's important to remember that the grass isn't necessarily greener – a traditional regular salary doesn't guarantee financial stability, with redundancy always a possibility for many employees. Many solo workers are actually more secure than some employees, having built a financial buffer into their planning to help cope with quiet patches.

Chasing payments can feel unpleasant, too, and if you hate it, and can possibly outsource it, do so as quickly as you can – there are plenty of virtual assistants online who are brilliant at this. Badgering for payment is probably one of the most energy sapping aspects of solo work, especially when a client is very late to pay, and someone who specialises in hounding late payers will be better at it than you and good at using the right legal terminology to create just the right amount of fear. Plus it creates a barrier between you and your client, meaning you never have to be directly angry with them yourself. If they get offended by your chaser's tactics, you can apologise, denying all knowledge. 'Oh I'm so sorry! I'll have to have a word!' And then send an email thanking your VA when the money finally lands in your account.

Money can be hard on relationships, too. As Alex Hannaford, the writer and podcaster, now in Texas, recalls. 'It's one of the biggest hot-button issues that can cause problems,' he told me. 'There have been times in my career where Courtney [his wife] had the regular checks every month. Particularly when we lived in London and things were more expensive, she would sometimes ask, "When are you getting paid by ... ?" And I've gone on the defensive, but also, I'm thinking, "Yes, when the fuck do I get paid by X?"'

'There is some research that shows, over the long term, if a business isn't doing well, it spills over to the life partner of the entrepreneur,' Professor Ute Stephan told me. 'And I think that's just worth appreciating – that when you have financial trouble in your work, it may have a negative knock-on effect on your partner.' While there is no obvious solution to the problem of slow payers, what can we do within relationships to defend ourselves against the damage money worries might cause? 'Be open about it, and appreciate that maybe there is some joint problem-solving that needs to be done,' she says. Keeping a financial burden hidden from your partner is a dangerous strategy – exhausting for you and highly stressful, and when revealed also shows a lack of trust and transparency between you. It's another problem with over-identifying yourself with your work. If you can separate the two, it's easier to tell other people that 'the business' isn't doing well financially, because you don't feel like you're confessing to a personal flaw.

Feeling stressed about money seems to be a feature of solo working life even when there's a fair amount of it about.[1] One way through this is to look for training in things like small business finance. In some areas, there are local schemes which provide such training free of charge. If you feel like you don't have time, think of it this way: the amount of energy you may currently be wasting on nebulous, unformed money worries will rapidly eclipse the time and energy required to go on a short course. If it sounds boring or intimidating, you are probably telling yourself that you don't have time to do it. But if you balance that time spent against the possibility of not being worried about money all the time, doesn't that sound like a pretty sweet deal? A few actual hours versus potentially hundreds of soul-sapping hours of worry? (There's also evidence to show that in many countries, self-employed people have no idea whether grants or funding exist to help them set up or grow their business, or help them recruit if they want to – one UK government scheme only reached 6 per cent of its intended soloist recipients recently, in part because they didn't know a thing about it.[2])

I said at the beginning of this book that I wasn't going to teach you how to do your taxes, and that is still the case. But there is one thing to say: your gross income is not your income at all. A quarter to a third, or more, of it belongs to your government and was never really yours. It's a system which almost seems designed to trip soloists up. But the one piece of critical advice I got when I went freelance was to put away part of each payment for tax (and any other deductions that your government might make), and leave it in a bank account which you do not otherwise use. It's terrifying and depressing to receive a tax bill and discover that you will have to work to earn enough to pay it off. To avoid this, I use a spreadsheet (downloadable from howtoworkalone.com, designed by my sister Katy, who – true story – actually likes using Excel spreadsheets) which you can use to work out how much money to winnow off from each payment you receive. I take a percentage for tax, another for savings and another for my pension contributions, and then I live off the net remains. I do it for every payment – even ones of just a few hundred pounds – because I pay tax on every single amount which comes in. It takes about 15 minutes every week and since using it, I've never been hit with a tax bill I can't handle. I never, ever touch the money in the tax account. In fact, my payments go into one account and once I've allocated all the funds, I transfer the remainder into a separate current account. That way, I'm never tempted to start spending from the gross income – I can only spend the net.

This is more like personal advice, rather than solo specific but I think it helps soloists feel more secure: knowing exactly what you're spending your money on gives you so much more control and you're less likely to spend it stupidly. For years and years, my bank account hovered around the zero mark, with my salary topping up my arranged (free) over-draft each month. When I took voluntary redundancy from the newspaper, I got a settlement which – frankly – helped me change my ways, as it paid off my overdraft and gave me some savings. Even so, it's only in the last few years that I've started paying close attention to my bank statements, and now I know precisely how much I have and where, at any given moment – a quite extraordinary shift, considering I used to actively avoid looking at my on-screen balance when withdrawing cash. The funny thing is, I worry far less now than I did when I just avoided looking, despite having less disposable income than I did ten years ago.

I use Monzo bank, which is really useful because it breaks down all your expenditure into sections – finances, groceries, eating out, entertainment, family, shopping and so on. (Many of the new challenger or app-based banks offer a similar budget breakdown, as do many of the app-based accounting programmes.) It was a stomach-lurching experience to see how much I was spending a quarter on eating out, but we are now saving (and I can't quite believe I'm saying this) *thousands* of pounds a year just through knowing how insane our spending was on everything from sandwiches to high-end restaurants. Once again, having the knowledge is what allows us all to make changes – prior to this I probably knew I was spending too much, but because I didn't know how much, I wasn't able to access the willpower needed to curb it. And because the intention was vague ('stop spending so much on eating out') rather than specific ('save thousands by eating out only on very special occasions') it was easy to ignore or work around, meaning the money-sapping, bank-balance avoiding behaviour continued. Perhaps, like making ourselves a good lunch, taking breaks from work and being kind to ourselves, part of this is about beliefs and mindset. We each have to get to a point where we not only believe we can take control of our money, but that we deserve to be in control, too.

How to set your rates, fees or prices

Rate setting can be a bit of a minefield whatever your field, so I asked Joanne Mallon, one of the UK's most experienced careers coaches, who has been helping freelancers with sticky issues like money for 20 years, for her advice (joannemallon. com).

- **Research** Mallon says, 'Find a few friendly allies in your business – join professional associations or online forums. It's not uncommon for independent

professionals to do this. Discuss fees where
appropriate, but don't just ask – be prepared to share
your rates too. Some other businesses will also have
their rates stated on their website, or websites such as
Bidvine will give you a broad estimate of what's being
charged in certain industries.' Gather data about what
others charge, and then make an assessment of what
your prices can look like based on your comparable
experience and skill level. If necessary, be sneaky – ask
a friend to make an enquiry of someone in a similar
field, if you don't want to ask directly. But many
people will be prepared to discuss their rates quite
openly, and I'd argue that where possible, the more
transparent we can all be about what we are paid for
what we do, the better. Although there will obviously
be work which has to be priced very specifically
(bespoke joinery, for example) other work, like social
media management or proofreading is slightly more
standardised, and fees sit within a given range, usually
based on a day rate.

- **Negotiate** That may mean that you ask for a little or
a lot more, especially from repeat clients, or as your
experience and status grows. 'In negotiations, avoid
being the first one to name a figure,' says Mallon.
'Your potential client will always have a budget or a
figure in mind, so find out what that is using open
questions. Ask 'What sort of budget/fee/rate did you
have in mind?' because this assumes that they've got
one. A line I like to use is 'Hopefully we can work out
a rate that we're both happy with,' which shows that
you're not looking to rip them off, but equally you're
not expecting them to rip you off either.'

The Problem with Money (Practical)

- **Have confidence** Believe that you deserve to be paid well – some people call this having a positive money mindset, which is an idea with a huge and growing following online. In its purest form, I think it's broadly a good thing, but it can drift uncomfortably (for me) close to ideas about affluence and abundance, which as we've seen above, have been shown to be unhelpful or unhealthy motivators for solo workers. 'It's worth being aware of your own issues around money and working those out so that you can make confident negotiations,' says Mallon. 'Try looking in the mirror and saying "My daily rate is a million pounds." Keep saying it over and over again until you stop laughing and believe it. Then when you do quote your actual rate, it will feel like an absolutely tiny amount and you will be able to ask for it confidently. Too often people quote a rate and it sounds like they're asking a question, as if the client is doing them a favour. Ideally you want to be quoting figures with the neutrality of saying your own phone number.'

- **Budget** Figure out what you need to live on, and work back from there. If you can't make enough to live on, you need to think about other income streams (not credit card or debt-based) so that you don't find yourself unable to meet your basic living costs. Some rate calculation websites suggest simply dividing up your living costs to work out what to charge, but Mallon disagrees. 'It's worth working out how much you want to earn per month or year, and using that to work out how many billable hours you need to be working. Remember that as an independent at least some of your time will be spent marketing and building your business, which will not be billable. However, a client is never going to pay you a fee just because you want or need it. Your other outgoings are nothing to do with the client. They'll pay your rate because they believe in you, your work and experience, so this is what to emphasise in your conversations with them.'

- **Refuse** If someone wants to pay you an unacceptably low rate – say no. Obviously this is harder at the very beginning of your career, and at that point it may be worth saying yes to a very few jobs on a lowish rate so that you can build a portfolio and increase your contacts. However, be aware that often big-name low-payers are well known, so you might need to balance this against your need and want for portfolio projects – you don't want your portfolio to signal to future clients that you may be inexpensive. Mallon agrees. 'Never be afraid to walk away from a potential client who gives you bad vibes or has unrealistic expectations of what their budget will achieve.'

- **Charge** The same is true of working for free, which, unless it is very strictly within the format of an internship, work experience or training, I would strongly advise against. It is almost impossible to convert a client who doesn't pay into one who does, and by working for free you will be unwittingly dragging the rates downwards for everyone else in your industry. In one of the freelance Facebook groups I am part of, it is common to see posts from new freelance writers about whether they should take on an unpaid job. They are always followed by dozens, if not hundreds of comments imploring the poster not to take the work because of the damaging effect it has on rates across the industry.

- **Swap** The same is not true of swaps, though. A legit skills swap is a completely different thing, can be extremely useful if you need help with something specific but out of your skill set. Swaps can also be a good way to navigate a potentially tricky situation if a friend asks you to do something for free – there's so much potential for an asymmetrical arrangement to go sour, but turning into a swap can even things out. That said, 'exposure' is not the same as a swap. A British tabloid newspaper once offered me exposure in return for writing them a 1,000-word article; I had at that point been a full-time journalist and editor for 12 years and frankly, it was offensive.

- **Charge enough** Counter-intuitively, being cheap doesn't always get the work. It is possible to charge too little, which can frighten a client into thinking you aren't experienced or skilful enough. Being slightly cheaper than your competitors can work in your favour, but being bargain-basement may be off-putting. 'The client who hires you because you're cheap will one day leave you for somebody cheaper, so don't feel that going low is the answer,' confirms Mallon.

How to charge

Hourly or daily rates versus project rates are contentious issues, and each has firm adherents. (This obviously applies less to you if you sell a product for a stated price, like jewellery.) There are downsides to both methods of rate-setting, so give whichever you choose a clear-eyed assessment over time, to be sure it's right for you. The downsides of daily or hourly rates are that they can make you appear more expensive than you are, especially if your client doesn't earn anything like what you're charging, themselves. Saying you cost £100 or £200 an hour, or £500 a day, can really freak out someone who only nets £1,500 a month in salary. That's because they're disregarding all the time in your week when you're not being paid at all, making the rate effectively spread over a longer time period than they realise, and because they aren't thinking about all your associated costs, like equipment. Charging a time-based rate also penalises you if you're quicker than others to get the work done ... although it also means clients are more likely to come back in the future. Other upsides include that if a project is bigger than it first appears, or the client continually expands the brief, you carry on getting paid.

Project rates are the opposite: an all-in fee might not be enough if the job has hidden depths, or a vague brief. For projects, I quote for the amount I think it will cost me (time wise) and then add an optional 25 per cent to be discussed as the project progresses, which keeps the client in the loop and prevents me working extra time, unpaid. At the very least, be sure to build in extra costs for things like unexpected revisions – it's usual to include one or two sets of revisions or changes into a quote, with any more being chargeable. This is just as true for painting and decorating, as it is for editing a book or magazine.

Whichever way you choose, get it all in writing, along with a clear brief, before you start work, whether you're tiling someone's fireplace or redesigning a website. If your client won't or can't give you a brief, write your own, based on your understanding of what they have said they want, and send it back to them to check. This means there's a paper trail of everyone's expectations, and they can tell you if you've got it wrong. (Or, more likely, that they've changed their mind. Or expressed what they wanted badly.)

If you're working on a project which is going to run for a while, especially if it will be full-time or exclude other work, it's acceptable and sensible to request part-payment upfront, or to bill in instalments – once a month, or even every week. It's far safer for you to work this way, because it means your financial eggs are not in one basket, a basket which could be months in arriving. Think about what could happen if the business you are working for fails in six months' time, or how you and your bank account will feel if you bill after three months, only to find they have a 90-day payment cycle?

18

What to Do When You're Not Working

By now, you probably won't be surprised to read that I suspect our biggest goal should be creating a working life which contains plenty of not-work. I want you to have whatever your version of success is, but I want you to have it alongside a life well lived. One in ten freelancers didn't take any time off at all last year.[1] More positively, one out of seven took 40 or more days – way above the 21 to 28 days most countries mandate for employees. Intriguingly, the data doesn't suggest that earnings affect time off taken – you would expect higher earners to feel they could take more time off, but they don't. What does have an impact is age: freelancers who are under 34 are more likely to take more time off. The same report showed (again) that there a host of good effects to be gained from time off – like improving relationships and reducing stress.

Taking time off when you're solo isn't easy – I'm not all that good at remembering to do it myself, and I've been marinating in the science of it for the last year. But, as Margaret Heffernan says, 'If you don't book a holiday, you won't take one. And I've also learned from other freelancers, musicians in particular, that when you book a holiday you can be certain you will almost immediately be offered a gig in that holiday period. There should be a name for it – "holiday buggering up"! But you have to stick to it,' she told me firmly. 'Because otherwise you won't take holidays for years and that leads to burnout.'

The science on holidays (rather than time off in general) is a little muddy, in truth. Some people seem to experience more stress in the run up to a holiday and/or a physical or mental crash when they finally reach it. Generally, holidays seem to have positive effects on long-term health and in the shorter term (two to four weeks) on general well-being – which I think could be an argument for taking more and regular holidays. Some small studies suggest performance and job satisfaction may be higher after holidays, and there's some evidence that mental flexibility is higher too.[2]

For soloists, it might not matter quite as much if we can't disconnect entirely from work – I do think it's harder to do than if you're taking traditional annual leave from employment (and it's hard enough, then). As long as we feel in control of when and how we engage with work on holiday, and it's strictly limited, it may not matter if we have to occasionally reconnect with it. That said, and regardless of the science, the holidays I have taken recently where I haven't had to check my emails have been blissful. It isn't always possible though, especially if you work with products on fixed schedules, with international clients or within extended teams – for Steve, for example, if he's got a shoot the week after a holiday, there will be several days of arranging to engage with in advance. But what the data does suggest is that mindless, regular email-checking does begin to undo all the good that a holiday can provide.

What should we do with our time off? (Which I am going to assume you will take, now, because of all the evidence I've already recounted elsewhere about time off and productivity, creativity, health, happiness and well-being.) The best evidence suggests we need a mixture of things. Quiet time, in which our minds can wander (and wonder). Some physical relaxation and some physical engagement. Exercise and rest. And the same for our brains – exercise and engagement, but in ways which are nothing to do with work.

Remember Tom Broughton from Cubbitts and his online chess? The reason it helped him get through the incredibly tough process of setting up his business was that he was engaging in what's known as deep play. Deep play is absorbing, skilful, satisfying – usually because it is something done with skill but with a binary outcome – win or lose, climb mountain, or not – and usually has a connection to the player's past. Broughton had played chess as a child and found that the attention he needed to pay to his games crowded out the anxieties he felt about his nascent business. Because the rules were clear – unlike in business – and he was unequivocally good at it (when you win, you win), it scratched something deep inside him which balanced out the discomfort in his working life.

He's not alone. Many well-known (and many not-at-all-well-known) entrepreneurs have a sideline in something which qualifies as deep play, which includes sports and endurance challenges like rock climbing and marathons. My friend and colleague John Vincent, co-founder of the 70-plus strong chain of LEON restaurants (and author of business book *Winning Not Fighting*) practises the martial art Wing Tsun; Richard Branson plays chess; Bill Gates plays card games to a predictably high level, including War and Bridge; Sandy Lerner, of Cisco, apparently likes jousting, which she does on horseback in full medieval dress; Tory Burch and Anna Wintour play tennis (not necessarily together); Condoleeza

Rice plays golf; the fashion designer Paul Smith has been collecting antique cycling ephemera since childhood, and dreamed of a cycling career until a nasty crash – he still cycles hard today at 73.

This isn't new news. The proverb 'All work and no play makes Jack a dull boy', was first recorded in print in the 1600s, and is probably much older. But today we not only know it for sure, we also know that making space in our lives for a rich not-working life, will make us better at our work, while getting it done in time to give us back our lives.

*

The world of work is changing incredibly fast, and it can feel hard to know quite what it might do next. But the one thing we soloists can do is get to know ourselves at work, our personalities, our rhythms and our needs. Then, as much as possible, we can protect ourselves from shocks, shakes and shifts, as well as learning how to construct a working life which suits our very unique and individual requirements. Be kind to yourself. You are not alone. (Come and join me in the @the_solo_collective, on Instagram.)

We may be solo, but we are in this together.

Notes

The Good Bits

1. Patrick Briône/IPA and IPSE report, 'Working Well for Yourself: What makes for good self-employment?', 2018, https://www.ipa-involve.com/Handlers/Download.ashx?IDMF=9a9fbd10–37ff–4a57–b9f5–3ce2045a4409

2. 'Independent consulting: a good gig in a changing world', Findings from the Eden McCallum LBS Future of Consulting survey 2018, https://edenmccallum.com/wp-content/uploads/securepdfs/2019/05/survey-report.pdf

3. Patrick Briône/IPA and IPSE report, 'Working Well for Yourself: What makes for good self-employment?', 2018, https://www.ipa-involve.com/Handlers/Download.ashx?IDMF=9a9fbd10–37ff–4a57–b9f5–3ce2045a4409

4. Dan Witter, Sangeeta Agrawal and Alyssa Brown, 'Entrepreneurship Comes With Stress, But Also Optimism', 7 December 2012, https://news.gallup.com/poll/159131/entrepreneurship-comes-stress-optimism.aspx

5. Patrick Briône/IPA and IPSE report, 'Working Well for Yourself: What makes for good self-employment?', 2018, https://www.ipa-involve.com/Handlers/Download.ashx?IDMF=9a9fbd10–37ff–4a57–b9f5–3ce2045a4409

6. Ibid.

Loneliness and Solitude

1. 'One can be the loneliest number – many UK freelancers feel lonely and isolated following leap to self-employment', Epson.co.uk, survey of 1000 freelancers, 2018, https://www.epson.co.uk/insights/article/

one-can-be-the-loneliest-number-many-uk-freelancers-feel-lonely-and-isolated-following-leap-to-self-employment

2. Katie Hafner, 'Researchers Confront an Epidemic of Loneliness', *New York Times*, 5 September 2016, https://www.nytimes.com/2016/09/06/health/lonliness-aging-health-effects.html

3. Cigna's US Loneliness Index, survey of 20,000 Americans, 2018, https://www.multivu.com/players/English/8294451-cigna-us-loneliness-survey/

4. Juliet Michaelson, Karen Jeffrey, Saamah Abdallah, 'The Cost of Loneliness to UK Employers', *The New Economics Foundation*, 2017, https://neweconomics.org/2017/02/cost-loneliness-uk-employers/

5. J. Holt-Lunstad, T. B. Smith, M. Baker, T. Harris, D. Stephenson, 'Loneliness and social isolation as risk factors for mortality: a meta-analytic review', *Perspectives on Psychological Science*, 2015;10(2), https://www.ncbi.nlm.nih.gov/pubmed/25910392

6. The Campaign to End Loneliness, Risk to Health, 2020, www.campaigntoendloneliness.org/threat-to-health

7. The JAMA Network Journals, 'Is a marker of preclinical Alzheimer's disease associated with loneliness?', *ScienceDaily*, 2 November 2016, https://www.sciencedaily.com/releases/2016/11/161102132631.htm

8. University of Surrey, 'Social isolation could cause physical inflammation', *ScienceDaily*, 5 March 2020, https://www.sciencedaily.com/releases/2020/03/200305132136.htm

9. Shawn Achor, Gabriella Rosen Kellerman, Andrew Reece and Alexi Robichaux, 'America's Loneliest Workers, According to Research', *Harvard Business Review*, 19 March 2018, https://hbr.org/2018/03/americas-loneliest-workers-according-to-research

10. Susan Cain, *Quiet: The Power of Introverts in a World That Can't Stop Talking*, p74, Viking, 2012

11. Sidonie-Gabrielle Colette, *Oeuvres Complètes*, Flammarion, 1948/1950 (various reprints thereafter)

12. A. R. Teo, H. Choi, S. B. Andrea, et al., 'Does Mode of Contact with Different Types of Social Relationships Predict Depression in Older Adults? Evidence from a Nationally Representative Survey', *Journal of the American Geriatrics Society*, 2015; 63(10), https://www.ncbi.nlm.nih.gov/pubmed/26437566

13. Michael Harris, *Solitude: In Pursuit of a Singular Life in a Crowded World*, p17, Random House, 2017

Notes

14. Brian A. Primack, Ariel Shena, Jamie E. Sidani et al., 'Social Media Use and Perceived Social Isolation Among Young Adults in the U.S', *American Journal of Preventive Medicine*, 6 March, 2017

15. John T. Cacioppo, Louise C. Hawkley, 'Social Isolation and Health, with an Emphasis on Underlying Mechanisms', *Perspectives in Biology and Medicine* 46, no. 3 (2003): S39–S52, https://muse.jhu.edu/article/168969

16. Michel Janssen and Jürgen Renn, 'History: Einstein was no lone genius', *Nature.com*, 16 November 2015, https://www.nature.com/news/history-einstein-was-no-lone-genius-1.18793

17. Ed Diener and Martin E. P. Seligman, 'Very Happy People', *Psychological Science*, 13(1), 2002, https://journals.sagepub.com/doi/10.1111/1467-9280.00415

18. Gillian M. Sandstrom and Elizabeth W. Dunn, 'Social Interactions and Well-Being: The Surprising Power of Weak Ties', *Personality and Social Psychology Bulletin*, 40(7), 2014, https://journals.sagepub.com/doi/abs/10.1177/0146167214529799

19. Gillian M. Sandstrom and Elizabeth W. Dunn, 'Is Efficiency Overrated?: Minimal Social Interactions Lead to Belonging and Positive Affect', *Social Psychological and Personality Science*, 5(4), 2014, https://journals.sagepub.com/doi/abs/10.1177/1948550613502990

20. Eric D. Wesselmann, Florencia D. Cardoso, Samantha Slater et al., 'To Be Looked at as Though Air: Civil Attention Matters', *Psychological Science*, 23(2), 2012, https://journals.sagepub.com/doi/abs/10.1177/0956797611427921

21. N. Epley and J. Schroeder, 'Mistakenly seeking solitude', *Journal of Experimental Psychology: General*, 143(5), 2014, https://psycnet.apa.org/doiLanding?doi=10.1037%2Fa0037323

22. University at Buffalo, 'Non-fearful social withdrawal linked positively to creativity: Not all forms of social withdrawal are unhealthy, research suggests', *ScienceDaily*, 20 November 2017, https://www.sciencedaily.com/releases/2017/11/171120174505.htm

23. Christopher R. Long and James R. Averill, 'Solitude: An Exploration of Benefits of Being Alone', *Journal for the Theory of Social Behaviour*, 33:1, March 2003, https://www.researchgate.net/publication/227867774_Solitude_An_Exploration_of_Benefits_of_Being_Alone

Notes

What Is Meaningful Work?

1. 'One-half of working population unhappy in job: Survey', *Canadian HR Reporter*, 2 May 2016, https://www.hrreporter.com/news/hr-news/one-half-of-working-population-unhappy-in-job-survey/281844
2. Jim Clifton, 'The World's Broken Workplace', *Gallup News/The Chairman's Blog*, 13 June 2017, https://news.gallup.com/opinion/chairman/212045/world-broken-workplace.aspx
3. Amy Wrzesniewski, Justin M. Berg, Jane E. Dutton, 'Turn the Job You Have into the Job You Want', *Harvard Business Review*, June 2010, https://spinup-000d1a-wp-offload-media.s3.amazonaws.com/faculty/wp-content/uploads/sites/6/2019/06/Turnthejobyouhaveintothejobyouwant.pdf
4. Adam Grant, 'Relational Job Design and the Motivation to Make a Prosocial Difference', *Academy of Management Review*, (32:2), April 2007, https://selfdeterminationtheory.org/SDT/documents/2007_Grant_AMR.pdf
5. J. Y. Kim, T. H. Campbell, S. Shepherd, A. C. Kay, 'Understanding contemporary forms of exploitation: Attributions of passion serve to legitimize the poor treatment of workers', *Journal of Personality and Social Pyschology*, 118(1), January 2020, https://pubmed.ncbi.nlm.nih.gov/30998042/
6. Jay Rayner, 'Is being a chef bad for your mental health?' the *Observer*, 26 November, 2017, https://www.theguardian.com/society/2017/nov/26/chefs-mental-health-depression
7. Robert Vallerand, Yvan Paquet, Frederick Philippe, Julie Charest, 'On the Role of Passion for Work in Burnout: A Process Model', *Journal of Personality*, 78, February 2010, https://www.researchgate.net/publication/43532701_

The Problem of Long Hours

1. Micheal Blanding, 'Having No Life is the New Aspirational Lifestyle', *Harvard Business School Working Knowledge*, 20 February 2017, https://hbswk.hbs.edu/item/having-no-life-is-the-new-aspirational-lifestyle
2. Silvia Bellezza, Neeru Paharia, Anat Keinan, 'Conspicuous Consumption of Time: When Busyness and Lack of Leisure Time Become a Status Symbol', *Journal of Consumer Research*, (44:1), June

Notes

2017, https://wwwo.gsb.columbia.edu/mygsb/faculty/research/pubfiles/19293/Conspicuous%20Consumption%20of%20Time.pdf

3. P. Afonso, M. Fonseca, J. F. Pires, 'Impact of working hours on sleep and mental health', *Occupational Medicine*, 67:5, July 2017, https://academic.oup.com/occmed/article/67/5/377/3859790

4. M. Virtanen, S. A. Stansfeld, R. Fuhrer, J. E. Ferrie, M. Kivimäki, 'Overtime Work as a Predictor of Major Depressive Episode: A 5-Year Follow-Up of the Whitehall II Study', *PLoS ONE* (7:1), 2012, https://journals.plos.org/plosone/article?id=10.1371/journal.pone.0030719

5. Akira Banna, Akiko Tamakoshi, 'The association between long working hours and health: A systematic review of epidemiological evidence', *Scandinavian Journal of Work, Environment & Health*, (40:1), 2014, https://www.jstor.org/stable/43187983?seq=1

6. Sendhil Mullainathan, Eldar Shafir, 'Freeing up intelligence', *Scientific American Mind*, Jan/Feb 2014 (9) (Adapted from *Scarcity: Why Having Too Little Means So Much*, by Sendhil Mullainathan and Eldar Shafir), https://scholar.harvard.edu/files/sendhil/files/scientificamericanmind0114-58.pdf

7. Ashley Whillans, 'Time For Happiness', *Harvard Business Review/The Big Idea*, January 2019, https://hbr.org/cover-story/2019/01/time-for-happiness

8. Laura M. Giurge, Ashley V. Whillans, 'Beyond Material Poverty: Why Time Poverty Matters for Individuals, Organisations, and Nations', Working paper 20–051, *Harvard Business School*, 2019, https://www.hbs.edu/faculty/Publication%20Files/20-051_9ccace07-ec9b-409e-a6aa-723f091422fb.pdf

9. Joachim Merz, Tim Rathjen, 'Entrepreneurs and Freelancers: Are They Time and Income Multidimensional Poor? The German Case', IZA Discussion Paper No. 9912, April 2016, https://www.iza.org/publications/dp/9912/entrepreneurs-and-freelancers-are-they-time-and-income-multidimensional-poor-the-german-case

10. Ashley Whillans, 'Time For Happiness', *Harvard Business Review/The Big Idea*, January 2019, https://hbr.org/cover-story/2019/01/time-for-happiness

11. John Pencavel, 'Recovery from Work and the Productivity of Working Hours', IZA DP No. 10103, July 2016 http://ftp.iza.org/dp10103.pdf

Notes

12. R. H. Van Zelst, W. A. Kerr, 'Some correlates of technical and scientific productivity', *The Journal of Abnormal and Social Psychology*, (46:4), 1951, https://psycnet.apa.org/record/1952-04231-001

13. Ron Friedman, 'Working Too Hard Makes Leading More Difficult', *Harvard Business Review*, 30/12/14, https://hbr.org/2014/12/working-too-hard-makes-leading-more-difficult

14. 'Report summary: Working Long Hours: a Review of the Evidence', *Institute for Employment Studies*, 2003, https://www.employment-studies.co.uk/report-summaries/report-summary-working-long-hours-review-evidence-volume-1-%E2%80%93-main-report

15. Roger B. Manning, 'Rural Societies in Early Modern Europe: A Review', *The Sixteenth Century Journal*, (17:3), 1986, https://www.jstor.org/stable/2540326?seq=1

16. Nicholas Boring, 'How Sunday Came to be Established as a Day of Rest in France', *Library of Congress law blog* (blogs.loc.gov/law), 2 September 2014, https://blogs.loc.gov/law/2014/09/how-sunday-came-to-be-established-as-a-day-of-rest-in-france/

17. John Maynard Keynes, 'Economic Possibilities for Our Grandchildren', 1930

18. Michael Huberman, Chris Minns, 'The times they are not changin': Days and hours of work in Old and New Worlds, 1870–2000', *Explorations in Economic History*, 44, 2007, https://personal.lse.ac.uk/minns/Huberman_Minns_EEH_2007.pdf

19. OECD Hours Worked Data, https://data.oecd.org/emp/hours-worked.htm

20. André van Hoorn, Robbert Maseland, 'Does a Protestant work ethic exist? Evidence from the well-being effect of unemployment', *Journal of Economic Behavior & Organization*, 91, July 2013, https://www.sciencedirect.com/science/article/abs/pii/S0167268113000838

21. Richard B. Lee and Irven DeVore, *Man The Hunter*, 1968 (from the chapter, 'What Hunters Do For a Living', by Richard B. Lee)

22. James Suzman, 'The Bushmen Who Had the Whole Work-Life Thing Figured Out', *New York Times*, 24 July 2017 https://www.nytimes.com/2017/07/24/opinion/the-bushmen-who-had-the-whole-work-life-thing-figured-out.html

23. Melanie Curtin, 'In an 8-Hour Day, the Average Worker Is

Productive for This Many Hours', inc.com, 21 July 2016, https://
www.inc.com/melanie-curtin/in-an-8-hour-day-the-average-
worker-is-productive-for-this-many-hours.html

24. 'Want a better work-life balance as your own boss? Study finds
self-employed people take just 14 days holiday a year', *The Telegraph*,
5 February 2018, https://www.telegraph.co.uk/news/2018/02/05/
want-better-work-life-balance-boss-study-find-self-employed/

Courage, Resilience and Doing Hard Things

1. Shawn Achor, 'Resilience Is About How You Recharge, Not
How You Endure', *LinkedIn Pulse*, 10 November 2019, https://
www.linkedin.com/pulse/resilience-how-you-recharge-endure-
shawn-achor/?articleId=6599380709478055936#comme
nts-6599380709478055936&trk=public_profile_article_view

2. Megan Jay, 'The Secrets of Resilience', *The Wall Street
Journal*, 10 November 2017, https://www.wsj.com/articles/
the-secrets-of-resilience-1510329202

3. Drew Magary, 'How to Write 10,000 Words a Week',
medium.com, 24 January 2020, https://forge.medium.com/
how-to-write-10-000-words-a-week-a7c63d97ea79

4. Megan Jay, 'The Secrets of Resilience', *The Wall Street
Journal*, 10 November 2017, https://www.wsj.com/articles/
the-secrets-of-resilience-1510329202

5. Gianpiero Petriglieri, Susan J. Ashford, Amy Wrzesniewski, 'Agony
and Ecstasy in the Gig Economy: Cultivating Holding Environments
for Precarious and Personalized Work Identities', *Administrative
Science Quarterly*, (64:1) 2019, https://journals.sagepub.com/doi/
full/10.1177/0001839218759646

6. Ibid.

7. Adam Grant, 'Productivity Isn't About Time Management. It's
About Attention Management', *New York Times*, 28 March 2019,
https://www.nytimes.com/2019/03/28/smarter-living/productivity-
isnt-about-time-management-its-about-attention-management.
html?auth=login-email&login=email

8. Martin Binder, 'The Way to Wellbeing', Centre for Research on
Self-Employment, 2018, http://www.crse.co.uk/sites/default/files/
The%20Way%20to%20Wellbeing%20Full%20Report_0.pdf

9. Tim Herrara, 'Micro-Progress and the Magic of Just Getting

Started', *The New York Times*, 22 January 2018, https://www.
nytimes.com/2018/01/22/smarter-living/micro-progress.
html?auth=login-email&emc=edit_sl_20191007?campaign_
id=33&instance_id=12888&login=email&nl=smarter-
living&regi_id=78598733&segment_id=17650&te=1&user_
id=5dd7fd2f86725daefa367c13872d6d25

10. Herrara was also building on an original blog post by James Clear:
jamesclear.com/physics-productivity

11. Iowa State University, 'No evidence that power posing works',
ScienceDaily, 1 October 2019, https://www.sciencedaily.com/
releases/2019/10/191001110824.htm

12. Robert Emmons, 'Why Gratitude is Good', *Greater Good Magazine*
(published by the Greater Good Science Center at UC Berkeley),
16 November 2010, https://greatergood.berkeley.edu/article/item/
why_gratitude_is_good

Focus and Flow

1. Tom Knowles, 'I'm so sorry, says inventor of endless online scrolling',
The Times, 27 April 2019, https://www.thetimes.co.uk/article/i-m-
so-sorry-says-inventor-of-endless-online-scrolling-91rv59mdk

2. Rob Asghar, '4 Ways Your Smartphone Is Making You Dumber',
Forbes, 10 November 2014, https://www.forbes.com/sites/
robasghar/2014/11/10/4-ways-your-smartphone-is-making-you-
dumber/

3. Ioanna Katidioti, Jelmer P. Borst, Marieke K. van Vugt, Niels A.
Taatgen, 'Interrupt me: External interruptions are less disruptive
than self-interruptions', Computers in Human Behavior, October
2016, https://www.sciencedirect.com/science/article/pii/
S0747563216304654

4. Linda Stone, 'Beyond Simple Multi-Tasking:
Continuous Partial Attention', essay on her site: www.
lindastone.com, https://lindastone.net/2009/11/30/
beyond-simple-multi-tasking-continuous-partial-attention/

5. Jiageng Chen, Andrew B. Leber, Julie D. Golomb, 'Attentional
capture alters feature perception', *Journal of Experimental Psychology:
Human Perception and Performance*, (45:11), 2019, https://psycnet.apa.
org/buy/2019-49303-001

6. Peter Kelly, 'Task interrupted: A plan for returning helps

Notes

you move on', *University of Washington News*, 16 January 2018, https://www.washington.edu/news/2018/01/16/ task-interrupted-a-plan-for-returning-helps-you-move-on/

7. Laura Vanderkam, *What the Most Successful People Do Before Breakfast*, p89, Penguin, 2013

8. Pam A. Mueller, Daniel M. Oppenheimer, 'The Pen Is Mightier Than the Keyboard: Advantages of Longhand Over Laptop Note Taking', *Psychological Science*, (25: 6), 2014, https://journals.sagepub.com/doi/abs/10.1177/0956797614524581

9. P. M. Gollwitzer, V. Brandstätter, 'Implementation intentions and effective goal pursuit', *Journal of Personality and Social Psychology*, 73(1), 1997, https://psycnet.apa.org/record/1997–04812–015

10. F. Sirois, T. Pychyl, 'Procrastination and the Priority of Short-Term Mood Regulation: Consequences for Future Self', *Social and Personality Psychology Compass*, 7:2, 2013, http://eprints.whiterose.ac.uk/91793/1/Compass%20Paper%20revision%20FINAL.pdf

11. Jooa Julia Lee, Francesca Gino, Bradley R. Staats, 'Rainmakers: Why bad weather means good productivity', *Journal of Applied Psychology*, (99:3), 2014, https://psycnet.apa.org/buy/2014–01192–001

12. Professor Jihae Shin and Professor Adam M. Grant, 'When Putting Work Off Pays Off: The Curvilinear Relationship Between Procrastination and Creativity', *Academy of Management Journal*, April 2020, https://journals.aom.org/doi/10.5465/amj.2018.1471

13. John Gierland, 'Go With the Flow', Wired.com, 09/01/96, https://www.wired.com/1996/09/czik/

14. Angela Duckworth, *Grit: The Power of Passion and Perseverance*, p44, Scribner Book Company, 2016

Be Your Own CEO

1. Ben Wigert, Sangeeta Agrawal, 'Employee Burnout, Part 1: The 5 Main Causes', *Workplace/Gallup.com*, 12 JULY 2018, https://www.gallup.com/workplace/237059/employee-burnout-part-main-causes.aspx

Inside and Outside

1. 'The Global Impact of Biophilic Design in the Workplace', report in *Human Spaces*, 2015, http://interfaceinc.scene7.com/is/content/InterfaceInc/Interface/Americas/WebsiteContentAssets/

Notes

Documents/Reports/Human%20Spaces/Global-Human-Spaces-Report.pdf

2. Ibid.

3. M. S. Lee, J. Lee, B. J. Park, Y. Miyazaki, 'Interaction with indoor plants may reduce psychological and physiological stress by suppressing autonomic nervous system activity in young adults: a randomized crossover study, *Journal of Physiological Anthropology*, 2015, https://www.ncbi.nlm.nih.gov/pmc/articles/PMC4419447/

4. 'The Global Impact of Biophilic Design in the Workplace', report in *Human Spaces*, 2015, http://interfaceinc.scene7.com/is/content/InterfaceInc/Interface/Americas/WebsiteContentAssets/Documents/Reports/Human%20Spaces/Global-Human-Spaces-Report.pdf

5. Ibid.

6. Olli Seppänen, William Fisk, Q. H. Lei, 'Effect of Temperature on Task Performance in Office Environment', 2005, https://indoor.lbl.gov/sites/all/files/lbnl-60946.pdf

7. Molly C. Bernhard, Peng Li, David B. Allison, Julia M. Gohlke, 'Warm Ambient Temperature Decreases Food Intake in a Simulated Office Setting: A Pilot Randomized Controlled Trial', *Frontiers in Nutrition*, 2015, https://www.frontiersin.org/articles/10.3389/fnut.2015.00020/full

8. David Wyon, 'Creative thinking as the dependent variable in six environmental experiments: A review', Proceedings of the 7th International Conference on Indoor Air Quality and Climate: Indoor Air '96, https://www.researchgate.net/publication/285320928_Creative_thinking_as_the_dependent_variable_in_six_environmental_experiments_A_review

9. Ulf Ekelund, Thomas Yates, 'Sit less – move more and more often: all physical activity is beneficial for longevity', *British Medical Journal Opinion*, 21 August 2019, https://blogs.bmj.com/bmj/2019/08/21/ulf-ekelund-and-thomas-yates-sit-less-move-more-and-more-often-all-physical-activity-is-beneficial-for-longevity/

10. Rebecca Seguin, David M. Buchner, Jingmin Liu et al., 'Sedentary Behavior and Mortality in Older Women', *American Journal of Preventive Medicine*, February 2014, https://www.ajpmonline.org/article/S0749-3797(13)00594-1/abstract

11. University of Utah Health Sciences, 'Walking an extra two

Notes

minutes each hour may offset hazards of sitting too long',
ScienceDaily, 30 April 2015, https://www.sciencedaily.com/
releases/2015/04/150430170715.htm

12. Gretchen Spreitzer, Peter Bacevice, Lyndon Garrett,
'Why People Thrive in Coworking Spaces', *Harvard
Business Review*, September 2015, https://hbr.org/2015/05/
why-people-thrive-in-coworking-spaces

13. Matthew P. White, Ian Alcock, James Grellier, et al., 'Spending at
least 120 minutes a week in nature is associated with good health
and wellbeing', *Scientific Reports* 9, June 2019, https://www.nature.
com/articles/s41598-019-44097-3

14. Frances E. Kuo, William C. Sullivan, 'Aggression and Violence in the
Inner City: Effects of Environment via Mental Fatigue', *Environment
and Behavior*, 1 July 2001, https://journals.sagepub.com/doi/
pdf/10.1177/00139160121973124

15. Florence Williams and Aeon, 'Why are Fractals so Soothing?', *The
Atlantic*, 26 January 2017, https://www.theatlantic.com/science/
archive/2017/01/why-fractals-are-so-soothing/514520/

Food and Drink

1. Jennifer Jabs, Carol M. Devine, 'Time Scarcity and Food Choices:
An overview', *Appetite*, (47:2), 2006, https://www.sciencedirect.com/
science/article/abs/pii/S0195666306003813

2. S. W. Sadava, M. M. Thompson, 'Loneliness, social drinking, and
vulnerability to alcohol problems', *Canadian Journal of Behavioural
Science / Revue canadienne des sciences du comportement*, 18(2), 1986,
https://psycnet.apa.org/record/1988-10967-001

The Power of Planning

1. 'Independent consulting: a good gig in a changing world',
Findings from the Eden McCallum LBS Future of Consulting
survey 2018, https://edenmccallum.com/wp-content/uploads/
securepdfs/2019/05/survey-report.pdf

The Curse of Comparison (and Why Social Media Sucks)

1. Angela Duckworth, *Grit: The Power of Passion and Perseverance*, p39,
Scribner Book Company, 2016

2. Mai-Ly N. Steers, Robert E. Wickham, and Linda K. Acitelli, 'Seeing

280

Everyone Else's Highlight Reels: How Facebook Usage is Linked to Depressive Symptoms', *Journal of Social and Clinical Psychology*, 2014, https://guilfordjournals.com/doi/abs/10.1521/jscp.2014.33.8.701

3. Erin A. Vogel, Jason P. Rose, Lindsay R. Roberts, Katheryn Eckles, 'Social comparison, social media, and self-esteem', *Psychology of Popular Media Culture*, 3(4), 2014, https://psycnet.apa.org/record/2014–33471–001

The Problem with Money (Psychological)

1. Richard Eisenberg, 'What Workers Crave More than Money', *Forbes*, 27 September 2016, https://www.forbes.com/sites/nextavenue/2016/09/27/what-workers-crave-more-than-money/#692db1ab3150
2. Timothy A. Judge, Ronald F. Piccolo, Nathan P. Podsakoff, John C. Shaw, Bruce L. Rich, 'The relationship between pay and job satisfaction: A meta-analysis of the literature', *Journal of Vocational Behavior*, 2 October 2010, http://www.timothy-judge.com/Judge,%20Piccolo,%20Podsakoff,%20et%20al.%20(JVB%202010).pdf
3. Sanford DeVoe, Julian House, 'Time, money, and happiness: How does putting a price on time affect our ability to smell the roses?', *Journal of Experimental Social Psychology*, March 2012, https://www.sciencedirect.com/science/article/abs/pii/S0022103111002897?via%3Dihub
4. Jeffrey Pfeffer, Sanford DeVoe, 'The Economic Evaluation of Time: Organizational Causes and Individual Consequences', *Research in Organizational Behavior*, 32, 2012, https://www.sciencedirect.com/science/article/abs/pii/S019130851200007X
5. Shawn Achor, Andrew Reece, Gabriella Rosen Kellerman, Alexi Robichaux, '9 Out of 10 People Are Willing to Earn Less Money to Do More-Meaningful Work', *Harvard Business Review*, 6 November 2018, https://hbr.org/2018/11/9-out-of-10-people-are-willing-to-earn-less-money-to-do-more-meaningful-work
6. Ashley Whillans, 'Time For Happiness', *Harvard Business Review/The Big Idea*, January 2019, https://hbr.org/cover-story/2019/01/time-for-happiness
7. UK Government statistics, https://www.gov.uk/government/statistics/number-of-individual-income-taxpayers-by-marginal-rate-gender-and-age

Notes

8. Ashley Whillans, Hanne Collins, 'Accounting for Time', *Harvard Business Review*, 30 January 2019, https://hbr.org/2019/01/accounting-for-time

The Problem with Money (Practical)
1. Martin Binder, 'The Way to Wellbeing', *Centre for Research on Self-Employment*, 2018, http://www.crse.co.uk/sites/default/files/The%20Way%20to%20Wellbeing%20Full%20Report_0.pdf
2. Ibid.

What To Do When You're Not Working
1. Inna Yordanova, 'Taking Time Off As A Freelancer', *IPSE Report*, 23 August 2019, https://www.ipse.co.uk/resource/taking-time-off-as-a-freelancer.html
2. Jessica de Bloom, 'Making holidays work', *The Psychologist/The British Psychological Society*, August 2015, https://thepsychologist.bps.org.uk/volume-28/august-2015/making-holidays-work

Select Bibliography and Further Reading

Achor, Shawn, *The Happiness Advantage: The Seven Principles of Positive Psychology that Fuel Success and Performance at Work*, Virgin Books, 2011

Bailey, Chris, *Hyperfocus: How to Work Less to Achieve More*, Macmillan, 2018

Cain, Susan, *Quiet: The Power of Introverts in a World That Can't Stop Talking*, Viking, 2012

Coplan, Robert J. and Bowker, Julie C. (eds), *The Handbook of Solitude: Psychological Perspectives on Social Isolation, Social Withdrawal, and Being Alone*, Wiley, 2014

Currey, Mason, *Daily Rituals: How Great Minds Make Time, Find Inspiration and Get to Work*, Picador, 2013

Day, Elizabeth, *How to Fail: Everything I've Ever Learned from Things Going Wrong*, Fourth Estate, 2019

Duckworth, Angela, *Grit: Why Passion and Resilience are the Secrets to Success*, Vermilion, 2017

Dweck, Carol, *Mindset: Changing the Way You Think to Fulfil Your Potential*, Robinson, 2017

Fetell Lee, Ingrid, *Joyful: The Surprising Power of Ordinary Things to Create Extraordinary Happiness*, Rider, 2018

Fried, Jason and Heinemeier, David, *Remote: Office Not Required*, Vermillion, 2013

Gannon, Emma, *The Multi-Hyphen Method: Work Less, Create More: How to Make Your Side Hustle Work for You*, Hodder and Stoughton, 2019

Geddes, Linda, *Chasing the Sun: The New Science of Sunlight and How it Shapes Our Bodies and Minds*, Wellcome Collection, 2019

Harris, Michael, *Solitude: The Pursuit of a Singular Life in a Crowded World*, Random House, 2017

Select Bibliography and Further Reading

Harvard Business Review (various), *HBR's 10 Must Reads: On Managing Yourself*, Harvard Business Review Press, 2011

Heffernan, Margaret, *A Bigger Prize: When No One Wins Unless Everyone Wins*, Simon and Schuster, 2015

Heffernan, Margaret, *Beyond Measure: The Big Impact of Small Changes*, Simon and Schuster, 2015

Morin, Tom, *Your Best Work: Create the Working Life That's Right for You*, Page Two, 2020

Mulcahy, Diane, *The Gig Economy: The Complete Guide to Getting Better Work, Taking More Time Off, and Financing the Life You Want*, Amacom, 2016

Newport, Cal, *Deep Work: Rules for Focused Success in a Distracted World*, Piatkus, 2016

Newport, Cal, *So Good They Can't Ignore You: Why Skills Trump Passion in the Quest for the Work You Love*, Piatkus, 2016

Pang, Alex Soojung-Kim, *Rest: Why You Get More Done When You Work Less*, Basic Books, 2016

Pink, Daniel, *Drive: The Surprising Truth About What Motivates Us*, Canongate, 2018

Ressler, Cali and Thompson, Jody, *Why Work Sucks and How to Fix It: The Results-Only Revolution*, Portfolio, 2011

Rock, David, *Your Brain at Work: Strategies for Overcoming Distraction, Regaining Focus, and Working Smarter All Day Long*, Harper Business, 2009

Shaw, Graham, *The Speaker's Coach: 60 Secrets to Make your Talk, Speech or Presentation Amazing*, Pearson Business, 2019

Vanderkam, Laura, *I Know How She Does It: How Successful Women Make the Most of Their Time*, Penguin, 2015

Vanderkam, Laura, *What the Most Successful People Do Before Breakfast: How to Achieve More at Work and at Home*, Penguin, 2013

Warr, Peter and Clapperton, Guy, *The Joy of Work?*, Routledge, 2009

Warr, Peter, *The Psychology of Happiness*, Routledge, 2019

Acknowledgements

Without Steve Joyce's encouragement (and patient, then not-so-patient discussion of the matter, over a very long six months), I'm not sure I would ever have been brave enough to go solo in the first place. But there are many other people who supported me on my solo journey and directly or indirectly contributed to this book:

My parents, Hilary Seal and Dave Seal, and my sister Katy Collett have listened and cheered me on in everything I've ever done. Thanks also to Jessica Hopkins, Marian Hodgkin, Elkie Mace, Carmel King, Charlotte Scott and Jon Thorne.

For their time, wisdom, guidance and knowledge: Brigid Schulte, Anna Blackwell, Tom Morin, Adam Grant, Alexandra Dariescu, Robert Kropp, Thomas Broughton, Nicholas Hooper, Brendan Burchell, Esther Canonico, Jackie Sykes, Dan Biddulph, Ilke Inceoglu, Andrew Brodsky, Alex Hannaford, Diane Mulcahy, Ingrid Fetell-Lee, Emma Morley, Heejung Chung, Victoria Moore, Levison Wood, Thomas Broughton, Dior Bediako, Jameela Donaldson, Margaret Heffernan, Nat Rich, Graham Shaw, Solveiga Pakštaitė, Joanne Mallon, Karen Eyre-White, Susan Ashford, Nick Bloom and Ute Stephan. (Naturally, any mistakes are mine alone.)

Thanks to my agent Antony Topping, for waiting a long time for this idea to grow into something real, and for telling Rebecca Gray at Profile Books and Souvenir Press about it; to Cindy Chan for making sure the whole thing made sense, and for giving up holiday time (along with Graeme Hall, Ali Nadal and many others in the Souvenir and Profile team) to get the book out quickly once we all realised that it could be useful sooner than we had originally planned.

Finally, thanks to my daughters, Isla and Coralie, who tolerate – just – the strange and erratic ways Steve and I do what we do, and who, more than anything or anyone else, have taught me that there is far, far more to life than work.

Index

Index

Index

Index

Herrara, Tim 123
Hive 244
Hodgkin, Marian 125–6
holding environments 112, 115–16
holidays 18, 266–7
Hollis, Rachel 233, 235
Holt-Lunstad, Julianne 28
Hooper, Nicholas 35, 121–2, 124, 141
hourly rates 263–4
house plants 197–8
Hoxby Collective 246
hunter-gatherers 86–8, 89
Hyperfocus (Bailey) 133, 163

I

Ideal Week exercise 142–4
identity 113–15
identity precariousness 113
Illinois Institute of Technology 79
inbox zero 74, 148, 150
India 198
Industrial Revolution 80, 81–2, 91, 94
internal/intermittent recovery 99, 101–2
interruptions 129, 130, 138–9
intrinsic motivation 49, 249–50, 252
introverts 31
Iron Man 227
isolation 7
    perception 34, 35–6

J

James, LeBron 104
Japan 72

Jay, Megan 103
Jesus 29
job crafting 63–4, 66
Jobs, Steve 161, 227
Joyful (Fetell Lee) 194
Ju/'haonsi' 86–7

K

Keinan, Anat 71
keyboards 201
Keynes, John Maynard 82–3, 85–6
King, Carmel 244
Korea *see* South Korea
Kropp, Robert 206–8
!Kung Bushmen 86

L

Lee, Richard B. 86
legitimate power 179
Lerner, Sandy 268
Leroy, Sophie 131–2, 138
lighting 80–81, 195–7
list writing
    present tense journal 233–5
    to-do lists 133, 141, 151–7
    to-remember lists 154–5
London School of Economics
    (LSE) 53, 54, 58, 107–8
loneliness 7, 27–8, 30, 36, 41, 249
    and social media 242

M

Magary, Drew 104–5
Mallon, Joanne 259–63
manners 178–9
Marvel 227
meal breaks 214–15, 216–17

Index

Index

Index

Index